Take the
to

1. **Are you in a relationship with someone other than you?**
   a) Yes
   b) No
   c) It's complicated.
   d) Relationships are for weak people.

2. **If someone asks you if you're happy in your relationship, you would say:**
   a) "He completes me."
   b) "We're in a good place right now."
   c) "It could be better."
   d) "No, not really. Can you help?"

3. **The last time you had sex was:**
   a) This morning
   b) Last week
   c) My memory doesn't go back that far.
   d) By sex, do you mean intercourse?

4. **You come home from work, the hallway's a mess, the refrigerator is empty, and no cocktail is awaiting you. You say: "_____, _____? It looks like _____. Why don't you _____ and I'll _____?"**
   a) Is everything okay, sweetie; / you had a hard day; / take a load off; / run a nice bath for you.
   b) Wow, what happened here; / someone didn't have time to clean up; / take care of the situation; / be down when you're done.

c) Are you serious, dude; / a petting zoo in here; / get to work for once; / pour myself a Manhattan.

5. **The most common fight you have with your partner is about:**
   a) Housework
   b) Kids
   c) Sex
   d) Fighting

6. **About how long does a typical fight with your partner last?**
   a) 15 minutes or less
   b) Between 15 minutes and an hour
   c) More than an hour, but less than a day
   d) We never stop fighting.

7. **The division of labor in your house is:**
   a) We split everything 50/50.
   b) In theory, we split everything 50/50.
   c) He picks up his socks every other Wednesday.
   d) I do everything because, otherwise, nothing would get done.

8. **When something's bothering you, you:**
   a) Bring it up immediately, work through the issue, and come to a mutually agreeable resolution
   b) Stew until he asks you what's wrong
   c) Post a status update for your 1,800 closest friends about what he did to hurt your feelings
   d) Interrogate him until he breaks

9. **The two of you communicate:**
   a) Extremely well
   b) Well

c) Moderately well

d) "Communication" isn't our strong point.

10. **Your definition of compromise is:**
    a) A give and a take
    b) I know I'm right, but I'll throw him a bone this one time.
    c) Okay, fine, but I'll remember this.
    d) Because I said so

11. **When you try to talk, in earnest, about your relationship, he usually:**
    a) Listens and responds
    b) Says "Sure thing!" and then sets the timer
    c) Goes to his "safe place"
    d) Sticks his fingers in his ears and says, "I'm not listening I'm not listening I'm not listening."

12. **The last nice thing you did for him was:**
    a) Can't say, this is a family book
    b) Encouraged boys' night out
    c) Braised pork shoulder—and potatoes!
    d) Woke up next to him

13. **Over the years together, you have:**
    a) Worked through rough patches and come out stronger
    b) Worked through rough patches that have left you both a bit scarred
    c) Struggled through rough patches, but are still together
    d) Come close to breaking up a few times, and still might

14. **Money is:**
    a) Something we share equally and that affords us a measure of happiness

b) Something we fight about occasionally

c) Something he thinks is self-replicating

d) Our undoing

15. **The quality I love about him most is:**

a) His mind

b) His body

c) His soul

d) Give me a minute

ANSWER KEY

Mostly A's: It sounds like your relationship is pretty good. Buy this book to keep it that way!

Mostly B's: Not bad, but plenty room for improvement. You should definitely buy this book.

Mostly C's: Cloudy with a chance of breakup. You need to buy this book.

Mostly D's: Glad I'm not you. This book might not help you, but you should buy two anyway.

"Comparing marriage to a business doesn't sound very romantic. But in [*It's Not You, It's the Dishes*], journalists Paula Szuchman and Jenny Anderson make a convincing—and creative—case for how the dismal science can help reconcile marital disputes. Applying economic research to anecdotes from couples around the country, Szuchman and Anderson draw on concepts such as the division of labor and game theory to help readers determine who should mow the lawn or how to persuade a homebody spouse to join you at the movies."

—*The Washington Post*

"*It's Not You, It's the Dishes* is one of the most delightful, clever, and helpful books about marriage I've ever seen."

—ELIZABETH GILBERT, author of *Eat, Pray, Love* and *Committed*

"Practical, compelling, and hilarious, *It's Not You, It's the Dishes* highlights economics-based strategies for couples coping with the inevitable annoyances of a relationship. How can you coax him to do chores without nagging? Or change her mind about important decisions, quit yelling at the kids, or step away from the computer? The minute I finished this book, I started to experiment on my husband."

—GRETCHEN RUBIN, author of *The Happiness Project*

"Apply economic principles to marriage and you will be happier is the message—and the more you think about it, the more it makes perfect sense. . . . Thinking of your marriage not as a love affair that is slowly getting buried under layers of family responsibilities, but as a start-up business that is adding skills by the day, makes everything look completely different. Rosy, even. And pretty sexy. Try it."

—*The Sunday Times*

"A brilliant and innovative book. And if you're a rational consumer, you really have to buy it: A few bucks to improve your marriage? That's just good decision making."

—A. J. JACOBS, bestselling author of *The Know-It-All*
and *The Year of Living Biblically*

"This book—by suggesting that people are not rational, but irrational—turns our thinking about relationships on its head. A stimulating, must read for all of us who want to better understand and improve our love lives."
—JOHN GOTTMAN, bestselling author of
The Seven Principles for Making Marriage Work

"Szuchman and Anderson describe 10 big economic principles and many more small ones to recognize or apply at home in service of a better relationship. . . . Happy is the student who learns economics through the teachings of Szuchman and Anderson."
—ANNIE LOWREY, Slate

"[This book] pretty much nailed it. . . . The authors are funny, smart and relatable—and the advice isn't just designed to make both parties happy; it's also simple enough to work. Even if your marriage isn't operating in the (emotional) red, consider this book a great investment."
—JENNA MCCARTHY, iVillage

"[*It's Not You, It's the Dishes*] is funny, smart and breaks down complex ideas about economics and relationships into easy-to-digest anecdotes about who does the dishes and how often married folks get laid. . . . They promise readers improved marriages with more sex, less strife and smoother handling of everything from bills to bedtime routines. Sounds impressive, right? It is. The authors interviewed dozens of married couples, as well as experts in economics and relationships. They know what they're talking about."
—SIERRA BLACK, Babble.com

"[*It's Not You, It's the Dishes*] delivers: Two accomplished journalists master a fascinating body of research I'd been hoping to learn more about, then weave it into a narrative that's a pure pleasure to read. Bravo."

—ROBERT H. FRANK, professor of economics at
Cornell University, and author of *The Economic
Naturalist* and *The Winner-Take-All Society*

"Paula Szuchman and Jenny Anderson say if you only treated your marriage like the business partnership that it is, many [common] issues just might solve themselves. It's behavioral finance for the bedroom and beyond. And it is both helpful and hilarious."

—TESS VIGELAND, *Marketplace*

"[*It's Not You, It's the Dishes*] is grounded in solid research, makes economics entertaining, and might just save a marriage or two."

—JAMES PRESSLEY, Bloomberg

"[*It's Not You, It's the Dishes*] lets you peer into other people's relationships and offers valuable lessons for your own. This is a fun and breezy read for anyone who wants to be both smarter about economics and wiser about love."

—STEVEN E. LANDSBURG, author of *The Armchair Economist*
and *More Sex Is Safer Sex*

"*It's Not You, It's the Dishes* offers couples real-life, commonsense solutions for some of the knottiest conflicts regularly experienced in marriage. Written with great wit and understanding, it is both very helpful and a pleasure to read. I recommend it highly."

—JOHN W. JACOBS, M.D., author of
All You Need Is Love and Other Lies About Marriage

It's Not You,
It's the Dishes

It's Not You, It's the Dishes

HOW TO MINIMIZE CONFLICT AND MAXIMIZE HAPPINESS IN YOUR RELATIONSHIP

Originally published as *Spousonomics*

PAULA SZUCHMAN & JENNY ANDERSON

Random House Trade Paperbacks
New York

2012 Random House Trade Paperback Edition

Published in the United States by Random House Trade Paperbacks, an imprint of
The Random House Publishing Group, a division of Random House, Inc., New York.

RANDOM HOUSE TRADE PAPERBACKS and colophon are trademarks of Random House, Inc.

Originally published in hardcover in the United States by Random House, an imprint of
The Random House Publishing Group, a division of Random House, Inc., in 2011,
as *Spousonomics: Using Economics to Master Love, Marriage, and Dirty Dishes*.

LIBRARY OF CONGRESS CATALOGING-IN-PUBLICATION DATA

Szuchman, Paula.
It's Not You, It's the Dishes: How to Minimize Conflict and Maximize Happiness in Your
Relationship / Paula Szuchman and Jenny Anderson.
p.   cm.
Includes bibliographical references and index.
ISBN 978-0-385-34395-4
eISBN 978-0-679-60440-2
1. Marriage—Economic aspects.   2. Marriage—Psychological aspects.
3. Economics—Sociological aspects.   I. Anderson, Jenny   II. Title.
HQ734.S997   2011   646.7'8—dc22   2010035287

Printed in the United States of America

www.atrandom.com

2 4 6 8 9 7 5 3 1

Book design by Chris Welch

For our husbands

Contents

Introduction

Robert, a handsome thirty-eight-year-old San Francisco entrepreneur, wanted to have sex last night. It had been a tough couple of weeks: A major investor in his energy drink company had bailed out, his marketing director had left to join a rival start-up, and this afternoon, the supplier of his secret Balinese ingredient threatened to double its cost estimate.

Joanne, Robert's wife, was not even remotely in the mood to have sex. She was beat. She'd spent the day on conference calls with grouchy New York traders, missed lunch, nearly rear-ended an Escalade racing to pick up her kids from soccer practice, and still had a stack of overdue bills to pay. She wanted to watch *24* reruns, eat a few Mallomars, and go to bed.

Should Joanne have had sex with Robert?

Robert would say yes. She's his *wife,* for Pete's sake—that's what she signed up for. Is it too much to ask his own *wife* to agree to fornicate with him on occasion, especially when he's totally strung out and the last time they did it was three weeks ago? Doesn't she realize he has *needs*?

Joanne's girlfriends, if asked, would tell her no way—she doesn't have to put out every time Robert comes knocking. She's not some concubine in his harem. She needs to set boundaries, listen to what her own libido is telling her. Doesn't he realize she's had a rough day, too?

But there's a third answer to the question: the economist's answer. The economist would advise Joanne to strip away all the simmering resentments and scorekeeping, the questions about who's more tired and who's less horny, and keep things simple with a basic cost-benefit analysis: Would the marginal cost of having sex with Robert—nine minutes of sleep, a third Mallomar—outweigh the benefits—an orgasm, a happy husband, a peaceful home?★

Welcome to a new way of managing your love life: using economics to minimize conflict and maximize returns on life's biggest investment—your marriage.

WHY ECONOMICS
(AND NOT, SAY, AROMATHERAPY)?

Many people think of economics as dull, wonky, and irrelevant to their daily lives. Those people are not entirely wrong. It's called "the dismal science" for a reason. Economists, it is true, have been known to write papers riddled with impenetrable equations, Greek letters, and words like autarky, satisficing, and monopsony.† But that's just so no one else can understand what they're saying.

At its core, economics is way simpler than all that. It's the study of

---

★There's no right or wrong answer to the question—it depends on a range of factors, from who's answering it to the lunar cycle. But if you're curious how Joanne replied, her answer was no, the marginal cost would *not* outweigh the benefits. She thus agreed to a quickie after dinner, fell asleep immediately, and left Robert to finish the dishes.

†In English: self-sufficiency (autarky); settling for what's good enough (satisficing); and a market controlled by one buyer (monopsony).

how people, companies, and societies allocate scarce resources. Which happens to be the same puzzle you and your spouse are perpetually trying to solve: how to spend your limited time, energy, money, and libido in ways that keep you smiling and your marriage thriving.

Think about it: Here you are, two ambitious, opinionated, stressed-out adults, trying to live in the same house together, prosper together, maybe raise kids together, and, with any luck, take pleasure in spending the rest of your natural-born lives together. This is not easy. For all intents and purposes, your marriage is a business, a business that flourishes in boom times but at other times feels like running a marathon the morning after a night of too many margaritas. It feels like work.

All kinds of work.

There's the administrative work that goes into maintaining some semblance of a home, which is a whole lot more complicated when two people are in the mix. Someone might consistently pick up after himself, for example, while someone else leaves a trail of apple cores, unmade beds, and sweaty gym clothes. If there are kids, then someone has to make sure those kids have done their homework and are fed, clothed, and in bed by seven, and sometimes that someone is unexpectedly doing it alone because the other person decided to go to happy hour with friends from work, and happy hour turned into dinner, which turned into a late-night beer-pong tournament.

There's the emotional work that comes with living with someone who's not you and who therefore has different preferences and styles of communicating. She might prefer to talk for three days straight if that's what it takes to resolve an argument, while you would rather fill your pockets with granite and walk into the ocean. He might like camping and you might like opera, and since there's only one free weekend to do something fun together, someone either caves or you both stay home and watch QVC.

There are the little things—the work of compromising on the perfect house, of calculating where to cut costs when money's tight, of deciding whether it's cruel to name your first child after Aunt Flo. And the big things—the work of being nice to each other after a terrible fight in which mean things were said, of staying up all night worrying if you made the right decision moving to the city for her new job, of letting him discipline the kids, of picking your battles, meeting halfway, letting things slide. In other words, when the going gets tough, remember that it's not you—or him—it's the dishes. Love isn't the problem—it's the business of love most of us need help with.

And for that, we need to dip into those scarce resources we mentioned earlier. We need to find the time, muster the energy, feel the love, weigh the costs of being flexible and the benefits of standing our ground.

This is where a little economic know-how comes in handy. By thinking like an economist, you can have a marriage that not only takes less work, but that feels like a *vacation* from work. The trick is to a) boost those precious resources, and b) allocate them more intelligently. Do that, and before you know it, you'll be on your way to a better return on your marriage.

We believe in economics because it doesn't discriminate between the sexes, between who's "right" and who's "wrong," who communicates better and who talks worse. It doesn't talk down to you or attempt to psychoanalyze. It doesn't care who won the last fight or whose turn it is to control the remote. Instead, it offers dispassionate, logical solutions to what can often seem like thorny, illogical, and highly emotional domestic disputes.

In this book, we'll show you how to apply basic economic principles to get the most out of your resources. Meaning: have more sex, wash fewer dishes, argue more effectively, have more sex, survive the lean years, negotiate more successfully, have more sex, and, believe it or not, get your spouse to do things he's never done before, like clean the gutters. Or listen.

WHY US?

Because we've spent the better part of the last decade toiling away in the trenches of *The Wall Street Journal* and *The New York Times,* where news about economics and business has been part of the air we breathe. Because we've covered financial meltdowns, crunched GDP data, pored through SEC filings, deconstructed jargony acronyms like TARP, RMBS, and ABS CDOs, and talked to some of the top dogs in finance and economics, including Tim Geithner, Hank Paulson, Lloyd Blankfein, and Buzz Aldrin (okay, so Buzz isn't a finance guy per se, but he went to the moon!).

And because we also, at a certain point, got married.

Which means we started grappling with the kinds of issues our married friends had long said they grappled with but we either didn't understand or smugly thought they should get over. Like how to find time for each other when you both work sixty hours a week. How to get along when one of you is pregnant and puking and the other one is . . . not. How to divide up the housework and bill paying without leaving blood on the floor. How to compromise when it's all his fault. How to keep being polite to your in-laws now that they're officially your in-laws. How to agree to disagree about what defines "too risky" when it comes to parenthood and motorcycles. How to keep the flame alive. How to give each other space. How to stop fighting in the car.

We wanted solutions.

HOW WE DID IT

We decided on a two-pronged approach: first economics, then love.

For economics, we hit the library, read the classics, maxed out our credit cards on Amazon, fell deep into the econosphere (who knew economists love to blog?), and boned up on the latest studies on everything from incentives to game theory to the art of the trade-off. We immersed ourselves in various schools of economic thought, including neoclassical, in which human beings are thought to act rationally, and behavioral, which borrows heavily from psychology and assumes we're not at all rational. We interviewed dozens of economists—some of them pretty famous—and squeezed them for all the wisdom they had, not only about their research, but about how to apply that research to marriage. They turned out to be a surprisingly romantic bunch, offering us advice like: Never let your own happiness outweigh that of your spouse. Always try to anticipate his next move before launching into a negotiation. Divide the housework not fifty/fifty, but according to who does what better. Don't be afraid to use incentives to get what you want. Be willing to lose an argument. Sometimes, go to bed angry.

Once we had a handle on the economics, we turned to love. We hired professionals to conduct our Exhaustive, Groundbreaking, and Very Expensive Marriage Survey, in which roughly one thousand people nationwide answered more than sixty probing questions about the highs and lows of married life. We asked them how they convince their partners to do things they don't feel like doing (answer: Have sex), why they have sex when they don't feel like it (answer: To get their partners to do things they don't feel like doing), whether they've gained or lost weight since they married (answer: Gained), how much they're saving (answer: Not enough)—and wish they were saving (answer: Much more)—for retirement.

Finally, we embarked on a coast-to-coast listening tour. Logging thousands of frequent-flier miles and countless hours in the car, we traveled the country in the name of research, talking ourselves into the living rooms of couples from New York to San Francisco, Minneapolis to Miami. We attended a weekend marriage workshop in

Seattle, where we questioned renowned experts John Gottman and Julie Schwartz Gottman about what makes relationships work (one answer: Overcoming "regrettable incidents"). We talked to bankers, doctors, coaches, writers, real-estate agents, comedians, lawyers, teachers, architects, chefs, engineers, English professors, construction workers, musicians, stay-at-home moms, and stay-at-home dads. We asked hundreds of complete strangers—as well as some close friends—to reveal intimate aspects of their private lives. And, with the help of a little food (and beer), they actually did!★

When it was all over, we were convinced: Economics is the surest route to marital bliss. For example, once you understand the concept of division of labor, you can solve your housework disputes once and for all. Feel like one or both of you has let yourself go lately, is maybe taking the other one for granted just a little bit? Moral hazard is the likely culprit. Problems sticking to your promises, planning for the long term? All a matter of making better intertemporal choices and then following through on them. The solution to circuitous arguments that seem to last all night: Stop being so loss-averse. And sex. Sex! One of married life's most persistent conundrums—merely a function of supply and demand.

The result of our efforts, we believe, is a relationship book unlike any other. *It's Not You, It's the Dishes* isn't squishy. Our approach doesn't require that you look each other in the eye until you weep tears of remorse. Or that you keep an anger log, a courage journal, or a feelings calendar. It's straightforward, no-nonsense, solutions based. It works. It's for anybody who wants a stronger, happier, more fun marriage and, while they're at it, wouldn't mind learning a few things

---

★Surefire ways to get people to tell you about their marriages: 1) beer; 2) pizza; 3) sushi; 4) talk to each partner separately; 5) ask how they met and what they liked about each other; 6) offer prizes.

about negative sloping demand curves and nerdy guys named Schumpeter.

A NOTE ON METHODOLOGY

Each of the case studies we present in the following chapters is real. Names and dates and identifying details, however, might not be. That's because hundreds of real-life people were kind enough to share some remarkably intimate information with us, and since we didn't want to be responsible for a wave of divorces or torched friendships, we promised them anonymity. Our own spouses, on the other hand, were promised no such thing, and they do make brief appearances in the chapters that follow. But being loyal practitioners of what we call "spousonomics," each did a cost-benefit analysis and concluded that the benefit of keeping us happy (translation: doing what it took to help us write our book) far outweighed the cost of keeping their idiosyncrasies (translation: lovable qualities) private.

It's Not You,
It's the Dishes

1

DIVISION OF LABOR

Or, Why You Should Do the Dishes

THE PRINCIPLE, PART ONE

Who should do what?

It's one of the first questions Fortune 500 companies, governments, and gas stations have to answer if they plan on getting anything accomplished.

Consider your local Hess station. It wouldn't exist without the truck drivers who delivered the concrete that was then poured and shaped into a foundation by a team of construction workers—not to be confused with the other team of construction workers who built the quickie mart, which is now staffed by a cashier in a green vest who sells the Ho Hos that were brought by the Hostess man with the "FBI: Female Body Inspector" T-shirt. There's the guy who fills the underground tanks with gas, and the guy who pumps that gas into your car. Don't forget the crane operator who lifts the number changer high up to the glowing Hess sign to swap out the number 7 next to "Premium" for a number *8* so that when you drive up, you can decide whether you want to spend $3.08 for a gallon of top-notch petroleum.

Every person has his or her job to do in order to create the final product: a functioning—and, if Hess is lucky, a prosperous—gas station. The fuel-pumping guy can't drop his hose and start delivering fuel, just as the number changer can't operate the crane without risking tearing a giant hole in the roof of the quickie mart, where the cashier sits, printing out lotto tickets and offering customers directions to the nearest IHOP.

This is what's called "division of labor," and it's what makes economies function.

Take a look around you. Every piece of furniture in your house, the boneless chicken breasts you eat for dinner, the car you drive, and the clothes on your back—they all owe their existence to a division of labor. Even the book you have in your hands right now came into being thanks to loggers, ink makers, printing press operators, glue producers, art directors, nagging editors, gifted writers, guys in suits who sign checks, and a group of deep-pocketed German publishers who pay the salaries of the suit-wearing check signers. There's no way those gifted writers could fell a tree or pay anyone's salary, much less their own. And maybe the ink makers could one day learn the art of glue producing, but it wouldn't happen overnight, and the glue quality would probably never be the same, and . . . well, you get the idea.

That businesses thrive when employees have specialized tasks is hardly a novel idea. It probably dates back to the cavemen, when certain hunters were prized for their good aim and others were aces at skinning and filleting bison. But in more recent times, the concept is often credited to Adam Smith, the father of modern economics.

In 1776, Smith published his now seminal work, *An Inquiry into the Nature and Causes of the Wealth of Nations.* Among the many insights that to this day form the basis of economic theory, Smith argued that the secret to a nation's wealth wasn't money, but labor, and specifically, a division of labor based on specialization.

To prove his point, he used the example of a pin factory, saying that

Adam Smith: An Extremely Smart Guy
You Should Know About

 Born 1723, Scotland. Philosopher, professor, private tutor, lifelong bachelor. Lived with his mother. Enjoyed talking to himself. Coined the term "invisible hand" to explain how markets are naturally efficient and self-regulating. Despite never having married, Smith was something of a Dr. Phil of his day, espousing untold insights into the often paradoxical nature of love. He believed, for example, that we are engaged in an eternal struggle between our passions on one side and a dispassionate "impartial spectator" on the other. He also believed we are driven by both self-interest and selflessness, or the urge to improve our own lives while also doing good for others. Kind of like when you want to stop on the way home to pick up flowers for your spouse but instead you stay late at the office to impress your boss.

many more pins could be made in a day if each of eighteen specialized pin-making tasks was assigned to specific workers, rather than each worker making an entire pin from start to finish. Ten workers, he said, could produce forty-eight thousand pins a day if they specialized, versus perhaps just ten pins without specialization: "One man draws out the wire, another straights it, a third cuts it, a fourth points it, a fifth grinds it at the top for receiving the head." And so on.

Seems evident now, at a time when many of us take specialization for granted, when we buy iPods in Kansas that were assembled in China with parts made in Japan and the Philippines, when we work in offices where some people are in charge of hanging art on the walls and others unclog toilets. But until Adam Smith put quill to parchment, no one had quite articulated the benefits of dividing labor into its component parts or made such a compelling argument for running the world this way.

THE PRINCIPLE, PART TWO

Now back to the question of who should do what. Division of labor is only part of the answer. It tells us that no one person should do everything and that each person should have a specialty. But it doesn't say anything about *how* we go about deciding who's best suited to hanging art or pumping gas, or which country should make the iPod's display screen and which the hard drive. For some ideas on that front, we turn to British economist David Ricardo, who, four decades after Smith's *Wealth of Nations,* came up with a theory called "comparative advantage."

The theory of comparative advantage says that it's not efficient for you to take on every single task you're good at, only on those tasks you're *relatively better* at compared with other tasks. (See: Michael Jordan's short-lived baseball career.) Or, as economists would put it, what matters is not your *absolute* ability to produce goods, but your ability to produce one good *relative* to another. Those are the things in which you have the comparative advantage.

Comparative advantage is the foundation of free trade. The idea is that instead of each country making everything it needs for its people, it should specialize in what it produces relatively better and then trade these goods and services with other countries. Countries develop specializations for any number of reasons. They might have control over scarce resources, like Saudi Arabia with oil. They might have millions of people willing to make flat-screen TVs for a pittance, as China does. They might have unique weather patterns, as Spain does, with its windy plains and burgeoning wind-turbine industry. Or they might be in the middle of nowhere: New Zealand, for example, saw a spike in tourism after the September 11 attacks, when travelers were looking for destinations terrorists would never think to go.

For David Ricardo, sitting in his Gloucestershire estate and ruminating on the notion of comparative advantage back in 1817, wind turbines and flat-screen TVs were the stuff of science fiction. Ricardo's theory was founded on the much more rustic example of England and Portugal trading wine and cloth. Ricardo said that even if Portugal could make both wine and cloth more quickly than England could, it was still in Portugal's interest to specialize in the one good it was *relatively* better at and trade with England for the other.

Pay attention, because we're going to tell you exactly how and why it pays to trade. First, take a look at the (hypothetical) amount of time it takes England and Portugal to produce one unit each of wine and knickers (cloth) when they do it all themselves and don't trade.

WITHOUT TRADE

Product	Portugal	England
1 pair of knickers	20 minutes	30 minutes
1 bottle of wine	10 minutes	60 minutes
Total time	30 minutes	90 minutes

Given how much faster Portugal is at making wine and knickers, you'd think Portugal should make everything itself, right? Wrong.

Here's why:

Going it alone, Portugal spends half an hour making a bottle of wine and a pair of knickers and England spends ninety minutes doing the same.

Let's say they decide to trade. Portugal makes two bottles of wine, since it's relatively faster at wine than at knicker making, what with all the grapes growing everywhere. England makes two pairs of knickers, since it clearly has more sheep than vineyards. Then they trade—one pair of knickers for one bottle of wine . . . and suddenly Portugal's got one of each for only twenty minutes of work. England had to put in only sixty minutes of work instead of ninety.

WITH TRADE

Product	Portugal	England
2 pairs of knickers	n/a	60 minutes
2 bottles of wine	20 minutes	n/a
Total time after trade	**20 minutes**	**60 minutes**

It's like magic. Only it's not magic. It's math. Very, very simple math, we concede—math that doesn't take into account all the other things the two countries make or the prices they could charge for their goods on the open market. It's also true that England's workers still wind up working longer hours compared with Portugal's workers for the same rewards, but it's undeniable that they've saved time *relative* to their pretrading workloads.

Ricardo's model illustrates a universal truth: There are great rewards to be had from trading smartly and great wastes of time and energy from trying to do everything yourself, or even from splitting things in half.

Which is what takes us to the topic you've probably been waiting for: your marriage. Think of your marriage as a business comprising two partners. You're not only business partners in the sense that you work together for the good of your company, you're also trading partners who exchange services, often in the form of household chores. How should you decide who does what? Who should specialize in shopping for orange juice and who in cleaning windows? Who should provide clothes that are freshly laundered and folded, and who should put food on the table at dinnertime? We all wish these kinds of questions had easy answers, yet household labor issues are often the most divisive that couples face. They don't have to be. Economics offers clear solutions. You're about to meet three couples, each of whom were nearly undone by all sorts of seemingly inane duties that they were dividing in all the wrong ways.

One couple, thinking that a fifty/fifty split was the way to go, made the mistake of having no specializations at all. Another couple miscalculated what their comparative advantages were, and a third couple discovered that specializations aren't static and can sometimes change as the marriage itself changes.

CASE STUDY #1

The Players: Eric and Nancy

Eric and Nancy had never heard of David Ricardo when they fell in love and decided to merge as lifelong trading partners. They weren't familiar with the theory of comparative advantage, and if it came up at a dinner party—which, frankly, it never did—their eyes would very likely have glazed over. Eric was a photographer for glossy cooking magazines, and Nancy designed a line of teen clothing for one of those apparel chains that have an outpost at every mall in America. They were more artsy than economicsy.

Yet economics—bad economics—dominated their lives. Without knowing it, they'd become a case study in how a bad division of labor can harm an otherwise well-matched couple. That's because Eric and Nancy split the work not on the basis of who did which job best, but on what seemed fair. And fair, in their view, was a strict fifty/fifty split.

They divided *everything* in half. They had a joint checking account into which their roughly equivalent salaries were deposited directly and from which they transferred the same allowances every month into their individual checking accounts to spend as they pleased. They had a mutt named Moo Shoo whom they took turns walking every other morning. When Eric cooked, Nancy cleaned. When Nancy cooked, Eric cleaned. They rotated laundry, bill paying, in-law calling, trash days. Eric was in charge of cleaning the upstairs bathroom. Nancy handled the downstairs.

On the outside, Eric and Nancy's system made them seem like the perfect modern couple. Their friends marveled at how they defied stereotypes: *Eric knows how to use a Swiffer! Nancy gives him so much space! He's so accommodating! She goes to Home Depot without him!*

There was only one kink: Eric and Nancy weren't happy.

The Problem: The Fifty/Fifty Marriage

Here's a puzzler: Think of a successful business whose employees work the exact same hours and do the exact same amount of work for the exact same pay.

Still thinking?

That's because, outside of assembly lines, there aren't many.

From your grocery store to your money manager's office to the website you get your news from, businesses are organized around specialization. Employees have distinct tasks that require different sorts of expertise and command higher or lower salaries. Bond traders know the bond market inside and out, stock traders are more proficient in stocks. There are people who sell the ads that appear on *The Wall Street Journal*'s website and people who write the stories, and neither group knows very much about what the other does all day.

Imagine what would happen if those ad guys started spending half their time writing articles and reporters spent half their time selling ads—all in the name of fairness. It would be a disaster.

The specialization model also applies to the broader economy. Some countries grow bananas, some produce cars, some make tank tops.

The same logic applies to marriage. In insisting on a "fair" division of labor, Eric and Nancy had created a monster. For all their focus on fifty/fifty, some days things could feel a little *too* egalitarian.

Like when the laundry hamper would overflow with dirty clothes and an exhausted Nancy would say to Eric, who was busy shopping for old camera equipment online, "I did the laundry last time—it's your turn."

Or when Eric, chopping onions for a lamb tagine, saw Nancy watching *Law & Order* and thought, "Wait a minute, why am I spending all this time on a fancy meal when all she ever makes is mac and cheese?"

Or the time Nancy's parents were coming for dinner and she and Eric spent the day arguing over whether Eric cleaning his office really counted as "housework" as much as Nancy mopping all the floors—since, said Nancy, his office wasn't a "communal living area."

This was life at Eric and Nancy's house. Each one constantly monitoring the other's workload, keeping mental bar graphs of who had done more and who had fallen behind, sounding the unfairness alarm whenever it seemed the split was starting to shift into the—gasp!—sixty/forty range. "Everything was a debate," said Nancy. "We spent so much time fighting over who was doing more and who needed to pick up the slack, it's amazing we got anything done at all."

"It got to the point where if I was dusting and Nancy was painting her nails, I'd drop the duster and check my email just so I didn't end up doing more than her," said Eric.

They posted two chore logs outside the kitchen and checked them frequently to ensure no one was cutting corners.

As you can see in the "basic chore log" below created by Nancy, even opening the mail counted as a chore. In fact, once Nancy realized how much time she was spending on the mail, she decided it was only fair to hand off making the bed to Eric.

Not to be outdone, Eric created an "advanced chore log" that included onetime jobs. These tended to be more time-consuming and intensive. Eric thought he was being especially clever when he delineated his tasks into "easy," "harder," and "pain in the butt," lest Nancy think that he was getting away with all the simple stuff.

Eric and Nancy knew on some level that they could be, to put it kindly, "petty" about the housework, but their paranoia invariably got the best of them. Nancy worried about becoming the stereotypical

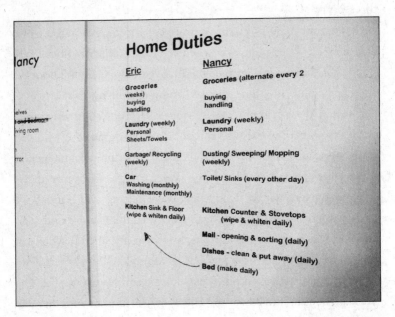

Figure 1: Basic Chore Log

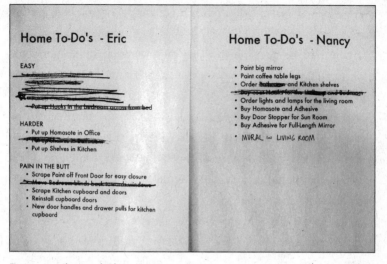

Figure 2: Advanced Chore Log

"housewife" who did everything for her husband—the very role she'd watched her mother play. And what did it get her mother? A bad back and a husband who never said thanks.

Eric worried about being taken for granted, too. He had his own baggage—old girlfriends who took advantage of his easygoing disposition and got him to cater to their every whim. Nancy wasn't like that, but baggage was baggage, and Eric was still on guard.

Yet by keeping score constantly, Eric and Nancy were becoming the worst of themselves. They were turning into the Bickersons.

The scorekeeping wasn't the only problem with fifty/fifty. There was also the fact that they didn't like the same jobs equally. Eric, for example, hated walking the dog. What was grosser than picking up dog poop? Nancy found walking the dog meditative, a chance to relax. When it came to laundry, Eric liked his whites and darks separated. Nancy threw everything in together, which deeply annoyed Eric.

So why was Nancy still doing laundry and Eric still walking the dog?

If you put the question to them, they wouldn't have a good answer. In fact, we did put the question to them, and here's what they said:

Nancy: "Eric isn't open to the idea that walking the dog can be pleasant. Also, he thinks if he complains about it enough, I'll give in and do it all myself. Not gonna happen. I just find it interesting that he thinks he should be able to enjoy the rewards of dog ownership without doing any of the work."

Eric: "It would take Nancy two extra minutes to separate the laundry. Two minutes! But no. She won't do it. It's like she's *trying* to get me to do the laundry myself. No way I'm falling for that."

Eric and Nancy had once seen themselves as "partners"—sharing a life, merging their worlds, creating a strong union. But over time, they weren't acting like partners, they were acting like bookkeepers. And that's just bad economics.

The Solution: Specialization and Comparative Advantage

Eric and Nancy needed to go back to the economic roots of marriage. For centuries, marriage thrived thanks to specialization. Husbands and wives did what each had the perceived comparative advantage in. Husbands specialized in selling encyclopedias and drinking Negronis. Wives specialized in casseroles and sublimated rage. How could either one argue about whose turn it was to do the laundry when the husband was out all day closing deals and wouldn't know a washboard from a checkers board?

In the past fifty years, as the market economy changed, so did the institution of marriage. Technological innovations like washing machines meant women didn't have to spend whole days doing laundry.

Readily available clothes at malls made sewing redundant. Frozen dinners and microwaves meant quicker, easier meals. Women entered the workforce en masse, while men were forced to step it up at home, make dinner for themselves occasionally, and learn how to change diapers.

Marriage, as the economists Betsey Stevenson and Justin Wolfers put it, began to shift from "a forum for shared production to shared consumption." Whereas a man and a woman used to join their lives together because they needed to, now they join together because they want to. "Modern marriage is about love and companionship," write Stevenson and Wolfers. "Most things in life are simply better shared with another person: This ranges from the simple pleasures such as enjoying a movie or a hobby together, to shared social ties such as attending the same church, and finally, to the joint project of bringing up children. Returning to the language of economics, the key today is consumption complementarities—activities that are not only enjoyable, but are more enjoyable when shared with a spouse."

So we get married because it's fun. And it is! Sometimes. But there's still plenty of work to do—and the problem is, there's no longer a clear delineation between jobs. Who takes care of the house, the kids, the bills, the entire business of the marriage—the who does what—has become a giant question mark. For all the progress we've made, too many of us are like Eric and Nancy, still bickering over who should do the dishes.

If arguing over chores seems petty to you, consider this: In 2007, the Pew Research Center conducted a survey that asked, "What makes marriage work?" The number one answer was faithfulness, followed by sex. Makes sense. But third, ahead of everything else, including kids, money, and religion: sharing household chores.

Other research backs this up. According to a 2009 survey of working women by the Boston Consulting Group, the second most common thing people argue about with their partners is household chores. That's behind money but ahead of sex, work, and raising kids. In our own Exhaustive, Groundbreaking, and Very Expensive Marriage Survey, 73 percent of women said they did more than 50 percent of the housework, whereas only 40 percent of men said they did more than half the housework (you have to at least give the men credit for honesty). Motivations for doing more than their share also differed: The most common reason cited by women was, "If I don't do it, it won't get done," while the most common reason for men was, "It makes me feel like a good partner."

Slightly disturbing that women tend to have a martyr complex about it, while men just want to be helpful, but whatever. The point is, Eric and Nancy weren't the only couple in America keeping score. And, hopefully, they're not the only couple that came up with a solution.

"If we were ever going to get along," Eric told us, "I knew we'd have to stop keeping score." To do so, they adopted one of the oldest ideas in economics: dividing things up by comparative advantage.

Like two countries, two married people also exchange goods and services, and each also brings to the table a different set of abilities and interests. By figuring out which of them has the comparative advantage in a range of tasks, from dishes to dog walking to bulb planting, Eric and Nancy could then decide who would specialize in what. And maybe, just maybe, they could reach détente.

As an example, Nancy was better and faster at both doing the dishes and tidying up around the house. She was focused and had an *I Dream of Jeannie* knack for finishing things in the blink of an eye. Nancy wasn't particularly proud of these attributes, but she knew she had them. And so did Eric. In econ-speak, Nancy had an absolute advantage in both dishes and tidying.

Coincidentally, the time it took Eric and Nancy to do each of these tasks was remarkably similar to the time we said it takes Portugal and England to make wine and knickers. Imagine that.

DAILY TIME INVESTMENTS

Task	Nancy	Eric
Dishes	20 minutes	30 minutes
Tidying	10 minutes	60 minutes
Total time	**30 minutes**	**90 minutes**

WEEKLY TOTALS

Task, Frequency*	Nancy	Eric
3 nights dishes	60 minutes	90 minutes
3 nights tidying	30 minutes	180 minutes
Total time	**90 minutes**	**270 minutes**

* Assumes Sundays are housework holidays.

Given how much faster Nancy is at doing dishes and tidying, chores that typically get done six days a week in her house, does it make sense for her and Eric to split those two chores? Not really, but neither does it make sense for Nancy to do it all while Eric stares at the ceiling.

What does make sense is a system based on comparative advantage. And Nancy has the comparative advantage in tidying, while Eric has the comparative advantage in dishes.

If instead of splitting each job, they specialize, Nancy would tidy up six nights a week and Eric would do the dishes. It would look something like this:

COMPARATIVE ADVANTAGE TRADING SYSTEM

Task, Frequency	Nancy	Eric
6 nights of dishes	n/a	180 minutes
6 nights of tidying	60 minutes	n/a
Total time	**60 minutes**	**180 minutes**

In a week's time, Nancy has saved herself thirty minutes and Eric has saved ninety minutes. The new system isn't "fair," according to their old definition of fairness, because technically, Eric is spending more time working than Nancy is. But was the old fifty/fifty system, when Eric was spending three hours more than Nancy on this stuff, any "fairer"? Eric and Nancy had simply assumed the old system was fair because neither one got stuck doing everything. In reality, they were losing months of their lives they could never get back.

"The magic of comparative advantage is that everyone has a comparative advantage at producing something," says economist Lauren F. Landsburg. "The upshot is quite extraordinary: Everyone stands to gain from trade. Even those who are disadvantaged at every task still have something valuable to offer."

In econ-speak, the extra total time Nancy and Eric now have—120 minutes, or 2 hours—represents the couple's collective gains from specialization, which can be illustrated with the handy graph. A "labor vs. leisure" graph typically illustrates a basic economic trade-off: The more you work (labor), the more money you make, but the less free time (leisure) you have. Conversely, the more you sit back and relax, the less time you have to dedicate to work and the less money you make. Simple. Obvious. Sublime.

Traditionally, in a graph like this, the y-axis (the vertical line) would show the amount of money you're making from your labor, and the x-axis (the horizontal line) would give you the amount of free time

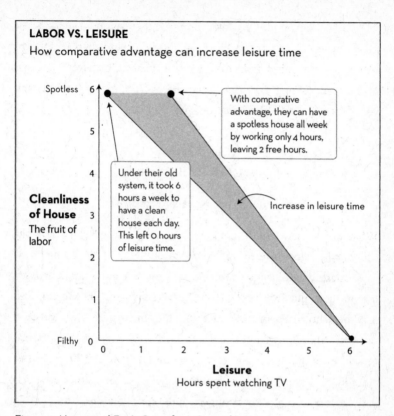

LABOR VS. LEISURE

How comparative advantage can increase leisure time

With comparative advantage, they can have a spotless house all week by working only 4 hours, leaving 2 free hours.

Under their old system, it took 6 hours a week to have a clean house each day. This left 0 hours of leisure time.

Increase in leisure time

Cleanliness of House
The fruit of labor

Spotless 6
5
4
3
2
1
Filthy 0

Leisure
Hours spent watching TV

Figure 3: Nancy and Eric's Gains from Specialization

you have. In our example, the labor is getting a clean house each week (well, not a totally spotless house, but one that's tidy and has clean dishes), and the leisure is Eric and Nancy's free time. The more time they spend cleaning, the less time they have to watch TV.

Without comparative advantage, it takes every minute of Eric and Nancy's free time to have a spotless house six days a week, leaving them with zero TV time. If they work enough to have a fairly clean house, they'll have two hours left over to watch TV. Fine.

But if they decide to use comparative advantage, it takes two fewer hours to have a spotless house, leaving them extra time to watch TV.

And keep in mind: TV is only one way they can use their gains—meaning all that extra time. They can also do other things they enjoy, like play Mastermind, sit in the backyard at sunset, or have sex. Moral of the story: Doing the dishes every night leads to more sex. Thank you, David Ricardo of Gloucestershire!

CASE STUDY #2

The Players: Nora and Andrew

What happens when a couple's situation changes and a well-calibrated comparative advantage system suddenly stops working?

Kids are what changed the equation for Nora and Andrew. They met in their mid-twenties when they were living in Philadelphia and had the whole "opposites attract" thing going. Andrew was born in western Pennsylvania and had never lived outside the state. Nora had moved every few years as a child, spending part of her life overseas. Andrew was good with his hands, watched Eagles games at sports bars, and had a tight-knit group of high school buddies he still hung out with every weekend. Nora spoke French and German, her friends were artists or unemployed or both, and she thought the Eagles were a baseball team.

They lived on the same block, and Andrew would spot Nora at the corner deli on weekday mornings picking up coffee and the paper. He thought she was cute and started saying hi to her, then expanded to discussions about the weather, until finally he asked her out.

On one of their first dates, Andrew asked Nora what she liked to do with her friends. She said they spent a lot of time at cafés ("This was in the early nineties," she said, "pre-Starbucks"), and she was shocked, yet charmed, when he said he'd never been to a café but would like to go to one with her someday.

"At first I was like, 'Where did this guy *come* from?' " Nora said. "But the way he was honest about it, not at all self-conscious, got my attention. We had such different life experiences, but Andrew never let himself be defined by his experiences—he's a naturally curious person." Over time, what really sealed the deal for Nora was that it was clear Andrew would make a great dad. "I saw him play with his nephews and he was so much fun with them," she said. "He was engaged. He'd get out in the middle of the room and wrestle with them. I loved that."

Andrew also saw in Nora a great mother who, he hoped, would one day be as devoted to their kids as his mom had been with him and his siblings. "Nora had this independent streak that I admired, but she wasn't extreme about it," he said. "She also wanted to start a family and be a part of something bigger than herself."

For the first three years of their marriage, they both worked outside the home—he as an airline analyst and she as a Web developer. At home, they'd created a system for dividing up the labor that worked—it took into account their skills and also their interests, a system very much built around the ideas of comparative advantage.

For example, Nora did the food shopping because she was more opinionated about what they bought, while Andrew kept the floors swept and the appliances dusted, jobs that played into his obsession with details. Nora took care of their social plans, and Andrew kept in touch with both sets of parents. Some things tended to be split down traditional gender lines, with Andrew taking out the trash, doing the recycling, and fixing stuff that broke and Nora doing the laundry, cleaning the bathrooms, and planting flowers in the window boxes.

During these years—years that Nora calls the "glory days"—they were committed city people, walking or biking to work, enjoying a car-free, kid-free, anti-suburban life. If they ran out of coffee or craved late-night pints of Häagen-Dazs, they could run downstairs to the deli, the same deli where Andrew had first spied Nora. But when Nora got pregnant, they started to see the city differently. Hiking up three flights of stairs to get to their cramped apartment no longer seemed romantic. The prospect of pushing a stroller up and down cobblestone streets also lacked charm. The choice of free inner-city schools or break-the-bank private schools was one they hoped never to face. Yes, they wanted to expose their kids to a vibrant city life, but they didn't want to exhaust or bankrupt themselves in the process.

So finally they did the thing that people do—six months before Nora gave birth, they moved to the suburbs. They found a hundred-year-old fixer-upper on the Main Line and set about fixing it up. Even though she was getting more pregnant and physically uncomfortable every day, Nora said, renovating the house was one of the most satisfying things she's ever done.

Then the baby came, followed two years later by twins. Nora decided to stop working full-time and to assume most of the responsibility for taking care of the kids. Andrew's job paid enough for them to live well on, and he fully supported his kids being raised by their mom instead of a nanny.

But what Andrew and Nora didn't consider was whether Nora had the comparative advantage in child rearing, in terms of ability, patience, and enjoyment. The decision was fueled more by factors like money (Andrew's job paid more than Nora's, so giving it up would come at a greater cost to the family than Nora giving up hers) and social norms: Both assumed, because of the way they were brought up, that moms were naturally better suited to child rearing than dads.

Further complicating things was that they never realized that Nora would end up assuming many of the household tasks Andrew used to do, simply by dint of being home more. Or that the amount of work around the house would quintuple. They had assigned new specializations based mostly on speculation.

IN PLAIN ENGLISH:

Speculation

A bad idea. In finance, people who "speculate" are typically people who want to make a quick profit. (Silly Bandz are hot? Let's buy a hundred thousand!) The problem with speculating is that it usually doesn't involve a ton of research, or forward-looking thinking, or even facts. It involves assumptions—optimistic assumptions.

Marriage is one of the biggest speculative ventures around. You have no good reason to think it'll pay off—roughly half of all marriages don't—but you buy into it anyway, hoping, assuming, betting the odds that you're one of the 50 percent for whom it will pay off. But here's the rub: The only way you stand a chance of success is if you treat your marriage like a long-term investment, sticking it out when the going gets tough, profits stagnate, and shareholders revolt.

"Every friend of mine who stayed home with the kids said housework became an enormous source of friction with their husbands because the balance of power shifted," said Nora. "Same with us. Andrew earned the paycheck, he paid the mortgage. Even though he never said anything overtly, the understanding seemed to be that since I was home, I'd do the housework."

In theory, Nora was fine with this. In practice, tensions started brewing immediately. She could usually get everything done, but all it took was one sick kid or one school holiday and Nora's finely calibrated system came toppling down. She would demand help from Andrew the minute he walked in the door. "I became my worst nagging self," she said.

Nora said there was too much on her plate, and none of it felt hugely rewarding. Since she had to feed the kids before Andrew got home from work at seven, she found herself making two dinners a night: one for the kids and one for the adults. Since she did all the kids' laundry anyway, she threw in hers and Andrew's, too—and then folded it and then put it away. She was now shopping for five, making more social plans for the kids than she ever dreamed possible, putting things away and then putting them away again when they reappeared, wiping mud off sneakers, fielding calls from her parents and in-laws, and even sewing missing buttons. Sewing buttons—what was this, 1952?

The Problem: Market Failure

The system Nora and Andrew had set up without actually discussing it first was this: The value of Nora's caring for the kids and taking care of the home was equal to the value of Andrew's paycheck. He worked outside the home in exchange for her working inside, and vice versa.*

But as Nora grew more resentful that so much stuff was falling in her lap—and really, let's not pretend her and Andrew's jobs were remotely equal—their system of exchanging goods and services (their market) was on the brink of collapse. Or, in econ-speak: Their market appeared to be failing. One sign of market failure: Nora was almost always in a bad mood, almost always her "worst nagging self."

In the real world, when markets appear to have failed, economists sometimes say don't blame the market, blame the *lack* of a market.

Steven Landsburg, an economist at the University of Rochester, gives the example of factories that pollute. Left to the free market, he says, factory owners will pollute the air, harming the environment and

---

*This is an admittedly simplified summation of a deep and complex, loving and committed relationship between two three-dimensional people. But it's also true.

Ten Signs of a Marriage Market Failure

- Burned-out kitchen lightbulbs that go unreplaced for six weeks.
- Military push-ups sound better than sex.
- A bottle of wine. Per person. Per night.
- A raised bump in the middle of the bed and sheets that haven't been washed since last obligatory lovemaking session, seven months ago.
- Indecision, especially around what to have for dinner, what to do Friday night, whether to go to bed at nine thirty or nine forty-five.
- Love handles, man hooters, braidable pubic hair.
- Eagerness to go to the dentist—on a Saturday.
- Another dive into *The Brothers Karamazov* to fend off romantic advances.
- Newfound interest in woodworking.
- Soul death.

the people living nearby. But is that a failure of the free market or a failure to *create* a market for air? If there's no market for air, you can't charge a fee for polluting it, which means there's no incentive for factory owners to use clean-burning fuel. Create a market for air, charge for polluting that air, and factory owners will have an incentive either to not pollute or to pay for the privilege of polluting. "Inefficiencies arise from missing markets," writes Landsburg. "Wherever there is an inefficiency, it is a good bet that a missing market is lurking (or more precisely, failing to lurk) in the background."

In Nora and Andrew's marriage, as in many marriages, there was no real market for child rearing. Unlike the chores they had so seamlessly placed values on and exchanged during their solo years, the endless kid-related work was never discussed or evaluated. And because of that, their division of labor no longer made sense.

The Solution: A More Efficient Market

Nora and Andrew had options. One, Nora could go back to work and they could hire a nanny. Two, Nora could go back to work and Andrew could stay home with the kids. Three, Nora could go back to work part-time, Andrew could do the same, and they could share the child rearing. All those options, however, would mean less disposable income. And neither of them liked that prospect one bit.

A fourth—and, we think, a better—option was to stick to their roles but to create a market, or more than one market, for some specific tasks that went into Nora's job. That required assigning a value to these tasks and then essentially trading with Andrew for things of similar value. For example, Nora said, a week of doing the food shopping for five, cooking for five, and doing the laundry for five was worth at least one night of going to the movies and hanging out with friends—two things she never got to do anymore. Andrew could come home early one night and she could take the night off.

"I had to get better at saying what I needed," said Nora. "And when I thought about it, what I needed wasn't actually that much. It was just, 'Hey Andrew, Saturday I'm seeing so-and-so and you have to be home.'"

That was the price she felt comfortable charging Andrew for her services as head of household chores. As it happened, that price was one that Andrew was more than happy to pay. The exchange helped them become a more efficient team.

When we say efficient, by the way, we're talking about a special kind of economic efficiency called "Pareto efficiency," and it's slightly different from the way most people think of the word. A Pareto-efficient situation is one in which nobody can be made better off

Vilfredo Pareto: He Loved His Cats

 Pareto efficiency is named for the late-nineteenth-century Italian economist Vilfredo Pareto. He helped pioneer the field of microeconomics, but he was far less precocious when it came to love. His first wife dumped him for their cook. He and his second wife shared a villa with more than two dozen Angora cats. It wasn't his wife who inspired his genius, but the cats, who would sit on his shoulders while he worked.

without somebody else being made worse off. It may not be perfect, but it's as perfect as it can be under the circumstances. If it's possible for one party to become happier without making the other party any less happy, then the situation is not yet Pareto-efficient.

Think of pizza. We're sharing a large pie that we decide to split in half: four slices each. After I eat three of my slices, I'm stuffed. You eat your four and you're still hungry. Should I give you my extra slice? If I don't, you'll be hungry, and I'll be no more satisfied than I already am. On paper, holding on to my slice is totally fair, since we're staying true to the original fifty/fifty agreement. But it's not efficient. That's because there's an option to make you happier without making me any less happy—the option to give you my extra slice. When I give you that slice, we've achieved Pareto efficiency.

Too often, couples divide their labor without regard to this kind of efficiency. They get wedded to one system, even when there are simple ways to change it so that one or both of them are happier without making a dent in the other's happiness.

10 Things I Can Do for You That Won't Make Me Any Worse Off—AKA, A Pareto-Efficient Marriage*

Paula came up with this list as an early Valentine for her husband:

1. Help with garbage night.
2. Join you in the 30-day meditation challenge.
3. Not remind you when you have to make up a work shift at the food co-op.
4. Use my Petzl head lamp when I'm reading in bed and you're already asleep.
5. Work on my tone of voice when I'm frustrated.
6. Pick my battles.
7. Entertain the notion that my way isn't the only way.
8. Try again to make braised pork shoulder.
9. Give Sonny & the Sunsets another chance.
10. Let things go.

*We're using the term Pareto-efficient loosely, so apologies to all you economists. Let's just say that if there are things you can do to make your partner happier—and it doesn't actually make you any worse off (and really, what makes you *that* worse off?)—then your marriage isn't yet Pareto-efficient.

Nora and Andrew were stuck in just such a system. As a result, Nora felt overworked and resentful, and Andrew felt frustrated and flummoxed by Nora's put-upon-ness.

"I always wanted to work with her to fix things, I just had no idea what she wanted. One minute she wanted me to put a kid to bed, and the next she wanted me to get out of the room and let her do it," Andrew told us. "Which is it, sister?"

For Nora, the answer had nothing to do with putting any one kid to bed and everything to do with getting more time for herself. "As long as I'm the one home, it's never going to be fifty/fifty," Nora conceded. "But it can still *feel* fair."

Life need not be a fifty/fifty split for each person to be happy. It could be sixty/forty, or seventy/thirty, or even ninety-nine/one, depending on the people, the situation, and the willingness to put away the calculator and give and take based on what really works best rather than what we think *should* work best.

In the fraught world of housework, looking for Pareto efficiencies is another way to redivide the labor and live happily ever after (at least until the next time life throws you a curveball—or another kid). Nora and Andrew, like Eric and Nancy, had achieved every economist's dream: They created new resources—in this case, time for Nora and peace in the house—out of apparent scarcity.

CASE STUDY #3

The Players: Sam and Ashley

Sam and Ashley were best friends for five years before they started officially dating. "It was very *When Harry Met Sally,*" said Ashley.

Within a few months, they were already talking about marriage. Why bother waiting, they figured, since they knew each other so well already? They went shopping together and bought an engagement ring with two wedding rings to match. Ashley suggested they attend a premarital counseling workshop to get a few tips. Both she and Sam didn't expect married life would be anything more than an extension of their long friendship and their brief courtship, but it couldn't hurt to get some pointers from the experts.

The workshop turned out to be useless—"a total waste of time," Sam said. The last hour of the workshop was the most painful, since that's when they failed their "compatibility test." The instructor said they each came from such dysfunctional families that they were unlikely to have successful families of their own, and that getting married was probably a bad idea unless they were willing to immerse themselves in years of counseling first.

Ashley and Sam got married a week later in a small ceremony in their friend's backyard.

Though she'd always heard the first year would be the hardest, Ashley said it was the opposite: "It was bliss. It was like having a slumber party every night with your favorite person." She can remember only one fight their first year as a married couple, and she can't even remember what it was about, though it might have involved one of them throwing a shoe, the other storming out, and then both of them coming back together to hug and kiss and apologize for causing the other person an ounce of unhappiness. Mostly they did what they'd always done together: go out to hear live music, linger at dinner parties, make pasta, take road trips, scour estate sales, and have sex a few times a week.

The second year: not so smooth. Neither one of them knew for sure how it all unraveled, but they started picking fights over small things, like the fact that Sam was always running late, disrespectful of other people's (namely Ashley's) time. Ashley would snap at Sam when he didn't come home from work until after eight p.m., and he'd tell her he didn't have a choice in the matter—it was *work*. "You always have a choice," Ashley would say. "And your choice is work over me." But the worst part for Ashley was how lazy Sam had gotten about the little things: He left his clothes strewn all over the bedroom; he didn't clean his breakfast dishes; he never glanced at a bill; he left the car littered with empty soda cans and potato-chip bags; and it never occurred to him that a full laundry hamper was a cue to, like, do the freaking laundry.

Sam had his share of gripes, too. Ashley was too tightly wound; she needed to "loosen up" and stop riding him about everything. Since when did she care so much about a few dishes in the sink or how neat the car was? He said she never gave him credit for all the stuff he *did* do—like mow their stupid lawn every week even though he hated lawn mowing, change the oil in the car (did Ashley even *know* the car required oil to run?), and routinely stop at the supermarket on his way home to pick up stuff for dinner. And who got up on Sunday mornings to make pancakes while *someone* slept in?

Sam and Ashley had nothing in common with our fifty/fifty couple Eric and Nancy except in one regard: They, too, had become the Bickersons.

Desperate, Ashley turned back to counseling. She signed them up for a thirteen-week workshop offered by the very same group that had warned them they'd fail as a married couple.

Which was why Sam was amazed when Ashley asked him to go. He had zero interest, not only because he'd sworn off those people after the first experience, but because he didn't want to argue about the fact that they were arguing. But then again, he also didn't want to argue about the fact that he didn't want to argue about arguing. In the end, he capitulated.

The Problem: Incentive Compatibility

Besides learning a few surprising things about their psyches—like that Sam was a natural "pleaser" who feared disappointing others and Ashley a "rescuer" who feared abandonment—they also pinpointed a key problem area that they never in a million years thought they'd have: housework.

Turns out Sam and Ashley's approach to dividing labor was similar to their approach to the rest of their marriage—dive in and ask questions later. It would never occur to them to sit down, make a list of chores, and divide them up carefully. Housework was trivial, something you figured out along the way. Love and friendship were all that mattered.

"If you see something that needs to get done, do it," Ashley said about her and Sam's philosophy on housework. "We're both adults."

Adults, yes. Good trading partners, no.

Part of the issue was that many of these chores required more effort as married people than as single people. Sam rarely bothered mowing the lawn when he was a bachelor, and Ashley had far fewer bills to pay and socks to fold when she was living on her own. Each may have had the comparative advantage in those tasks—Sam could mow a lawn faster than Ashley because Ashley wasn't sure how to turn the mower on, and Ashley was a quick folder because she'd worked summers during college at The Gap—but that didn't mean they *liked* doing them. And because they didn't necessarily like their jobs, they didn't "just do it," as Ashley assumed they would.

Since the labor was divided based on comparative advantage, the system should have worked. But in practice, their lack of enthusiasm for their chores meant they had no incentive to do them—which in turn meant their comparative advantages were moot.

In the real world, no matter how good a worker is at her job, she still needs an incentive to *do* the job. It's called a "job"—not a "pleasure cruise"—for a reason. That incentive might be a paycheck, or a letter of praise from the boss, or a chance to get ahead. If any of those incentives moves her to work hard, then the system is "incentive-compatible."

When it comes to marriage, an incentive-compatible system can't involve salaries or letters of recommendation. There's no climbing the corporate ladder in the business of love. What it can involve is the security of knowing that the other person will do the job without being asked, prodded, pushed, or pressured. Each person has to know that the other will get the job done because he or she actually *cares* about the results. In this case, caring about the results is the only incentive that works.

Unfortunately, we don't always know what we'll care about until we're thrust into each other's lives. Ashley, for example, didn't know she cared so much about an overgrown lawn until she had neighbors whose lawns were always perfectly trimmed. Sam didn't know how much he enjoyed home-cooked meals back when he was a bachelor and never home for dinner.

Now that they'd been living together for a while, Sam and Ashley were discovering new things they really cared about—and things they didn't. In the process, they also realized that housework wasn't a trivial part of marriage you figured out as you went along.

The Solution: Learning a Few New Tricks

Back in the day when David Ricardo was sitting in his great room puzzling out the mysteries of global economics, comparative advantage seemed like a pretty straightforward approach to trade. Sure, England could put up greenhouses and make a go at becoming the world's number one wine producer, but that would require an investment so massive that the costs would outweigh the benefits. Better to stick with sheep. And Portugal could hire a team of crack geneticists to clone a superbreed of sheep that could grow new wool every hour, but there was no such thing as cloning back then, and DNA wasn't discovered for another fifty years.

Point is, times have changed. Technology has made it easier than ever for countries to launch new specializations. Classic example: the "South Korean Miracle." After the Korean War, poverty and unemployment in South Korea were widespread and Seoul's infrastructure was nonexistent. The country had few natural resources to tap. For all intents and purposes, it specialized in nothing. But over the next three decades or so, the country grew into one of the world's largest economies. The secret: Korea's leaders figured out what the country had the potential to excel at and put all their energy toward that goal. The country invested in industries, courted foreign investors to help foot the bill, and ultimately became one of the biggest exporters of manufactured goods, including cars, electronics, textiles, chemicals, and ships.

Korea gained the comparative advantage in something it previously had no advantage in at all—all because it made a determined investment. In other words, you *can* teach an old dog new tricks.

Columbia economist Jagdish Bhagwati coined the term "kaleidoscopic" comparative advantage: "Today, you have it; but in our state of knife-edge equilibrium, you may lose it tomorrow and regain it the day after. Boeing might win today, Airbus tomorrow, and then Boeing may be back in play again. It is as if the design of trade patterns that you see now gives way to another, as if a kaleidoscope had turned."

In the era of the egalitarian marriage, old specializations that long defined husband and wife can be similarly upended. For Sam and Ashley, their comparative advantages had turned into comparative headaches. They needed to invest in new specializations. If Korea's agricultural economy could become a manufacturing economy, Sam could certainly develop a talent for paying the bills, and Ashley could very well learn how to operate a lawn mower. Call it the "walking a mile in your spouse's shoes" path to a better division of labor.

Shelly Lundberg, a professor at the University of Washington who studies the economics of households, told us that her husband, who also happens to be an economist, made a strategic investment in learning to give their kids baths when they were infants. It's a scary job when you've never bathed a newborn, but he told himself that if he didn't become an expert in at least one key child-rearing task, his wife would end up having the comparative advantage in everything having to do with the kids—and worse, he might take advantage of that. "His technique, which he now recommends to all new dads, short-circuited the conversation so many new parents face: 'Why can't you do this thing?' 'Because I don't know how to!' " says Lundberg.

The first strategic investment in Sam and Ashley's life came the day Sam taught Ashley how to use the mower. Initially intimidated by the machine, Ashley took to the job quickly, loving the control and sense of completion that came after finishing each row. Since Sam didn't *like* mowing the lawn, Ashley eventually took over the job.

In exchange, they picked something of hers he could take over: the bills. Sam was scared of bills and budgets. He claimed to be "bad" with money. But Ashley sat patiently with him at the computer and showed him how she paid the bills online and did the taxes every year.

It took a few months before Ashley could learn to trust that the bills were being paid on time, but eventually she reveled in her newfound freedom. She hated paying the bills and would always rather be out doing something with her hands than sitting in front of a computer. Did we mention Sam was an Internet addict? That at least meant he had the patience for staring at a computer screen.

Under the new system, Sam made sure they stuck to a budget, and Ashley made sure their lawn was never an overgrown embarrassment. With a little effort, they'd gained new specializations—and, even better, they were incentivized to act on them.

THE BOTTOM LINE

1. **Are you Portugal or England?** Do you make a mean cocktail or do you find cleaning the hamster cage meditative? Assign chores based on your comparative advantage—what you do best *relative* to other chores.

2. **Specialize.** It saves time, which none of us seem to have enough of. Think of what you could do: Sleep late. Go to the movies. Have sex. Any of this sound familiar?

3. **50/50=dead end.** We understand the impulse, but keeping score can turn a once high-functioning couple into the Bickersons.

4. **Improve your efficiency.** Is there a simple change that will make your partner happier without making you any worse off? So he's in charge of garbage night, but he dreads it. It probably won't kill you to help him out on the nights you're not doing anything else.

5. **Learn some new tricks.** Specializations can and should change over time. No matter how awesome you are at scrubbing pots, or how effortlessly he pays the phone bill, switching it up sometimes can keep you both on your toes.

2

LOSS AVERSION

Or, The Upside of Going to Bed Angry

THE PRINCIPLE

t's one p.m. on Monday, and the markets have been rising since the opening bell. Tech stocks, up 1 percent. Financials, up 2 percent. Consumers—Best Buy, Macy's, Costco—up, up, up. The trading floor is buzzing. "This is the real deal," you hear a trader say. "A rally with fuckin' *legs*!"

You call your guy at Goldman and bark an order: "I want one hundred knock-out at a fifty-four limit with five-cent discretion." (Translation: Buy me one hundred thousand shares of Coca-Cola, stock ticker "KO," aka "knock-out," at $54 plus or minus five cents.) You hang up the phone, sit back, and watch the tape. Coca-Cola rises and you're feeling like a genius. A rich genius. In half an hour you've pulled in two hundred large.

Then, faster than you can say Pepsi Light, the stock starts to dip. Down twenty-five cents, down fifty cents, down $1. This is odd. You ask the dude next to you if he's seeing what you're seeing. Yeah, he says, apparently the state legislature is talking about a soda tax. Some guy on C-SPAN says passage of the bill could be imminent.

Not good.

But it's okay, you tell yourself. Those jokers at the statehouse never get anything done. You call your guy at Goldman back: "Keep buying. Another fifty thousand."

The stock continues to fall. Another dollar. Two. Analysts start turning negative. Three. You're getting hammered. The stock is now at $51.

You need to recoup those losses. You're desperate to get that money back. So what do you do? You buy more. A lot more. The stock will rebound and then you'll be back on top. It's Coke! Carbonated sugar water! It *has* to rebound.

It doesn't rebound.

By four p.m. you've lost more than $400,000 of your boss's money. "Ouch," says a colleague as he stops by your desk. "Why'd you load up on so much Coke? Kinda obvious it was gonna tank, no?"

Maybe it would have been obvious to you, too, if you hadn't fallen prey to one of the more destructive forces in economics: loss aversion, otherwise known as an intense fear of losing.

Who doesn't hate losing? Losing feels bad, whether it's money, a relationship, a job, or an argument. We do whatever we can to avoid that bad feeling. You don't have to be an economist to know that. But in recent years, economists started asking a different set of questions: Can the very act of losing—or even just anticipating losing—affect our behavior? Can losing make us irrational, prone to rash decisions, aggressive, or defensive?

What economists found, through dozens of lab experiments and real-world data crunching, is that our aversion to loss is so intense that it leads us to behave in strange, often destructive ways. It turns out we hate losing even more than we love winning. Economists have quantified the difference: Losing hurts precisely twice as much as winning thrills. Meaning: You'd have to win $200 to make up for the pain of losing $100.

Loss aversion can explain why people make decisions that seem unwise, like holding on to assets that are losing value or betting the

house when they're down in blackjack or stubbornly refusing to negotiate the sale price of their house even when no one's buying.

Figure 4 illustrates how off-kilter our reaction to gains and losses
can be. The spot where the horizontal and vertical lines intersect is
called "the reference point," or the point from which we measure
gains and losses. You can see how in the lower left quadrant, a small
loss relative to the reference point results in a steep drop in satisfaction, while in the upper right, a small gain brings happiness, but not at
the same fast rate.

The mind of Jérôme Kerviel probably looked very much like this
graph. Remember Jérôme? He was the "rogue trader" whose extreme
aversion to loss wound up costing French banking giant Société

Figure 4: Your Brain on Loss Aversion

Générale billions in 2008. Jérôme didn't *mean* to lose that much money, of course. All he *meant* to do was hedge some futures for the European equity market indexes (*so* not a big deal in the world of international finance) and to practice judo in his spare time. Then he got his first big win: $600,000 on a bet that European markets would fall in the summer of 2005. He spent the next year and a half placing larger and larger bets, with some whopping gains here and there, including $38 million in February 2007 and $700 million five months later.

But when his luck turned in early 2008, it turned sharply. One Friday, as the markets were sliding, Jérôme was trading frantically, trying to recoup his losses. He bet the house, bet the house again, and kept on betting. By the end of the day, he had not only recouped nothing, he was down $2.2 billion. By the time he was caught that weekend, the total losses were even higher: $7.2 billion. Yes, *billion*.

As summed up by Andrew Lo, a professor of finance at the Massachusetts Institute of Technology who has studied the role of emotions in trading: "When you are threatened with extinction, you act like nothing matters."

It is this desperation—and the billions of dollars at stake every day in the stock market—that makes loss aversion such a fascinating and fertile field of study for behavioral economists.

In the late 1970s, in a series of now legendary experiments, psychologists Daniel Kahneman and Amos Tversky demonstrated how loss aversion works. In one experiment, they asked a group of students to choose between two bets:

> a bet with a 100 percent chance of winning $3,000.
> a bet with an 80 percent chance of winning $4,000 and a 20 percent chance of winning nothing.

IN PLAIN ENGLISH:
Behavioral Economics

A branch of economics that looks at how psychological factors influence economic decisions. Behavioralists would say people don't, on the surface, act "rationally," as the neoclassicists would have us believe, but do things that either make no sense or work against their own best interests. Among the key tenets of behavioral economics:

- We change our minds on a whim.

    Did I say Porsches were the ultimate douche wagons? That wasn't me. I totally want a Porsche—look, Bob got one, and it's awesome!

- We make rash decisions when we're losing.

    I can't believe that guy outbid me—I'm winning that crocodile rug if I have to bid $1 million for it.

- We choose lesser, immediate gains over greater, future gains.

    Kids' college fund or Bowflex? Security of future generation or six-pack abs? Abs.

- We're overconfident.

    This $2 million condo is a sure bet. Who cares if it's on a Superfund site—Florida real estate never loses its value.

- We fear change.

    What was so wrong with the old Tropicana label?

Behavioral economics sounds like economics but looks a lot like psychology. Just ask a psychologist—or don't, since she's likely to give you an earful, starting with the fact that the first behavioralist to win the Nobel Prize in Economics, Daniel Kahneman, is in fact a psychologist.

Eighty percent of the students said they would take the $3,000 bet even though the second option had a higher expected payoff. They preferred a sure win over a possible win. Or put another way, they didn't want to risk walking away empty-handed.

Then Kahneman and Tversky framed the question differently, asking the students to choose between the following:

a bet with a 100 percent chance of losing $3,000.

a bet with an 80 percent chance of losing $4,000 and a 20 percent chance of losing nothing.

This time, 92 percent of the students chose the $4,000 bet, even though it meant potentially greater losses. That "100 percent chance" of losing was so terrifying, they were willing to put themselves in danger of losing much more.

Now study both scenarios. See how when the choice was between two gains (in the first scenario), the students didn't want to take risks, but when the choice was framed as two losses (in the second), they were much more inclined toward risky behavior that could potentially lead to greater losses? That's loss aversion in action. It skews reality.

Loss aversion is why the average consumer tends to notice price increases more than decreases. When have you ever noticed that a gallon of gas was *cheaper* than it was the last time you refueled? Yet the minute gas goes up a tenth of a penny, you're outraged at all the money you're being forced to spend. Or what about when you're stuck in traffic on the highway, losing precious minutes you could be spending nursing your first cocktail of the evening, and you get off at the nearest exit hoping the local roads will be moving faster, only to lose even more time stopped at all the red lights?

If you're like us, now that you know what loss aversion is, you'll start to see its dirty fingerprints all over your life—and that includes your personal life. Because here's the punch line: Loss aversion is messing with your marriage. When loss aversion kicks in, you're liable to stay up all night arguing because you don't want to lose a fight. You'll refuse to compromise because it means giving up what you want. You won't apologize because you don't want to lose face. And you'll fail to appreciate the good stuff that's right in front of you because all you can think about is how much more fun married life *used* to be.

CASE STUDY #1

The Players: Amy and José

Amy and José had been married for more than ten years. She was a private school principal, and he was an associate in a commercial real estate law firm. They were one of those New York City couples who never slowed down and seemed to be able to manage ten thousand things at once, including two kids, two houses (one in the city and one on the beach), one nanny, four sets of parents, and even a couple of charity boards. They prided themselves on never getting bored or boring. While some of their cohorts stayed home Friday nights watching *Dora the Explorer* in their Crocs and bathrobes, Amy and José booked babysitters and spent weekend nights at new restaurants and on the benefit circuit.

"When things were good, we were hot," said Amy, who liked to brag that she and José still had sex three times a week. "But when things were bad between us, it was World War Three."

This is a fight Amy remembered vividly: José came home from work cranky because he'd spent the day in pointless meetings and had no time to finish writing a talk he was supposed to give the next day at an industry conference. With the looming anxiety of looking like an idiot in front of two hundred of his peers, he did what any respectable father, husband, and six-figure earner would do: He opened a beer, plopped down on the couch, and turned on ESPN.

Amy had also had a long day, after which she made dinner, cleaned up, and got the kids bathed, dressed in PJs, read to, and, finally, in bed. Watching José sit on the couch the whole time, acting as if there were no one else around, made her want to throttle him.

After the kids were tucked in, she returned to the living room and stood in front of José, blocking his view of the TV. José let out the sigh of the eternally afflicted.

"Just because you had a bad day doesn't mean you get to tune the rest of us out," said Amy.

José grunted.

"And by the way, next time the kids are hungry, *you* feed them."

You can imagine the rest.

"*Jesus Christ,* Amy. Give it a break."

"No, *you* give *me* a break, José."

"I told you: I had a hard day."

"I had a hard day, too. But I'm sick of being the one who gets stuck doing all the work."

José turned off the TV. "I can't deal," he said. "I'm going to work on my presentation."

"Wait, what? We're talking."

"*We're* not talking. *You're* yelling. *I'm* being yelled at."

"José, we're not finished. It's not about who's yelling, it's about you pulling your weight."

"Fuck this," José said as he got off the couch and started making his way toward the bedroom. Amy followed him, getting more angry the more he tried to shut her out. She was relentless, giving him what for as he walked up the stairs.

"I told him he was self-centered, took me for granted, worked too hard, didn't listen, and couldn't handle conflict," Amy told us. She said he never took any initiative when it came to noticing that it was bedtime and maybe the kids would like him to say good night. She said he had his head up his ass half the time, and the worst part was that whenever she tried to get him to man up, he ignored her even more, thereby confirming all her previous accusations and further fueling her rage.

Whew.

José said some stuff, too. He told Amy she was impatient, short-tempered, and always on the offensive, talking to him more like a principal disciplining a tenth grader than like a caring wife. "I told her she was condescending, and I reminded her how much I *hate* being condescended to, and I said something about how she never lets me get a word in and doesn't realize how stressful my job is."

Their fight had gone from the mundane—Amy could have used some help feeding the kids—to the catastrophic. It became a global shakedown of every issue that had been percolating in their marriage for the past few years. They argued for hours, going around in circles, saying the same things fifteen different ways, each intent on convincing the other one of their rightness at all costs. José's presentation never got done. Amy was too riled up to sleep.

The Problem: Compounding Losses

It's not that Amy and José were blind to each other's perspectives or that they had no empathy for the other's point of view. But at a certain point, after they'd invested so much in the dispute, neither one of them could stand the thought of losing. What they didn't realize was that by digging in their heels, they were playing a losing game. They were making character assassinations they normally wouldn't have made, that they didn't necessarily mean, and that they would later regret.

Such fights were not uncommon in their house. They'd typically be followed by a few days of a mutual silent treatment, followed by a slow thaw, followed by the inevitable rapprochement and make-up sex. They never talked about what had happened, they just moved on. "We would basically get tired of hating each other," said Amy.

Then, as soon as things were getting good, another epic showdown undid them. And over time, the vicious cycle chipped away at the relationship. Amy and José's loss aversion during any given argument—an aversion they weren't even conscious of—was compounding their long-term losses.

Most stock traders aren't aware of their aversion to loss, either, which is often why they make bad decisions. They hold a stock that's losing money and will probably keep losing money, given the bad health of the company, or they sell a stock that's going up in price for fear that it'll drop tomorrow.

THE PEOPLE SPEAK . . .
About Fighting

In our Exhaustive, Groundbreaking, and Very Expensive Marriage Survey, 71 percent of respondents said when they're fighting with their partners they sometimes feel that "it's a losing battle." Yet that doesn't stop a number of them from fighting the good fight:

- 53 percent said they keep arguing even after they start repeating themselves.
- 34 percent said they keep fighting even after they can't remember what they were originally fighting about.
- 34 percent said they keep fighting even after they know they're wrong.

In other words, once we're in, we're *all* in. It's like former Alaska governor Sarah Palin said in an interview with Charlie Gibson in 2008 during her vice-presidential run: "Charlie, you can never blink." And look how well that worked for her.

Or take Lehman Brothers. Remember them? The gold-plated investment bank was worth billions in 2007 and then collapsed in a toxic heap less than a year later. At the time, there was a lot of blame going around, and much of it fell on the firm's overexposure to real estate. As home owners and office tenants started defaulting on their mortgages, Lehman's investments deteriorated in value.

But part of what brought Lehman to its knees in those final months was simple loss aversion. Starting in the spring of 2008, when it became clear that the firm was in trouble, the company's CEO, Richard Fuld, scrambled to stanch the bleeding. Behind the scenes, he looked for buyers, discussed mergers, and raised capital to pay off debts. Buyers were interested, but at prices Fuld considered too low—accepting such offers would be too great a loss. In September, Lehman went bankrupt and Fuld lost a bundle—hundreds of millions in Lehman stock, the firm he had helped to build, and what was left of his reputation.

We can never know for certain, but many now say things could have gone differently had Lehman admitted its losses, taken the necessary, albeit painful, write-downs, and secured a buyer before it was too late. Lehman might have survived, the Great Recession might have been mitigated, Sarah Palin might have sailed quietly into a four-year career as vice president, and millions of unblinking Americans might have lived happily ever after in their exurban subdivisions.

The Solution: Sleep on It

For now, we'll settle for how Amy and José managed to live happily ever after.

It was Amy who initiated the change. And coincidentally, her approach was the same as that used by David Einhorn, president of the multibillion-dollar hedge fund Greenlight Capital, when his loss aversion kicks in. Einhorn told us that when he gets mad at the management of a company he's invested, oh, millions and millions of dollars in, and he starts to worry that the company is tanking because of managerial decisions he doesn't agree with, he puts the file in a drawer and takes a time-out. Rather than sell stocks in the company right away—which would be an emotional response fueled in part by his sense that losses were imminent—he sleeps on it. More often than not, he says, he feels clearheaded in the morning. That's not to say the company's problems disappear overnight, just that he's more open to coming up with solutions that might stave off potential losses.

Amazing to think that such an old-fashioned solution—sleep on it—could address a modern problem like losing millions of dollars.

Or losing a fight. After the hundredth late-night scream-a-thon with José, Amy decided something wasn't working. Even when she felt she had valid reasons to be upset, her anger only seemed to make things worse: "I would start out feeling so confident that I was right and that José had to see that, and then hours later I was still screaming."

On her mother's advice, she decided to invoke something she called the twenty-four-hour rule. Whenever she got mad at José and her desire to win kicked into high gear, she kept it to herself for at least twenty-four hours. Her goal wasn't to bottle up her emotions—she couldn't have that type of personality even if she tried—but to see how those emotions registered twenty-four hours after they first cropped up. If a day passed and she was still fuming, she'd broach the subject ("broach the subject" being the phrase she preferred over "lay into unsuspecting husband"); if she wasn't quite so upset, she'd drop it altogether and ride the wave.

It's hard to exaggerate how big a change this was for Amy, who had spent her life believing that all arguments needed to be resolved right away and that it was never good to carry around anger.

The first time she tried it, she said, she felt as if she were "going to explode—literally" as she got into bed next to José, intent on saying nothing about how he'd once again forgotten to bring home enough cash to pay the sitter. "It was the only thing he had to remember," said Amy. "But then again, the fact that he didn't remember things was the whole problem."

Still, Amy didn't waver. She said nothing. In the morning, she also said nothing. Oblivious to the machinations in Amy's head, José rolled over, still half-asleep, and squeezed her hard, kissing the back of her neck, she said, "in just the right places." That night, José handed her the money unprompted and apologized for forgetting it the previous day. "Miracle," said Amy.

A few months later, the twenty-four-hour rule had greatly diminished both the frequency and the intensity of their arguments. Amy challenged some very ingrained ideas she had about conflict resolution—namely, that to resolve things you need to have conflicts. She also put aside her fear of losing a disagreement—of José not seeing that she was doing more than he was, or that something he said or did hurt her feelings, or not getting an apology in exactly the way she wanted to be apologized to—in favor of a more measured approach. After all, José wasn't a total idiot, and she'd married him for a reason. But sometimes pounding the point home to him made him less inclined to listen.

Here's where economists and psychologists might agree. "A time-out is a great idea," says clinical psychologist and family therapist Gerald Weeks, especially when couples "cannot deal with each other rationally." With his patients, Weeks sets some rules for time-outs. First, each person can unilaterally call a time-out when they need to.

Second, the person calling the break has to set a time limit of not more than a day. Third, both people have to spend the time-out thinking about what it was about the disagreement that led to all that anger. "You are not to think about blaming your partner," he says. Think instead about why you each responded the way you did. And finally, when you come together, talk calmly, without making accusations.

Amy and José still argue—and there are plenty of occasions when Amy is still legitimately upset after twenty-four hours and she confronts José about it. But whenever they do argue, Amy will try to catch herself if she crosses into the realm of loss aversion. That's when the argument stops being about how hurt she is and starts being about winning.

"That's when I call a self time-out," she said. Even though her whole body is telling her to keep fighting until she can claim victory, a voice in her head will remind her that if she tries not to lose and keeps going, she's bound to lose more—more goodwill, more trust, more sleep—than she stands to win.

CASE STUDY #2

The Players: Paula and Nivi

Speaking of professional fighters, Paula (one of the authors of this book and someone who should know better) and her husband, Nivi, fought for the first full year of their marriage. About a La-Z-Boy.

Let's rewind. It wasn't just the La-Z-Boy. Before that, there was the couch Paula had bought at an auction. She thought it had personality. Nivi thought it was a torture device, since when you lay down on it, the busted springs bored into your spinal cord like a million little drill bits. And before the couch, there was Nivi's hook obsession, in which, despite Paula's protests, he lined the walls with hooks to hang his clothes on. Closets were dumb, he said, since you had to rifle through them to find the shirt you wanted—how much easier was it to have a wall of shirts, clearly visible on their hooks? There was the Tchotchke War of Attrition, involving figurines Paula had accumulated from every country she'd ever visited and that Nivi kept "accidentally" knocking over and breaking; the Bathroom Cabinet Thirty Days' War, wherein Nivi took the liberty of throwing out all the stuff in the bathroom he deemed "old" or "useless" without asking Paula first and which included her $200 teeth-whitening molds she was saving for a rainy day; and the still-fraught Kitchen Cabinet Intifada, in which Nivi's ceremonial (that is, dust-gathering) Japanese tea-drinking equipment would routinely appear front and center in the cabinet, blocking access to Paula's prized Fiestaware bowls.

But nothing did quite as much damage as the La-Z-Boy. Paula loved that chair. She'd owned it for nearly a decade, and she'd dragged it with her every time she changed apartments. She'd cuddled in it with her bipolar cat before she had to give him up for adoption for being too bipolar. She'd sat in it listening to depressing Joni Mitchell songs after a long, drawn-out breakup. That chair wasn't just a chair; it was a trusted friend. Upholstered in a soft, worn-in, mud brown velour, it had great lumbar support and a footrest. It was the most comfortable seat in the house. How could anyone think otherwise?

Apparently, Nivi could. When he looked at the chair, he didn't see good ergonomics or the warm patina of lost youth. He saw an ugly, frayed, cat-piss-stained brown lump in the middle of his living room. He said Paula was overly sentimental about her possessions and that her love for the chair was "unhealthy." He said that every time he looked at it, he cringed. He said it made him unhappy.

Which Paula thought was insane. How could merely looking at a chair make a person unhappy? Wasn't Nivi being a little melodramatic? And the chair was just the tip of the iceberg. Was it a coincidence, Paula wondered, that all her favorite things—her vintage sheet music collection, her Little League trophies, her many, many pairs of sandals—happened to be the things Nivi wanted to put in storage until they could "find a bigger apartment"?

Sure, Paula and Nivi might have been having the kind of spat all newlyweds have, the kind that the long-married would profess to be way past. Arguing over furniture and shoes? Who has time? Turns out a lot of people have the time. During our interviews with couples who had been married anywhere from three to thirty years, we heard one story after another that bore more than a passing resemblance to Nivi and Paula's. One couple fought for six months over a bathroom renovation—funny, because she wanted everything new and he preferred their old fixtures. Another couple ended up in foreclosure—not funny, because the wife refused to budge on the sale price of their home even as the real estate market was tanking (they had other issues).

But getting back to our heroes. The La-Z-Boy battle came to a head one day when Nivi and Paula spent a weekend in upstate New York and walked past a yard sale. There on the grass was a recliner. It was worn-in and upholstered in a mud brown velour. It had a footrest and, by the looks of it, decent lumbar support. The price: $20.

Paula looked it over. "They're crazy if they think they can get twenty bucks for that thing."

Nivi was shocked. Here was someone who stubbornly refused to give up her own eyesore, saying this replica eyesore was hardly worth a dime.

"So, um, Paula, how much would it take for you to sell your chair?" Nivi asked.

"It would take a lot," she said, thinking. "Maybe five hundred dollars."

The Problem: The Endowment Effect

Paula was suffering from something economists call "the endowment effect," in which we put an irrationally high value on our own stuff. It's a behavioral quirk that stems from our aversion to loss—when something's ours, we endow it with more meaning than things we don't own. And so we'll go to extremes not to lose it.

The endowment effect is why we'll charge $5—no negotiations!—for a used economics textbook at our yard sale, but we won't pay a penny more than $2 for the same textbook at a yard sale down the block. It's why we believe our house is worth $420,000, but we think our neighbor is batshit if she believes she can get more than $320,000 for hers. It's why mail-order companies offer free shipping for returned merchandise—they know once you see how good you look in that pirate costume, the odds are you won't want to give it back.

The classic example of the endowment effect comes from an experiment involving coffee mugs. Two groups were asked to assign a value to the mugs—but the people in the first group were told the mugs were theirs, they owned them, while the second group wasn't. The people in the first group (the owners of the mugs) tended to price the mugs higher than those in the second group. They also wanted to keep their mugs when they were given the option to trade them in for cash. The second group—the group that didn't own their mugs and so hadn't "endowed" them—chose the cash option.

In another study, car buyers (actually, volunteers who played the role of car buyers for the sake of the experiment) were told to buy fully loaded cars and then take out the options they didn't want or need. A second group was told to buy cars with no options and then add those they wanted or needed. Big shocker: The first group ended up with more options on average than the second. Once they'd bought into the bells and whistles, they were reluctant to give them up—that would mean losing something they owned.

In Paula's case, it wasn't just that she loved the chair—it was that she couldn't stand the pain of *losing* the chair. Losing it meant losing everything the chair had come to symbolize: her independent single days, her freedom to buy what she wanted and decorate how she wanted, and her ability to sit around doing nothing all day without having to consider the needs of someone else. The endowment effect pulls back the curtain on how very badly we don't want to lose things. Or money. Or people. Or times in our lives.

But was the chair worth another year of fighting with Nivi?

The Solution: Reframing

This is where marriage counselors might trot out the wisdom of "picking your battles" or "learning to compromise," and both are good rules of thumb. But they don't get to the heart of why we're having these battles to begin with. Very often, we just don't want to lose. And that aversion to loss can be triggered by the high value we place on things that are dear to us.

But how to unendow something? It's hard to stop caring about something you're attached to.

One technique is to reframe the question: Are you losing a La-Z-Boy or gaining a happy home? Are you losing something sentimental or gaining a chance to buy something beautiful?

Sometimes our sense that we're losing stems simply from the way a choice is framed. Earlier in this chapter, we discussed Kahneman and Tversky's experiments testing whether people would take riskier bets depending on how they were presented. In another experiment that tested for the effect of framing, they asked people to choose between different strategies for saving lives:

A Few Words on Loss

- "Second place is really the first loser."
  —George Steinbrenner, Dale Earnhardt, et al.
- "The very thought of losing is hateful to Americans."
  —General George Patton
- "You're never a loser until you quit trying."
  —Mike Ditka
- "What a waste it is to lose one's mind—or not to have a mind."
  —Dan Quayle
- "You're here, sir, because you are a loser!"
  —Judge Judy

Subjects were told to imagine a scenario in which an outbreak of a rare disease is expected to kill six hundred people. They were given a choice between two plans:

> Plan A had a 100 percent chance of saving two hundred lives.
> Plan B had a one-third chance of saving six hundred lives and a two-thirds chance of saving no lives.

Seventy-two percent chose plan A, in which there was the greatest certainty of saving some lives.

Then they were asked to choose between these two plans:

> Plan A carried a 100 percent chance of four hundred people dying.
> Plan B carried a one-third chance of no one dying and a two-thirds chance of everyone dying.

Seventy-eight percent chose plan B, which seemed to them like the only plan that offered some certainty that no one would die.

Notice, however, that in both presentations plans A and B are exactly the same; they're merely framed differently. The first presents the options in terms of who lives and the second in terms of who dies—in other words, as potential gains or potential losses. Invariably, subjects gravitated toward the gains.

Frame a choice differently and you might change your mind about which path to take. You might also feel more open to compromise. That's because our willingness to compromise has a lot to do with whether we think we're losing or whether we see the potential for a gain.

Nivi knew Paula well enough to know that telling her she was nuts for loving her chair wouldn't get him any closer to his goal. What would work? A spreadsheet charting use of the chair over time vs. usefulness of another piece of furniture—say, a new desk at which Paula might write her book like a civilized person instead of on the couch, which was giving her neck pains? A spreadsheet might seem like the height of dorkiness, but it was an approach Nivi suspected Paula might find endearing.

"I thought she would appreciate that I was making an effort and not just insulting her chair," said Nivi. "For the hundredth time."

He showed her the spreadsheet—sucker that she is, she found it endearing—and suggested they replace the chair with something they purchased together, as a couple. He mentioned he'd seen a vintage Danish modern desk at her favorite furniture store. Perfect inspiration for an author.

Paula's study of economics paid off. She weighed the costs and benefits of fighting for the chair and came to the conclusion that it was time to give it up for the sake of harmony. Of course, as an amateur economist she also knew there was no such thing as a free lunch.

How Lanie Finally Learned to Let Go

Harold, an attorney in Miami, told us he discovered the value of reframing when it came to a repeated (and ignored) request he'd been making to his wife for twenty-five years: Could she please get rid of that white flapper dress with the holes in the front that she wore every morning when she took their dog, Bailey, for a walk? For more than two decades, Lanie's answer was no. There was nothing wrong with the dress, she said. It was comfortable.

"But you're embarrassing the dog," Harold would say.

And: "You look like a bag lady."

And: "We have plenty of money for you to buy a new white flapper dress if you insist on wearing a white flapper dress to walk the dog."

Nothing worked. Talk about the endowment effect. One day, Harold, who prided himself on his powers of persuasion in front of a jury, came up with a plan. He waited until they were preparing to renovate the bathroom and closet in the master bedroom, a time when, by necessity, they had to empty everything out of the closet. They spent the weekend on it, and Harold gave it a very specific name: a "renewal event." It was a chance, he told Lanie, to take stock of all their old stuff and start fresh with the stuff they liked. When he came upon the white dress, he held it up casually and wondered if, you know, maybe it was time to finally throw it out? Lanie looked at it, and looked at it again, then said a little prayer and told Harold to go ahead and toss it. "To new beginnings," Harold said, thrilled his wife wasn't going to look like the neighborhood trollop anymore.

There Ain't No Such Thing as a Free Lunch

Also known as TANSTAAFL, the phrase has been the mantra of free-market economists since about the time free-market guru Milton Friedman wrote the book on it in 1975. Things that seem "free" never are—somebody always pays. A free Paul Simon concert might be free for *you*, but it costs Paul Simon time he could be spending making money at a paid concert. Free diaper delivery is plenty costly to the environment (fumes from FedEx trucks, plastic diapers in landfills). A second pair of socks free at The Gap is so obviously not free that it's not even worth explaining. And a concession from a wife to a husband will always end up costing that husband something, someday.

So when Nivi recently asked how mad she'd be if he came home with a second dog, she told him she wouldn't be mad at all—she'd just go right out and buy herself a new La-Z-Boy.

CASE STUDY #3

The Players: Rob and Ellen

Rob and Ellen met shortly after college at a Halloween party where they were the only two people who didn't bother to wear costumes. They stood in the corner all night talking, and a week later they went on a date. The conversation was easy, there were no awkward pauses. A few days later, they went out again. The second date flew by. They kissed.

Months passed. They met each other's friends, they spent a long weekend at Lake Tahoe. Gradually, their old routines started to slip away: Sunday mornings they slept late instead of going to the gym;

Saturday nights they cooked at home instead of meeting friends at a bar. The sex was magical, frequent, multiorgasmic. They felt so *connected*. At work, they got distracted thinking about the night before. They couldn't stop smiling. Their co-workers noticed and were jealous. "I remember that whole time as if it were a dream," said Ellen.

But it wasn't a dream, it was the honeymoon period, or what psychologists call "limerence," an involuntary state of intense romantic desire. Call it falling-in-love-ness. Or she's-the-one-ness. Limerence isn't a crush. It's deeper, more long-lasting, and fairly obsessive. Scientists have found that people in so-called limerent states have levels of serotonin—a chemical in the brain that affects mood—akin to people with obsessive-compulsive disorder. In other words, we really do fall crazy in love.

A year passed. Rob and Ellen met each other's families. They took a vacation together, a week surfing in Mexico. And they hit another milestone: They had their first major argument. Ellen canceled a long-planned trip because her sister needed help moving into a new apartment. "She acted like she didn't have a choice in the matter," said Rob. "And like how dare I be upset about her bailing on a trip *we paid for* to help her sister unpack boxes." ("He took that whole thing way too hard," said Ellen.) The honeymoon period was officially over, but they were still very much in love. Privately, each started to wonder if the relationship was headed toward marriage.

They were twenty-seven years old. Rob worried he hadn't slept with enough women yet. Ellen worried about having to consult with Rob whenever she wanted to buy a new toothbrush holder. Rob told himself he'd never give up his Sunday pickup basketball games, not even for his future kids or the love of his life. Ellen wanted to live abroad someday, and she knew Rob was a born-and-bred Californian who would never go for it.

Inevitably, Rob and Ellen started to talk about the prospect out loud.

"What are your thoughts on marriage?" Rob asked one night as they drove to a friend's party.

"Are you asking me to marry you?" said Ellen.

"No," said Rob. "I'm just wondering what you think of the idea in general."

"In general," said Ellen, "I support marriage."

"Marriage to me? Or marriage as a concept?"

"Both, I guess."

They rode the rest of the way in silence.

The next morning at breakfast, Ellen restarted the conversation. "Do you want to talk more about the monumental, life-changing thing you brought up in the car yesterday and then didn't mention again?"

"What thing?" asked Rob.

"The thing about you asking me to marry you," said Ellen.

"I never asked you to marry me," said Rob.

"Yeah, but you're considering it," said Ellen.

"It's crossed my mind."

"Well, it's crossed mine, too—should we talk about it *for real*?"

And then, like the two grown-ups they desperately wanted to be, Rob and Ellen finally talked about getting married. They both wanted to have kids—Rob said he always wanted to have three, Ellen thought one would suffice. They both worried about losing their independence and wanted to have a marriage that didn't involve completely losing their individuality.

They figured they'd work it out. They took the plunge.

Married life wasn't exactly the way Rob and Ellen thought it would be. It was love, but it wasn't limerence.

For starters, there were money issues. Between her small salary working at a friend's clothing store and Rob's teaching income, and the high cost of living in San Francisco, how would they ever afford kids or anything roomier than their cramped rental apartment?

Ellen thought about going back to school for psychology, and Rob was supportive. He loved teaching and wanted Ellen to find something she loved, too. But two years into her master's program, Ellen started having doubts. "Sitting in a room and listening to people's problems all day sounded too depressing," she said. She considered switching to a PhD program and focusing on research but couldn't bear the idea of spending five more years in school and then facing a job market so competitive that she'd be lucky to land a position in Walla Walla.

While she was figuring out her next move, Ellen got pregnant. "We weren't trying, but we also weren't *not* trying," said Ellen. She managed to finish her master's and figured she'd find any job that put her degree to use—guidance counselor, librarian, Girl Scout leader, party organizer, life coach—but then she didn't land a job before the baby was born.

Living on one teacher's salary was doable . . . until Ellen got pregnant a year later. Now they were both stressed about how they would make ends meet. And Ellen stayed up wondering if she'd ever be more than a stay-at-home mom. She and Rob spent nearly nine months arguing.

For all the joys in their lives with two kids, Rob and Ellen started to miss the old them. The them that had magical sex. The them that went to the movies, that got eight hours of sleep, that never argued about money.

In her darker moments, Ellen wondered what it would be like if they separated. "I would go through worst-case scenarios," she said. "What if we stopped having sex altogether? Would that mean I would never have sex with *anyone* again, or would I have an affair? Could I have sex with someone else and still love Rob?"

Rob loved his kids but had moments when he missed the simplicity of having just one. "One kid was easy," he said. "We could still have some time together on weekends. But two kids was a whole different ball game. It was work and parenting, work and parenting, all the time. It was relentless."

Rob and Ellen had stumbled on a mystery millions of married people have yet to solve: Why does something we try so hard to attain, that we want so badly, sometimes disappoint?

The Problem: Status Quo Bias

Economists would diagnose Rob and Ellen's condition as a case of "status quo bias," an outgrowth of loss aversion that leads us to strongly prefer the known and familiar over the unknown and unfamiliar. Any change means losing, and that's something our monkey minds aren't very good at.

"The significant carriers of utility are not states of wealth or welfare, but changes relative to a neutral reference point," writes the economist Richard Thaler.

Or in plain English, our happiness isn't about where we're at right *now*, but where we're at compared with where we were *yesterday*.

In economics, the status quo is often a fixed number—like the purchase price of a stock or the sale price of a house or an annual income. Because we're programmed to fear losing, any movement away from the status quo can feel like a bad thing—even when it's simply a natural progression or part of a necessary cycle.

To see how status quo bias works, let's go back to the example of the stock price. A trader who buys a stock at $10 will often exhibit a bias for that price—he will believe that's the price the stock is worth, period. So when it closes the next day at $8, he'll despair. He'll refuse to sell—even amid growing evidence that the company is floundering—until the price goes back up to $10. (Remind you of our trader who

Status Quo Bias Warning Signs

Things you might find yourself saying that suggest you're stuck in the past:

- He never used to work this hard.
- Just because we have kids now doesn't mean we need to see his parents more often.
- We always had sex at least twice a week.
- She used to like all my friends.
- Bali. Now *that* was a vacation.
- We need to live in the city or the country, but not the suburbs because the suburbs have always been scary to me.
- The only way to keep a clean house is to have a housekeeper like my parents had when I was growing up.
- People like us don't go on cruise ships.

lost big on Coca-Cola?) Because he's loss-averse, he can't imagine accepting anything less than the status quo. Day after day, that price might keep dropping, giving him more opportunities to cut his losses, but he'll stubbornly refuse to sell.

What's confounding about status quo bias is that the same thing happens if the stock goes up in price. A gain of $2 will also make our trader queasy. Instead of reveling in his gains, he'll worry that his stock could drop below $10 someday soon, and he'll sell before that can happen. Meanwhile, the next day it goes up to $14 and he kicks himself. Studies show that traders hold on to losing stocks more than winning ones. "More money has probably been lost by investors holding a stock they really did not want until they could 'at least come out even' than from any other single reason," writes Philip Fisher, author of *Common Stocks and Uncommon Profits.* On the other hand, the best time to sell a winning stock, says Fisher, is "almost never."

The problem is that our preference is for yesterday's status quo, which by definition is gone, disappeared, dead. Nothing to do with the present. Today, the status quo might be very different, yet we can't always accept or appreciate what we've got today since we're focused on the past. In Rob and Ellen's case, they didn't recognize the "new them" as the new status quo—they just longed for the "old them." Limerence was the old status quo, but Rob and Ellen were nonetheless still clinging to it, still seeing it as the reference point against which they compared everything else in their lives.

In Figure 5, we've taken some serious liberties with the original

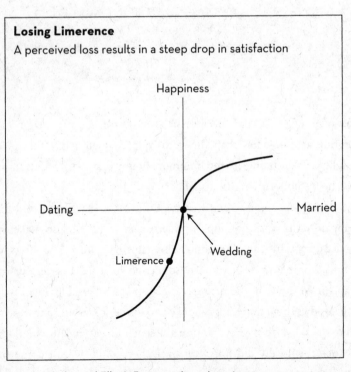

Figure 5: Rob's and Ellen's Brains on Loss Aversion

loss aversion graph from earlier in the chapter. But we're trying to make a point, which is to show how Rob and Ellen perceived the end of their limerent period as a loss, even though many people would argue their marriage had been a huge gain. And so would they—on a good day. But when they looked back at how euphoric they were during their honeymoon period, they *perceived* a loss, and that made them feel deeply bummed.

The Solution: Active Decision Making

Without a working time machine, what could Rob and Ellen do?

For one thing, they needed to recognize that they didn't have the problem they thought they had. Not having great sex every day after five years of marriage and two kids was not a problem. Not kissing and hugging each other each time they said hello and goodbye was not a problem. This was normal.

Their problem was that they *thought* they had a problem.

They got married, felt a certain way, and then felt differently. So they panicked. They had fallen into the trap of expecting limerence to be permanent, but it's only one stage in the life of a relationship, a relationship that's dynamic, changing day to day, minute to minute. Limerence was the status quo at the time—not in the present day. While Ellen and Rob were telling themselves they needed to recapture something that no longer existed, they were letting the gains of their marriage pass them by. They might as well have been hunting unicorns.

Some people solve this kind of dilemma by having an affair, thinking that will make them feel young and hot again. Others walk out in search of something they think will be more fulfilling.

Smart people get real.

"One of the first things I tell couples who come to see me is that the past is the past, and they are not allowed to bring up the past unless they can tie it directly to the present," says psychologist Stephen Koncsol. "It's very hard for most people to do that."

Or as an economist might put it: Anchoring to old reference points like limerence or making out in the rain outside your cousin's house or singing karaoke at that weird bar in Chinatown all night won't lead to optimal decision making. When life changes, you need to change with it.

We're not saying it'll be easy. You're habituated to seeing things a certain way, and shifting that view even slightly can feel like climbing Mt. Everest. Of course it's disappointing that you don't have thirty minutes of foreplay each time you have sex, and of course you see it as a sign the fire has died, and of course it means that you've lost something magical that you'll never get back and you're withered and lazy and not even plastic surgery will get rid of your thutt and why do you bother having sex at all?

But here's where you need an economist in the bedroom. Standing over your old, naked bodies as you both sit in bed, working on your word jumbles and privately wondering how and when your lives took a sharp turn down celibacy lane, the economist will snap his fingers and lecture you on a deceptively simple concept called "active decision making." This means exactly what it sounds like: taking an active role in the decisions that affect your life rather than sitting back and letting those decisions call the shots for you.

True, economists don't usually discuss active decision making in the context of sex or marriage. The topic comes into play more often in the study of health care economics, contract theory, and retirement savings. Should I choose my employer's PPO health plan, an HMO, or just go with the default management chose for me? Should I put 3 percent or 6 percent in my 401(k), or should I let the company decide for me? Cancel my *Popular Woodworking* subscription or let it automatically renew even though I never read it?

For years, economists believed people would address such questions by choosing the option that seemed most rational. You want to use an out-of-network doctor, you'll choose the PPO. You want to have a roof over your head when you're eighty, you'll put money in your 401(k). But study after study has shown that people are more inclined to stick to the status quo than to make a change for the better. Going with the default—also known as "passive decision making"—saves us time and saves us from having to think too hard, but it doesn't lead to optimal outcomes. So we don't save, we get the health plan that costs us more, and we pile up magazine subscriptions at the expense of old-growth forests.

We've found active/passive decision making to be hugely relevant to marriage economics. For one thing, we get passive about keeping the flame alive. We choose sudoku over orgasms, *The Wire* over conversation, a glass of Yellow Tail over time on the treadmill. It takes an active choice to get out of these routines. And for another, we get passive in our view of the marriage. It'll never be like it was, so why bother?

Rob and Ellen were doing a bit of both. They weren't making the active decision to get out of their rut and spice things up. They also weren't making the active decision to see the gains in their marriage rather than just the losses. In order to reset the status quo to the present time, they needed to *decide* to do so.

So maybe some things had gotten "worse"—they were having less sex, seeing fewer non-animated movies, shaving rarely. But what had gotten better? What gains had they seen that they weren't maximizing?

To answer these questions, they needed to take action and gather some data (economists love data, and so do we). Rob and Ellen didn't actually chart the data, but we recommend doing so, if only to make it easier to wrap your loss-averse head around. Sit down together, pour yourselves some wine, and write out something like this:

Yesterday's Status Quo	Today's Status Quo
Late nights dancing at the bar to a-ha	*High Noon* and takeout on the couch
Sunday morning in bed with the paper	Sunday morning in bed with the kids
Forty-mile bike ride followed by beers and burgers	Forty minutes at the playground followed by PB&J
Naps	Nap time
Dates	Date nights
French bulldogs	Two beautiful children
Vacations in rustic beachside cabanas	Vacations at Disney
Talking trash	Discussing retirement plans
Existential dread	Existential dread
Big Love	*Bob the Builder*
Spending all day in boxers and man-clogs	Getting dressed
Multiple orgasms	One real orgasm, two fake
Marijuana	Ambien

Now be honest: The column on the left doesn't comprise losses, just different sorts of activities from those on the right. When Rob and Ellen talked through their own list, they were reminded of the best of their marriage, the times spent throwing croutons to the ducks with their kids or curled up on the couch eating Thai food and watching old movies.

It also reminded them of some things from their past lives that they could resurrect if they took some initiative. They could take a long weekend at the beach alone and leave the kids with Rob's parents. They could get a babysitter and go smoke pot and listen to Steely Dan records with their friends Neal and Cynthia, who still did that sort of stuff. They couldn't envision a leisurely Sunday morning—not for a few more years, at least—but Ellen did force herself to sign up for the AIDS ride along the California coast. And Rob joined a bowling league. They had lost a few fun, romantic things along the way, but overall, life was pretty sweet, losses and all.

THE BOTTOM LINE

1. **Go to bed angry—wake up happy.** You don't need to resolve every argument before you go to sleep. What you need to do is sleep—sleep is great!—and see how you feel in the morning.
2. **Establish a 24-hour rule.** We're talking grown-up time-outs. Loss aversion means we act crazy when we sense we're losing, so we do stupid things, grasp at straws and insult our mother-in-law. Calling a time-out for yourself can give you the time you need to calm down and find the middle ground.
3. **Let go.** We're not Buddhists, but those guys do have a point about clinging. Of course, you don't want to give up your La-Z-Boy, or your honeymoon period, or your freedom to get drunk on White Russians every night—but instead of focusing on all those "losses," consider the "gains" of marriage, and let go of the little things.
4. **Embrace change.** Not to go all Dr. Phil on you, but change is your friend. We humans prefer the status quo, meaning the known and familiar, over the unknown and unfamiliar. But trying new things makes your brain happy the way sunny days make your brain happy. With no risk of skin cancer.
5. **The default is your enemy.** Default to Budweiser, you'll never get to know the joys of Magic Hat. Default to another night of TV and you'll never discover your love of live ukulele music. You get the drift.

3

SUPPLY AND DEMAND

Or, How to Have More Sex

THE PRINCIPLE

Let's talk for a minute about . . . the negative sloping demand curve. What's that, you say? You thought we were going to talk about *sex*? You thought you were going to learn how to light a fire under your bed and now you feel duped by some economic law of a distinctly nonsexual nature? Well, bear with us. This chapter does feature intimate details of other people's sex lives and it *is* guaranteed to increase the frequency of high-quality action with the person you love. But to get there, we first have to talk about the very unsexy-looking graph on the next page.

Don't roll your eyes: It could save your sex life.

Figure 6 demonstrates something very simple: When the cost of something gets too high, you want less of it. When the price of milk shoots up, for example, you'll drink your coffee black. When the price of gas hits $4, you'll start riding your bike more. When a pack of cigarettes costs $8, chewing gum starts to look more appealing. And when the cost of sex becomes too high, you'll opt for a mindless night of TV and jelly doughnuts. Important point: By the "cost" of sex, we don't mean the literal cost of *paying* for sex. We mean what it costs

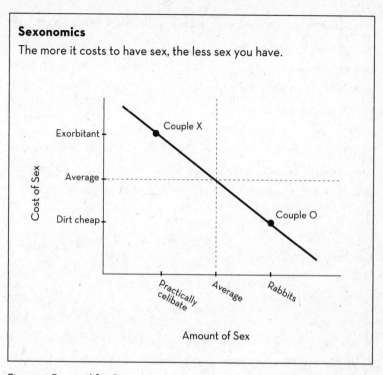

Sexonomics

The more it costs to have sex, the less sex you have.

Figure 6: Demand for Sex

you, as in what you have to give up to get it—the fifteen minutes of sleep you'll miss out on, the emails you won't have time to reply to, the last-minute run to the supermarket to make sure little Johnny's lunch is stocked with organic applesauce.

Now, let's visit our graph. On the vertical axis, you have the cost of sex; on the horizontal axis, the amount of sex. Notice what happens when you lower the cost from average to dirt cheap: You go from average to screwing like rabbits. Raise the cost to exorbitant, and you're in the practically celibate zone.

We've placed two couples, X and O, on the diagonal "demand curve." Couple X has attached a prohibitive cost to sex—in terms of time, energy, missed work—it just takes too much effort. So they do it only once a month. Couple O has brought their costs way down by having quickies the minute the kids go to bed and telling each other when they're in the mood instead of wasting time being coy. Couple O has sex a few times a week.

Wouldn't it be nice to be in couple O's shoes?

The problem is, as the married years tick by, most of us seem to move toward X and away from O. We're not ready (or qualified) to declare a nationwide sexual emergency here, but on our listening tour

THE PEOPLE SPEAK . . .
About Sex

Although we'd all love to be couple O, we also feel the need to warn you: Don't try too hard to be them or you'll drive yourself nuts. Listening to what everyone else is up to in the bedroom—and comparing yourself with them—is a path to ruin. The economic term for this is "market noise," meaning the chatter out in the ether about which companies are hot and which are not. Market noise often has no grounding in reality, which is why the rule of thumb is to ignore it.

Because we're human, however, we can't resist the noise. In our Exhaustive, Groundbreaking, and Very Expensive Marriage Survey, we learned that most people are inundated with noise:

- 51 percent talk to their friends about their sex lives.
- 58 percent talk to their friends about their friends' sex lives.
- 60 percent read articles and books about improving their sex lives.
- 53 percent watch TV shows discussing other people's sex lives.

we certainly picked up on the fact that couples aren't having as much sex as they would like. More than 78 percent of participants in our Exhaustive, Groundbreaking, and Very Expensive Marriage Survey said they had sex daily or at least two to three times a week when they were first married or committed, compared with 28 percent who do now. Yet a majority—54 percent, to be exact—said they wished they were having more sex.

This isn't trivial stuff. A growing body of research suggests there's a link between sex and marital happiness. According to the Pew Research Center, American adults rank a "happy sexual relationship" as the second most important factor in making a marriage work, behind "faithfulness." And according to the General Social Survey, which tracks the social behavior of Americans, more sex corresponds to three factors: 1) being younger (under thirty); 2) having been married fewer than three years; and 3) rating one's marriage as happy.★ In our own survey, 92 percent of the people who have sex two to three times a week report being satisfied or very satisfied in their relationships, compared with 56 percent of those who have sex every few months.

"There is a feedback relationship in most couples between happiness and having sex," Denise Donnelly, an associate professor of sociology at Georgia State University, told *The New York Times*. "Happy couples have more sex, and the more sex a couple has, the happier they report being."

So why not do it? What's stopping you?

The answer we got, pretty much across the board, was that you have too many other things to do. Couples, both young and old, from blue states and red, are working more, obsessing over their kids more, and focusing on their marriages less. In our survey, the number one

---

★Married people have 28 to 400 percent more sex than unmarried people, at various ages. So no matter how bad you think it is, being single would not solve your problem.

Sex After Sixty

In one ongoing study of sex and aging, 62.6 percent of women and 67.5 percent of men ages fifty-seven to sixty-four reported having sex at least two to three times a month. Not bad. Of course, the different percentages mean one of three things: 1) someone is lying; 2) men are having sex with other men; or 3) men are having sex with younger women.

Who can say?

The good news is, by age sixty-five, the discrepancy seems to have righted itself, with a heartening 65.4 percent of both men and women ages sixty-five to seventy-four reporting they have sex two to three times a month.

Also, according to people we spoke to, sex can get better the older you get:

- An empty nest means less chance of getting caught mid-orgasm by a kid who opens the door worried that Daddy's hitting Mommy, or vice versa.
- With menopause, no worries about birth control.
- No one to stop you from doing it on the washing machine.

reason people reported not having sex was "Too tired," followed closely by "Not in the mood" and "Angry."

Some couples said they'd given up or stopped worrying about it, figuring that in a world with so much divorce, having your best friend lying in bed next to you is just as good as having an orgasm every night. As the critic Caitlin Flanagan wrote in the *Atlantic:* "There is nothing like uninterrupted cohabitation and grinding responsibility to cast a clear, unforgiving light on the object of desire." Her prescription: have more sex.

That's our prescription, too, and we have a strategy for getting there: Lower the costs. Do that, and the quantity demanded will rise almost instantly. With the help of some very agreeable couples, we've come up with three ways to do this.

One is being more transparent—transparency being a prerequisite for any market to function efficiently. This includes things like not making the other person guess whether you're in the mood to watch golf or to get it on.

Two is resetting your habits. Once we get into a pattern—whether it's not exercising or not flossing before bed—it's hard to break that habit. When we're newlyweds, we tend to have good sex habits. Then life gets complicated. We're not the copy boy, but the president of Dave's Drills and Hammers, we have two kids, four hundred bills, and a bunion—and we get out of the habit. Getting back in is merely a question of reducing the initial start-up costs.

Three is sending informative signals to your partner about exactly what you want when you want it. Signaling can help avoid the awkwardness of asking for sex, or refusing sex, or getting shot down after asking for sex.

We focus on three couples who put these strategies to work. These aren't couples who had been having consistently great sex, year in and year out, though we did meet a few people like that in our travels (to you guys, we salute you, we envy you, and we sort of wish you didn't exist). Instead, we picked couples who had never had great sex and who turned things around, or who hit a long, dry patch and clawed their way out. We found one couple who spent eighteen years arguing about their very different sex drives and finally, thanks to some simple signals, found a reasonable compromise. We met another couple who realized, years into an otherwise fulfilling relationship, that each had no idea what turned the other on. And we found one pair of overachievers who jump-started their sex life by inviting their compulsive goal setting into the bedroom. Different problems, same solution: Lowering costs to up the action.

CASE STUDY #1

The Players: Heidi and Jack

The first time Heidi and Jack had lunch together, it was hardly stars colliding. In fact, Heidi spent the entire time talking about her fiancé, who lived in Northern California and whom she saw once a month. "I could tell Jack was into me, and it stressed me out, so I started blabbering about Dave." She talked about how she and Dave had weathered three years of law school together, which she took as a sign of how "strong" they were, and another two years living on opposite coasts. "We totally complement each other," she told Jack. "I'm kind of a slacker, and Dave is a doer. He has an MBA *and* a JD. He pays his rent. He actually calls me at the end of every month to remind me to pay my rent."

"It was so obvious she wasn't in love with this guy," Jack told us.

Jack didn't say this to Heidi at the time, of course. Or at least, not in so many words. Rather, he talked about his most recent relationship and how it seemed like a perfect match on paper. She was well educated, ambitious, attractive, and a great tennis player. Even Jack's mother approved. But at the end of the day, the relationship lacked lightning bolts, he told Heidi. This was an ideal lead-in for Jack—who likes to talk and to use terms like "lightning bolts"—to deliver a soliloquy on love. About how it should be powerful. Intense. "Mindblowing."

Heidi told Jack he'd watched too many movies.

But his words stuck with her. That night, she thought about Dave—warm . . . reliable . . . predictable . . . unimaginative . . .

Dave. And then she thought about Jack, whom she hardly knew but who seemed warm, too . . . but also spontaneous . . . adventurous . . . sexy.

A few weeks later, Heidi ran into Jack at a going-away party for someone in their office. It was late and cold, and they ended up on the roof together. Jack said he was happy for their friend, who was exiting the rat race to spend a few months in Nepal. Heidi said she thought he was nuts. "The job market is dead," she said. "He'll never get a job as good as the one he has now when he gets back."

Jack told her she was just as straitlaced as Mr. Pay-Your-Rent-on-Time Dave.

"I am not," Heidi said, feeling bold after four mojitos. "I can be very, very bad."

"Okay," he said. "Then kiss me."

She kissed him—and she liked it.

According to Jack, he and Heidi had the kind of cosmic connection he didn't have with other women. "We were soul mates," he said. (Yes, he used that term.) They laughed at the same dumb *South Park* jokes and liked random adventures, like a day trip to northern Pennsylvania to track down the nation's best key lime pie (according to a website dedicated to key lime pie). They biked everywhere. To breakfast. To work. To his parents' house thirty-five miles away.

Not everything was perfect, Jack conceded. "She was cautious in bed, but I figured it would take time."

"He talked a lot when we had sex," said Heidi. "Lots of dirty talk. Sometimes it was sexy and sometimes it was overkill. But it's hard to tell a guy to shut up when he's telling you how hot he is for you." She figured if she didn't say anything back, he'd pick up on the fact that she didn't like it and would eventually stop (he didn't). A few times she almost said something about it, but each time felt too awkward.

Sex issues aside, Jack and Heidi told us they were happy, way happier than most couples they knew at the time. One problem was Mr. Reliable, whom Heidi hadn't conjured the guts to dump. Three months after her first kiss with Jack, Heidi finally decided to fly to Menlo Park and break up with Dave. After that, she would call her father and tell him that she wasn't going to marry the man of *his* dreams.

And then she chickened out.

"Heidi is the least confrontational person you will ever meet," said Jack. "She couldn't do it. Here we are, totally a couple, and she's telling Dave she can't come visit because of work, because she has to see her grandmother, because there are clouds in Kansas. She even gave in once and visited him. And she came back without dumping him! I don't even want to know what happened. She said she loved me, so I hung in there and it all worked out. But, Christ, she didn't make it easy."

"I was lame," said Heidi. "I can admit that."

For the next five years, Jack and Heidi lived together, worked together, spent every weekend together, and traveled to offbeat places together, from Mendoza, Argentina, to the Aeolian Islands off the coast of Sicily. The subject of marriage came up frequently, but each assured the other that being married wasn't the be-all and end-all. "I always said I didn't need a piece of paper to stay committed to Heidi for the rest of my life," said Jack.

"I didn't care about it, either," said Heidi. "I was just relieved to be happy." When Jack realized that Heidi meant it—that she really didn't want to get hitched—he proposed.

They got married in a bar.

All was good except for the fact that their sex life continued to be average, despite Jack's hopes that it would improve with time. Sometimes he thought it was because Heidi was shy, and if he could get her to trust him, she'd relax and let down her guard. Other times she seemed distracted, as if she were thinking about work or who knows what, and he'd seriously debate snapping his fingers and asking her if anyone was home. Even in the midst of their initial whirlwind secret affair, Heidi—in her honest moments—would admit to feeling relieved the nights Jack didn't want to have sex and wondering, when they did, whether it wasn't supposed to be more fun.

Talking to us about it, they were surprisingly open about just how mediocre it had been.

"I remember the first time we had sex," Heidi said. "You were doing all these . . . weird moves." She waved her hands, discolike.

"That's because you never seemed that into it," he said. "So I felt like I had to try stuff." Jack said it wasn't just with sex that he had to be the instigator. "I'm writing her poetry and showing her how much I love her, and she's this super-self-protective person, sharing nothing. I was always trying to figure out what she wanted."

But Heidi seemed happy, and both of them admitted that in a weird way, their happiness masked the fact that their sex life wasn't great. "There was no one I wanted to spend time with more than Jack," said Heidi. "He was my best friend. I was like, how bad could it be?"

The Problem: Opaque Markets

One night they had friends over for dinner. They were all sitting out on the deck, drinking heavily, when their friend April announced that she had a question about sex. Was the stated national average of twice a week true? Because that's what she read in a magazine. Suddenly everyone was (ill-advisedly) comparing notes.

"It's about twice a week for us," one woman said.

"Wow. Impressive," said another. "It's more like once a week for us."

Jack couldn't remember the last time he and Heidi had had sex. They looked at each other and shared a very uncomfortable moment.

Later that night, after everyone went home and the pre-hangover started to assert itself, they argued. "Why do we never talk about our sex life?" Jack wanted to know. "Or lack thereof?"

"What is there to talk about?" said Heidi. "I'm not in the mood to do it twenty-four/seven like you are. That's me. It has nothing to do with you."

Jack disagreed. He said that since he was her husband and they'd agreed to spend eternity together, it had a lot to do with him. She stonewalled, even saying at one point—unconvincingly—that they had a great sex life and he was making a big deal out of nothing. Finally, he suggested they go to therapy.

"Therapy?" Heidi asked. "For *what*? We're happy!"

Again, Jack disagreed. He said he wasn't happy. He said he'd started worrying about their sex life constantly. He said he loved her, but he could already feel himself growing resentful, and if they didn't get help—soon—he wasn't confident they'd make it.

Heidi agreed to try one session and see how it went.

In their first session, Debbie, the shrink, asked Heidi about her parents' marriage. "How did I know you'd ask me that?" Heidi replied.

Heidi's mother was distant and unhappy, and her father was charming yet domineering. She never once saw her parents fight—or hold hands. As an only child, Heidi learned to work things out on her own. "I had erected the Great Wall of China around me. That's why Jack was so refreshing. He was open. I didn't know open. But I also didn't know how to respond to open. In the bedroom or anywhere else."

Heidi started to see that her bedroom self was a magnified version of her everyday self. "Jack was an open book when it came to his feelings and talking about what was on his mind, but I wasn't, and that meant that Jack's openness could only go so far," said Heidi. "If he was upset at me for flaking on him, he'd tell me, and then he'd feel better. But I didn't get mad. I didn't tell him that his dirty talk sort of skeeved me out. Or that I didn't think it was cool the way his parents talked about their sex life in front of us."

Heidi and Jack suffered from what could be called an "opaque marriage market," a market in which neither one knew what the other valued. That made the exchange of goods—emotional goods, in their case—impossible.

There are few better examples of the dangers of opaque markets than the financial crisis of 2007–2009. At its root, the problem was that too many people bought houses they couldn't afford.

But there was another factor: Banks had taken those suspect mortgages and bundled them into complex financial products with names like "collateralized debt obligations" (CDOs) and then written insurance against these CDOs in the form of something called "credit default swaps" (CDSs). (Warren Buffett referred to derivatives like these as "financial weapons of mass destruction.") The upshot: The market was flooded with products that even the engineers who created them didn't fully understand.

As long as the market kept rising, banks made buckets of money. Then the whole thing imploded, and the fallout was made even worse by the fact that the market was opaque: No one knew who owned these financial products, what they were worth, or how institutions priced them. Regulators had no idea where the risk was concentrated.

They found out the hard way that the risk was concentrated at supposedly rock-solid firms like Merrill Lynch, Citigroup, and AIG—the banks and insurance companies taxpayers subsequently bailed out to avert a total global meltdown. Opaque markets meant massive profits for those companies and Armageddon for the rest of us.

The Solution: Transparency

In marriage, as in the financial system, opacity can cloak disasters waiting to happen. If you never talk openly and honestly about your lackluster sex life, it'll become the Thing That Never Gets Talked About. It will never get better. It will become your personal $36 trillion credit default swap market, humming along until one day it goes bust.

Transparency is the cure for opacity. Let in a little light, pull back the curtain. Same deal whether it's collateralized doodads or marriage.

In therapy, Jack and Heidi got transparent about a lot of things—her relationship with her father, her decision to stay in a bad relationship for six years before Jack, and, eventually, the nuts and bolts of their own sex life. "We talked about small things," Jack said. "Like, does it feel good when I tickle you? Do you like it when I kiss your hands?"

Over time, Heidi started doing some of the talking in the bedroom, asking Jack to try things she was into instead of following his lead. "I used to say 'That's good' to things when we were having sex even if I wasn't into it. I thought that's what you were supposed to say."

The best example of how opaque their market had become related to some fairly straightforward positioning.

"It's early in the relationship, we're having sex, and Heidi gets on top," Jack said. "I shift her around because I have a muscle cramp or something—I can't remember—and apparently, her takeaway is that I don't like it when she's on top."

What kind of heterosexual male, Jack asked us, doesn't like a woman on top? Heidi admitted she found it hard to believe, but she nonetheless wondered if it might not be Jack's thing. Also, her confidence was shaken. Maybe it was her fault. Maybe she wasn't doing it right. She was embarrassed, so embarrassed that she never made the same move again. From then on, she avoided being on top. If Jack even tried to wiggle his way onto the bottom, Heidi would quickly wiggle her way to the side. Jack would be secretly disappointed, but Heidi was so cagey and insecure about sex that he didn't push her. "I'll let her drive the bus," he thought to himself.

Then, one day in therapy, Heidi said something about how she liked being on top and thought it was weird that Jack wasn't into it.

Jack practically choked on his Altoid. "What do you mean, you love being on top? You never get on top."

"That's because you practically tossed me off the first time we ever tried it."

Jack couldn't believe what he was hearing.

"I assumed you didn't like it," she said. "And then I felt even more self-conscious about it."

Therapy ultimately tore down a lot of walls for Heidi and Jack and allowed them to start communicating more about what they needed and what they did and did not want in the sack. In this way, they gradually lowered the cost of their sex life. They were more transparent, so there was no guessing, no mystery, no anxiety.

"At the heart of intimacy is self-disclosure," says John R. Buri, psychologist and author of *How to Love Your Wife*. "We become most intimate with those who are most transparent."

He said it himself—and he's a doctor!

Transparency—whether it's about how often you like oral sex or how much it annoys you that he won't shave on weekends or how well cooked you like your burger—helps prevent small issues from ballooning. Leading a transparent life allowed Heidi to be open to new ideas. Like toys. And teddys. "Guess what? Jack's into lingerie," Heidi told us. "I always assumed the faster we were naked, the happier he was."

One night they were watching a movie with an intense sex scene and Heidi found herself getting turned on. She asked Jack if this was what porn was like. Jack said it was close (trying not to sound too expert on the topic).

"Should we watch some?" she asked, much to Jack's shock and awe.

"It took me a while to be honest about what I liked," said Heidi. "But when I did, the sex got so much better."

How much better? we asked.

"We have sex all the time now," she said.

How often?

"Like every other night," she said.

Jack coughed. "Try twice a week, tops."

We didn't say it was a perfect market, just a substantially more transparent one.

CASE STUDY #2

The Players: Connor and Lindsay

Here's a conversation—or rather, an approximation of a conversation—we heard Connor, a molecular biologist, and Lindsay, an epidemiologist, having in their Washington, D.C., town house. (We were there, by the way, to talk about marriage.)

"I read the coolest article this morning," Connor said. "About pregnant women who live near cornfields where pesticides are used."

Lindsay looked intrigued.

Connor continued. "Apparently, farmers tend to apply larger amounts of pesticide in the spring, during planting season, and nine months later, the rate of birth defects in the area rises."

"Interesting. But did they rule out all the other variables?" asked Lindsay. "Maybe more poor people get pregnant in the spring, and we know there's a relationship between poverty and poor prenatal health care. Or maybe women who get pregnant in the spring spend more of their pregnancy outdoors, and there are air pollutants or other health risks that have nothing to do with pesticides."

"They factored all that stuff in," said Connor. "They ran their analysis through multiple regressions, and the trend lines seem strong. Even when you factor in race, poverty, and health risks, proximity to a cornfield is a huge predictor of birth defects. Plus, there's no spike near organic fields where pesticides aren't used."

We cleared our throats and gracefully shifted the conversation to more pressing issues, like how Connor and Lindsay met.

"In graduate school," said Connor.

"In a depressing corner of the medical library," said Lindsay. "He asked me if I had an extra pen. Extremely obvious. But he was cute, so I went along with it."

They had coffee, talked HIV and tuberculosis (her research) and the use of fertilizers in the developing world (his work). It didn't take long before they were spending the bulk of their time together. Talking about infectious diseases and fertilizers and occasionally other stuff.

"I could talk to him about death and dying for hours and he wouldn't think I was morbid," said Lindsay.

They talked about how they planned to save the world. Getting vaccines to rural villages. Microfinance for farmers. Convincing governments to care. And it wasn't all talk. In 1998 they graduated, got married, and spent the next three years at least two continents away from each other, on dangerous and exciting assignments in far-flung corners of the world. "I did Nigeria and then Somalia and then Botswana, while he did a fellowship at Harvard, a stint in South Africa, and then Vietnam," said Lindsay. "We spent some weekends together here and there, but we didn't spend a lot of *continuous* time together."

Both described their relationship at the time as perfect. "Being apart allowed us to focus on our work, but we also had someone to come home to," said Connor, admitting that "home" was a loosely defined term and "someone" usually meant a disembodied voice on the other end of the phone.

They were passionate. High-achieving. Proud of each other.

"Lindsay's greatest coup was containing a measles outbreak in Mogadishu," Connor said. "She had to negotiate with a bunch of warlords to land a plane to get vaccines to the villages. They ran through the airport wearing bulletproof vests. One of the warlords changed his mind after they'd landed."

"That took some improvisation," said Lindsay.

A few years into their long-distance marriage, they decided it was time to actually be, like, married. They convinced their organizations to post them, at the same time, in India. Their time there was like an extended honeymoon. "Best three years of my life," said Connor. Lindsay concurred.

In 2005, Lindsay got pregnant. They took Lola to Nepal and Bangladesh. They brought her to work and traversed the continent with her before she was two.

But when it came time for her to go to school, both Connor and Lindsay decided to move back to the United States. They took jobs with the government, put Lola in a Montessori school, and felt their exciting old life slip away.

Along with their sex life.

The Problem: Bad Habits

For the first ten years they were together, Connor and Lindsay described their sex life as "good."

"I wouldn't say we were wildly adventurous, but we had sex often and we generally clicked," he said. "We didn't *think* about sex. We just did it."

But by the time they had Lola and moved to D.C., they were starting to get out of the habit. They found themselves talking about it
more than doing it.

"We haven't had sex in a long time," Lindsay would say, as if Connor weren't aware of that fact.

"Okay, then let's have sex tonight," Connor would reply.

But when it came time to do it, Lindsay would always have to
work. "If I don't get this done, I'll get killed tomorrow," she would say.

There's a theory in economics called "rational addiction," and the
gist of it is that we get addicted to things—alcohol, gambling, porn,
crystal meth, cigarettes, loser boyfriends—by engaging in them over
and over again, and we stay addicted to them because we feel the benefits outweigh the costs. So a heroin addict *knows* heroin is habit-
forming and deadly but has decided he'd still rather be high and
addicted than not high and not addicted. In other words, being an addict is a completely "rational" decision in the sense that the addict has
considered the long- and short-term pros and cons. According to the
theory, the same applies to what might be considered "good" addic-
tions, like working, listening to music, having sex with your spouse, or
loving someone so much that you want that person to become your
spouse.

The Nobel Prize–winning economist Gary Becker, who came up
with the term "rational addiction" (and who, as it happens, also made
a name for himself studying the economics of marriage), said the best
way to overcome an addiction is going cold turkey. In the same way
we pick up habits by continued use over time, we can also kick those
habits—and develop new ones—by deciding the benefits no longer
outweigh the costs.

What does this have to do with Connor and Lindsay? Everything.

Connor and Lindsay used to be addicted to sex—not literally, but
in the economic sense of being in the habit. The benefit of having sex

outweighed the cost. Then the equation changed. For whatever reason, the benefits were no longer as clear and the costs had grown. So they broke the habit, and suddenly they had a new habit: not having sex. Another new habit: talking endlessly about the reasons they weren't having sex.

Remember our old friend, the negative sloping demand curve? Well, by talking their sex life to death, Connor and Lindsay were further jacking up the price of sex. In order to have sex, they had to talk about it first, and that cost them time and energy they could have spent, well, having sex.

Lindsay blamed the fact that living in D.C. had made them boring and bored. She said her job exhausted her. She thought maybe seeing each other every day inured them to each other. Connor blamed Lola for draining them of all their vitality. ("Sure, blame the innocent child," said Lindsay.) Connor also thought they weren't eating right. Not enough vegetables and too many processed foods were making them less energetic in general.

Lindsay had another idea. "I think it's the water," she said one night. "The industrial solvents might be worse than we thought."

"The *water*?" said Connor, who at that moment realized how insane their conversations had become. "Jesus, Lindsay."

The Solution: Resetting Habits

Connor knew their problem wasn't the water or the mercury levels in the air or a lack of green vegetables. Or, for that matter, their jobs. It was them. They were talking their libidos to death.

Ever the pragmatist, he suggested they set a sex goal of three times a week, and for the next few months force themselves to stick to it. "We need to get in the habit of having sex rather than sitting around talking about the reasons we never have it," he said.

Connor was thinking like an economist. To see what motivates people to change their habits, Gary Charness, an economist at the University of California at San Diego, and Uri Gneezy, an economist at UC San Diego's Rady School of Management, ran an experiment in which they paid people to go to the gym. They paid some people to go once and others to go for longer periods. Then they stopped paying both groups and watched what happened. They found that money did motivate people to go to the gym, but perhaps even more interesting, the couch potatoes who had no record of prior gym attendance kept going even after they weren't being paid anymore. The money helped them overcome their inertia, or their "start-up costs." Then, once they were in the habit, they kept going.

Lindsay was skeptical of Connor's plan. "Three's a lot," she said, eventually agreeing to it only because as a scientist, she added, she was always game for testing out a hypothesis.

We'll admit it: When Connor first told us about Operation Hat Trick,★ we were skeptical, too. Three is a big—some would say insurmountable—number in a busy, post-honeymoon life. But Connor and Lindsay were determined, and determination is a very good thing when it comes to keeping the marital bedsprings bouncing. They were also realistic. They set a goal of three times a week; they didn't set a goal of three steamy, foreplay-filled, candle-wax-and-lavender-oil massage sessions a week. That would have been way too costly.

Lindsay equated it to getting back into shape after having a baby. "The beginning was the hardest part," she said. "I love to run, but when I started running after I had Lola, it was hard. It wasn't how I remembered running, as some great release. I was grinding it out.

★A hat trick is three goals in ice hockey.

That's sort of what it was like with sex. The first few times weren't spectacular. But then it started to feel natural again."

Once they committed to three times a week, they found ways to make it happen. They tried having sex after Lola went to bed (an argument in favor of set schedules for kids if there ever was one) and *before* they ate dinner. They realized if they waited until after the meal and after they'd done the dishes and after they'd paid the bills and started the to-do list for the weekend, they were way too tired. But if they did it before, they were motivated by hunger to get the job done.

They tried to rekindle their old Sunday morning staple. It didn't work—having sex at seven a.m. before Lola got up was not like having sex at ten a.m. But they did figure out that having sex during Lola's nap on weekends worked (and Connor, being a guy, would then nap afterward).

"The idea is, if one person initiates, the other should at least try to respond," Lindsay said. "It doesn't always work. Sometimes I really do need fifteen more minutes of sleep or we're too hungry. But we try to meet the goal every week."

"We have more sex now," said Connor. "Not great sex. Good sex. Since we have it a lot, we worry less about the quality."

Connor and Lindsay reminded us of that Woody Allen line: "I've never had the wrong kind of orgasm. My worst one was right on the money."

If you're feeling dubious, we don't blame you. "Just have more sex" is advice you'd get from Nike, not economists. But judging from our own survey, people are more interested in lamenting the absence of sex than in finding ways to have more of it. For example, more than 77 percent of respondents agreed or strongly agreed with the statement "The amount of sex diminishes over time." Yet 76 percent said they disagreed or strongly disagreed with the statement "The amount of sex *should* diminish over time."

Come on people, get moving!

THE PEOPLE SPEAK . . .

About Being in the Mood

A surprising number of couples are doing their level best to keep their sex lives strong—even when they'd rather be knitting. In our Exhaustive, Groundbreaking, and Very Expensive Marriage Survey, we asked how often people get it on when they're not in the mood, and we were quite pleased to see that 47 percent said they "sometimes" do and 11 percent said they "frequently" do. Good effort, guys!

They also shared some of the likely reasons they would do it when not necessarily in the mood:

- It will make him or her happy: 83 percent.
- You believe you'll end up enjoying it in the end: 75 percent.
- You don't want to hurt his or her feelings: 62 percent.
- It will earn goodwill: 48 percent.
- He or she did something to deserve it: 45 percent.
- You feel guilty: 36 percent.

Maybe you'll like it. Or maybe making your partner a little happier will be worth the effort. Or maybe you'll get some of his (or her) killer pancetta-wrapped monkfish if you start his (or her) day with a happy ending. Not a bad deal.

CASE STUDY #3

The Players: Seth and Monica

Seth and Monica have been married for thirty-six years. And for most of those years, the song of their sex life has remained the same: She can take it or leave it, while he, as Monica put it, "gets turned on opening a door."

When it comes to the act itself, they're also different. Seth tends to rush through it, while Monica prefers to go nice and slow. "Seth's idea is you get in bed and have sex," she said. "My idea is that you touch and kiss and talk and cuddle. You set it up."

"Her idea of 'setting it up' is a little too elaborate for us mere mortals," said Seth.

When they met, Seth was thirty-four years old, divorced with one kid. Monica was single and ten years his junior. They were both English teachers at a private school in Massachusetts—he was the department head, and she was fresh out of graduate school. She showed up in his office one day asking for advice on how to teach Willa Cather's *My Ántonia*. "She claimed she wanted to know what I thought of Ántonia and Jim's relationship, but it seemed like a ruse to talk about other things, like teachers who were being mean to her and students who thought they were entitled to anything. And maybe to flirt with me."

He asked her to dinner. "We drank a lot of wine, talked about books, my life in Florida, his kid, his divorce, and by the end of dinner, he told me he wanted to sleep with me," said Monica. "No warning, no kiss. Just, 'I'd like to make love to you tonight.' "

Monica made him wait.

"Six months!" said Seth.

"I thought it would be nice if we actually got to know each other," said Monica.

When it finally happened, Monica was impressed with Seth's technique. "He was clearly an experienced lover," she said. She wouldn't elaborate except to say take her word for it: Seth knew what he was doing.

But skills alone didn't make Monica any hornier than she normally was—which was about one-fifteenth the level of Seth's horniness.

Through the years, even after their two kids were grown, sex remained an issue for them. Seth almost always initiated, and Monica either acquiesced or vetoed. "Seth was usually ready to go," said Monica. "I couldn't have initiated it even if I'd wanted to." Seth said he would have been all for Monica taking the lead, but he had resigned himself, grudgingly, to the fact that it might never happen.

They tried talking about the problem. They listened to each other, spoke in calm voices, and used the "I" word ("I feel like you are always thinking of having sex with me when sometimes I would rather have a pleasant conversation about the weather") instead of "you" ("You know what your problem is? Your problem is you're frigid!"). They were mature that way.

But when it came to sex, they didn't come close to a resolution. Seth complained that Monica rejected him all the time, which made him feel, well, rejected all the time. Monica complained that Seth's constant need for sex made her feel guilty. She said she would get into bed ready to curl up with a book and Seth would edge his way over, put his arm around her waist, and start kissing her. "In ten seconds he'd be ready to go," Monica said. "I'd be faced with this situation of having to say yes—even though I didn't feel like it—or saying no and disappointing him."

The Problem: Coordination Failure

To avoid this situation, Monica would plot her evenings. Go to bed before Seth. Have an extra glass of wine so she'd pass out on the couch. Decide to bake brownies at ten p.m. "I had a friend years ago, I'll never forget this," Monica told us. "She told me she wore her ugliest old nightgown to bed every night so her husband wouldn't want to have sex with her. That story always stayed with me. It struck me as incredibly depressing." Yet she knew her own late-night bake-a-thons were no different.

It wasn't that they didn't have sex. They did. And once in a while, it was really good.

Like this one year when, for their anniversary, Seth said he was picking her up from work and told her to bring nothing more than a toothbrush and a set of clean clothes for the next day. Seth surprised her with a room at an ocean-view hotel, a pair of gold-and-pearl earrings, and reservations at a small, candlelit restaurant. "I was like, 'What have you done with Seth?' " said Monica. "We had an amazing, amazing evening. I remember sitting by the window in our room after dinner, and as I looked out, I could swear there were two full moons. It took me awhile to realize it was the moon and the reflection of the moon. Then we had the best sex I can ever remember."

Why? we wanted to know. What had changed?

"I don't know. I was in the mood, that's all."

But as soon as they got back home, Seth reverted to acting like a sixteen-year-old with a raging boner. "The first night back I'm thinking, 'I need a night to recover,' and there's Seth, in bed, ready to go. I couldn't do it."

Once again, Seth felt rejected and Monica felt guilty.

No question, there's the issue here of different libidos. But economists might also point to a coordination failure, which is a whole lot easier to address. A coordination game is one in which two or more parties are faced with an identical set of choices. The outcome of the game can vary depending on what each party decides to do, with some outcomes being beneficial to all parties, others to just one party, and still others to neither party.

Coordination games are played more often than you might realize. When a fly ball is hit between two outfielders, one player has to call it. That's a coordination game. Same when four cars pull up—at the exact same moment—to an intersection with a four-way stop sign. Or when a bachelor walks into a bar hoping to find the right bachelorette among a sea of cosmo-sipping candidates, or when buyers of rare Venetian glass seek out sellers of rare Venetian glass, or when business school applicants are researching which MBA programs attract the best and brightest. Or when Seth is attempting to discern if tonight is a night Monica will want to put out.

Coordination failure can happen when people make decisions based on *assumptions* about how other people will behave. It's what happens when each outfielder assumes the other will catch the ball, so neither catches it and the runner scores a double. When all four cars go at once. When Seth makes his move . . . and strikes out.

See, Seth preferred having sex to not having sex. That was a given. But if sex wasn't going to be in the cards, he would rather have known ahead of time and avoided the moment of rejection. The issue was that he never knew when Monica might reject him (sadly, it never occurred to him that no one bakes at night unless they have a very good reason to), so he couldn't coordinate his moves—those moves being a) jump her bones, or b) tuck in for the night with a Philip Roth novel and a glass of seltzer. And because his preference was always sex, he had to try move A without knowing how it would be received. Thus, coordination failure.

At the end of the day, this meant sex was very costly for both Seth and Monica. He spent a lot of time and energy fretting over whether he was making the appropriate move and then feeling like a loser when he didn't, and she wore herself out trying to avoid him or reject him.

Monica and Seth needed to find a way to lower their costs. And moonlit evenings at expensive hotels were not a viable long-term solution.

The Solution: Signaling

Coming home after the hot anniversary sex, Monica was deflated. She had loved the sex, loved the intimacy. Why couldn't she feel like that more often?

She called her sister and confided what had happened: "We had this incredible, sexy night, but now it's back to the same story, the same guilt."

"Can you pinpoint what was different about that night?" her sister asked.

"I loved the romance. Not the earrings and the roses and the hotel. But the planning. The setup. He really thought about it. Also, it was the first night in I don't know how long that I initiated sex, which felt great."

"Sounds to me like you need to try to have sex on your terms sometimes," her sister said. "Maybe you liked it more because it was your idea."

This seemed about right to Monica.

She decided to experiment with taking the lead and, if it worked, to see if that alone would make her feel like having sex more often.

One Saturday morning, she got up before Seth, brushed her teeth, went downstairs, and made herself a cup of tea, which she always did. Then she went back upstairs, chucked her nightgown on the floor, and got back into bed—which she never did.

Seth, who was still dozing, noticed she'd returned. He also noticed she was naked. "I was confused," he said. "Saturday morning was not a time we ever had sex." He moved toward her, cautiously. Then she placed her teacup on the nightstand. It was all R-rated from there.

Ever since then, whenever Monica makes a cup of tea and gets back in bed, Seth knows it's go time. By moving slowly—something about Saturday mornings and teacups implies a slow start anyway—Seth helps Monica get in the mood. Tea has become a signal for Seth—one that Monica gets to send.

Signals remove inefficiencies created by coordination failures. The founders of eHarmony, for example, built an online marketplace in which total strangers can signal their likes, dislikes, and favorite music.

Ebay sought to solve the issue of how Venetian glass collectors can find one another by creating a space where buyers and sellers get reliability ratings. And when magazines rank business schools, those lists signal to students which schools are likeliest to attract high-profile employers. Economists have shown that the *U.S. News & World Report* college rankings have a large effect on where students apply.

Open for Business

On our nationwide listening tour, couples told us about the signals they use to let the other person know they're in the mood. The signals ranged from the standard stuff—get undressed, offer a back rub—to the downright strange:

- "She's naked and not in my college track T-shirt."
- "He's quiet. He usually talks a lot."
- "He's nice. Really nice. Extra inquisitive."
- "He throws back a few gin gimlets before dinner."
- "I usually put a condom on. That seems to give her the idea I want a little more than good conversation."
- "One of us says, 'Let's take a nap!' "
- "He'll say, 'Is it Special Time?' "
- "We call it 'booty duty.' We're each allowed to call for sex whenever we want. It's been an ironclad rule since we had our third kid, which means no one calls for it very often."
- "Irony. We say, 'We're not having sex. Just snuggling.' Then we usually have sex."
- " 'Wanna do it?' usually gets the message across."

As for Seth, he developed some signals of his own. Monica had talked so incessantly about how much she loved their anniversary night at the beachfront hotel that it occurred to Seth she might like other romantic excursions, too (smart guy, that Seth). He started planning something special every month or two: buying theater tickets, cooking an elaborate meal, lighting a fire instead of turning on the TV, reading to her from one of his favorite novels. "Girly stuff," said Seth.

Whatever the activity, Monica recognized that he was making an effort. "If it were up to Seth, we'd stay home and play Scrabble every night," said Monica. Now, on nights when she gets an earful of Byron, a fire, and some sparkling wine, she knows exactly what Seth is looking for, and she tries to be responsive.

The sex is still more infrequent than Seth would like. But he looks at their Saturday mornings and the every-so-often special night as a chance to prove to Monica how good it can be. If he can show her, time and time again, that the benefits outweigh the costs, the better the odds that she'll gear up again to pour herself a cup of tea.

THE BOTTOM LINE

1. **Stop being so aspirational about sex.** Keep costs down (make it easy) and demand will rise. We're all for the occasional five-hour medieval role play, but most of the time, a quickie will do.

2. **Get into the habit.** Economists and drug addicts alike will tell you that the more you do something pleasant, the more you want to keep doing it. So as long as you are having sex and not shooting heroin, you're in business!

3. **Speak up.** If you've never told your spouse just how you like it, how can you expect him to read your mind? A little transparency goes a long way, and we're not just talking see-through nighties.

4. **Don't wait until you're in the mood.** For anyone who's been married more than, say, ten minutes, waiting until you're in the mood is like waiting for a total lunar eclipse: It happens, but very rarely, and you can't always get there in time.

4

MORAL HAZARD

Or, The Too-Big-to-Fail Marriage

THE PRINCIPLE: PART ONE

You're sick. You don't know what's wrong with you, only that your stomach hurts. It hurts after a stressful day at the office and sometimes in the middle of the night. And after you exercise. And when you have tacos for dinner. Or pasta. Or ice cream. Or nothing at all. Come to think of it, there's no discernible pattern— it just hurts and you want it to stop hurting.

So you go to your doctor, just as you always do when you're sick. Your doctor does the full work-up, asking questions about your lifestyle and diet. Well, she says, shrugging, it could be stress, or maybe irritable bowel syndrome, or a food allergy. Maybe you're lactose intolerant! Finally, she says she doesn't see anything wrong with you and suggests, if you're really worried about it, that you go see a gastroenterologist.

And thus begins a year-long saga involving doctors, acupuncturists, allergists, and even, at one desperately low point, a hypnotist. You subject yourself to invasive and expensive procedures, including a CT scan, an endoscopy, and a colonoscopy. You deprive yourself of bread, dairy, eggs, and tuna fish. You wince as tiny needles are inserted into your ankles, earlobes, and forehead to open your chakras. You take prescription pills, probiotics, Tums, and Pepto-Bismol. At the end of the year, you still have no diagnosis. But oddly enough, your stomach feels better. Maybe it needed time. Who knows.

Your total out-of-pocket expenses for the year of living gastrically: about $300. Total paid by your health insurance provider: about $60,000. Not that you know or care what your insurer paid. It's not your problem. That's why they call it "insurance," right? If you've got it, why not use it?

No reason, unless you care about something called "moral hazard," the danger that people with insurance will behave differently—sometimes taking greater risks—from those without it. Look at you, you had no qualms about racking up thousands in doctors' bills (for a stomachache that, let's face it, was never going to kill you) because it wasn't your money you were risking.

In contrast, your friend Dina, a freelance art therapist who coincidentally also had mysterious stomach problems but had no insurance, went to a walk-in clinic, was prescribed an endoscopy, found out it would cost her $2,500 and decided to try lemon-ginger tea instead. Dina's problems didn't go away immediately, either, but like yours, hers got better with time and a concerted effort to eat better and reduce stress. Total out-of-pocket expenses for Dina? Just $3.50 a week in teabags.

IN PLAIN ENGLISH:
Moral Hazard

Give an inch, take a mile. Bet the house, wait for a bailout. Go directly to jail, get out of jail free.

We use the stomachache example because health insurance is one of the first places economists look for moral hazard. Remember the whole healthcare reform business that passed Congress by a hair in 2010? That it passed at all was a miracle given the intense resistance in the United States to anything remotely "universal" in the world of health care. Behind much of the opposition: moral hazard. Since the late 1960s, opponents of universal care have argued, among other things, that 46 million uninsured Americans aren't a big deal, since these people go to the doctor only when they really need to, thus keeping costs down for everyone. In contrast, the 255 million insured Americans waste both private and government insurers' money because they go to the doctor whenever they have a splinter they're too wimpy to deal with at home.

Long before it became the bogeyman of health insurance, moral hazard was the province of fire insurers, who are credited with introducing the term in the nineteenth century. Back then, insurance companies distinguished between two ways fires could occur: natural hazards, like lightning or short circuits, and "moral" hazards, which stemmed from human behavior. These could be deliberate (arson), accidental (knocking over a candle), or the result of "interested carelessness" (throwing a lit cigar into the newspaper bin—oops).

Moral hazards were seen as preventable, whereas lightning was an act of god.

Though we might like to think of ourselves as upright citizens, the fact is that any time there are no consequences for our actions—any time there's a safety net, or a $1 million policy burning a hole in our pockets—we all have the potential to be "moral hazards."

Think about it: If I don't have fire insurance and I leave a cigarette burning in the ashtray and the house burns down, I lose everything.

If I do have insurance, I get a fat check in the mail to build a new house. Under which situation do you think I'm more likely to put out the cigarette?

Similarly, if I'm not married, I will make damn sure I work out every day so I can keep fit and attract an equally fit husband. If I'm married, I might be tempted to stop going to the gym and grow a new ass. What's my husband going to do? Divorce me?

But wait, we're getting ahead of ourselves.

About a century after fire insurers coined the term "moral hazard," Kenneth Arrow, a Nobel Prize–winning microeconomist, was commissioned by the Ford Foundation to look at ways to improve U.S. health care policy. At the time, insurance policies cost a small fortune yet often covered less than they do now.

Arrow blamed moral hazard. Insurance companies, he said, were trying to protect themselves from customers who would be tempted to take advantage of their coverage and rack up unnecessary bills. Arrow's report didn't change the world overnight, but it is credited with bringing the idea of moral hazard back into the public consciousness and inspiring a wave of fresh research into its causes, effects, and potential remedies.

One big difference between Arrow's discussion of moral hazard and that of nineteenth-century insurers was that Arrow didn't frame the issue as one of *morality*—it wasn't a question of whether policyholders were intrinsically good or bad. Rather, it was a question of incentives. If people were allowed to rack up medical bills with no penalty or burden of sharing the costs, they would rack them up—there was no incentive not to.

In the years since, economists have cried moral hazard in all sorts of situations, often as an argument against programs that have the potential to help people. Some commonly cited moral hazard traps:

- Unemployment benefits

  Why should I look for a job when the government is paying me to drink Boone's Farm and drive around in my sweet new Eldorado?

- Welfare

  Ditto re: Boone's and Eldorado.

- Disability insurance

  Go back to work just because I can walk again? Yeah, right—I still have six weeks of paid time off coming to me!

- Warranties

  Shoot, I spilled a glass of water on my keyboard. Oh well, I'll call Apple and they'll send me a brand-new one!

- Government bailouts

  Citibank to itself: Should we or shouldn't we lend this person with no credit history $5 million to buy a new house? You know what? Let's go for it—if he defaults, we can always get Uncle Sam to bail us out.

THE PRINCIPLE: PART TWO

So what about the moral hazard lurking in another kind of insurance policy—the one you got the day you were married? The one that says you'll be taken care of in sickness or in health, if you lose all your money or win the lottery, if things get better or take a turn for the worse? The policy delivered by the state in the form of a marriage license that says at long last you can stop going to singles bars and trying to get the perfect cleavage shot to post on your Match.com profile because you've finally nabbed the One and he or she isn't going anywhere, hallelujah?

Oh, what sweet relief—and what a moral hazard minefield—lurks in that policy.

During our interviews with couples, we saw the moral hazard safety net popping up again and again:

- "I can yell all I want and he can't leave me!"
- "She never used to fart so much while we were dating."
- "I don't know why he's put up with my bullshit for so many years."
- "He seems to have forgotten how to cook anything more complicated than Steak-umms."
- "I would pick up my dirty socks, but I don't because I know she'll do it for me. Is that bad? That's probably bad."
- "I'm of the belief that failure is not an option," said one husband of his marriage, before going on to compare himself with the Spanish conquistador Hernán Cortés, who burned down his ships after landing in Mexico, then ordered his men to conquer the Aztecs or die trying.

Our interviews confirmed what other research says about the blindness of love. According to the General Social Survey, 90 percent of Americans in love say they'd rather suffer than see someone they love suffer; 79 percent say, "I would endure all things for the sake of the one I love"; and 72 percent say they can't be happy unless they place the happiness of their loved one ahead of their own.

This selfless aspect of love, as awesome as it can be, is also the very thing that can create moral hazard. Promise to endure All Things for the sake of your spouse and you're giving him a free pass to do what he wants.

We also saw moral hazard in the more mundane, everyday aspects of marriage: spouses who had let themselves go, gotten lazy, gotten boring, tossed romance out the window, stopped picking up after themselves, stopped pulling their weight, stopped considering the other person's feelings, started taking each other for granted. To some extent, such stories show the natural progression of any long-term relationship. We feel a level of comfort we don't feel with anyone else on earth, and we're relieved that we no longer have to work to impress someone we're trying to date. Love will carry the day, right?

Not if moral hazard is in play.

Without repercussions, without consequences, without the right incentives to behave responsibly—we're all liable to take unwise risks.

Fortunately, there are ways to lessen those risks. In this chapter, we'll touch on three.

The first involves turning spouses into investors. Moral hazard tends to be a problem when people don't feel invested in what they're doing or what they have. It's not as though I own the company, an employee might tell himself, and then proceed to take midday naps in the conference room. Fearing such moral hazard, companies can offer their workers stock options, a stake in the company that, with any luck, will motivate them to work harder. Restaurants put up photos of their best servers, landlords offer tenants the option of renting-to-own, writers have the potential to earn royalties on their books. The message: We're all in this together.

A second solution is regulation, which might entail setting limits. To discourage banks from risking their depositors' money willy-nilly, the government can impose regulations that set limits on what banks can do. For example, institutions must hold a certain amount of money in case there's a rush on their banks.

And a third solution is creating the right incentives. As Kenneth Arrow discovered, in the absence of consequences, we have an *incentive* to behave irresponsibly. If my health insurance covers Lipitor prescriptions, I have less of an incentive to eat healthy foods. Insurers try to change these so-called perverse incentives—incentives that have the opposite effect of their intent—by imposing things like co-payments and deductibles. Their intent is to make you think twice before running to the doctor every time your face looks puffy.

Co-payments for your spouse? A marriage deductible? Regulators in the living room? Absurd, you say? Not when you see how these three couples made it work for them.

CASE STUDY #1

The Players: Beatrice and Troy

When Troy looked at Bea, even after twenty-three years of marriage, he saw a beautiful woman, a devoted mom, a rock who had stood by him through tough times. He saw someone who had supported his musical career even as it stagnated and who always made him feel that he could, with a little focus, rise to new heights.

Bea used to see Troy in a similarly exalted way. He was sexy, full of surprises, reliable but never dull, and a gifted songwriter whose lyrics often brought tears to her eyes.

They had met at a Grateful Dead show in Nevada, and though they were both free spirits—interning at head shops, talking to their spirit warriors in sweat lodges—Bea always had her act together way more than Troy did. She had been raised by a single mom who worked nonstop to give her kids a good home, an education, and solid values. Slacking off was never an option. "There was always this good-girl voice in the back of my head telling me to not get *too* high, use condoms, and make sure there was a sober driver in the group," said Bea.

Troy, on the other hand, was the youngest of five, coddled and babied from the moment he came out of his doting mother's womb. People had always done things for him, beginning with his mother and older sisters and continuing on with his girlfriends in high school and college and then, finally, with Bea. "The role came way too naturally to me," said Bea. And since they had so much fun together, for a while she didn't even notice that she had become the de facto CEO of their marriage.

It was hardly a tough job. They never stayed in one place for very long, living in cities like Boulder, Reno, and Taos and taking odd jobs along the way. They even followed the Dead for a few months, with Bea's CEO duties amounting to little more than mopping up bong water from the backseat. Troy was such a bon vivant, so loving and affectionate, that Bea never minded taking care of the logistics. She thought they complemented each other perfectly.

But life, of course, has a way of settling down. They eventually moved to the Midwest, had a kid, and then had another. They bought a small house and day by day, year by year, acquired the same thousand-pound luggage the rest of the world carries around—mortgage bills, cable bills, electricity bills, credit card bills, water bills, gas bills, vet bills, unpaid taxes, playdates, Legos, *Star Wars* figurines, clogged drains, insurance premiums, Costco memberships. Life became a lot more complicated, a lot more expensive, a lot more . . . like life.

Bea had a steady job as an office manager for a doctor, and Troy did what he always did—pursued his not terribly lucrative dream of becoming a rock star. He had a band and played some gigs, taking temporary construction jobs when money was tight.

When the kids got sick, Bea took them to the doctor. When the faucets leaked, Bea called the plumber. She bought the food, cleaned the guinea pig cage, and cheered on the sidelines during the boys' soccer games while Troy scratched himself and pointed out cool cloud shapes. Troy knew he had it good. "Without Bea," he was fond of saying, "I'd probably be passed out on the side of the road somewhere."

Bea tried to be understanding. "He was always the baby in the family," she said. "I told myself it wasn't his fault, it was a problem of his upbringing." But there were times when it seemed Troy was being deliberately childish, and she would lose her cool. She told us about an incident when she came home late and Troy was lying on the couch watching TV. She asked him if he could put out the recycling before going to bed.

No response.

"Troy, did you hear anything I just said?" Bea asked.

Troy looked up at her and smiled. "What? Oh, I'm sorry, babe, I didn't hear you."

At that moment, something snapped in Bea. "It's stuff like that that made me question our entire marriage and what I was doing with my life," she told us.

Bea grew more and more bitter. She knew Troy loved her and she knew he appreciated her, but that wasn't enough anymore. She was tired. She was raising two kids. Life was a lot more demanding than it was when they lived out of their van and the biggest challenge was where to park for the night so the cops wouldn't chase them away. She had a nine-to-five job, and while managing an office and filing insurance claims wasn't 100 percent soul crushing, it was pretty close to 99 percent.

Which would all be okay if her home life didn't amount to a second job with an ungrateful employee. It suddenly occurred to her that Troy had become someone who lived in her house rent-free and occasionally paid his way by toasting Pop-Tarts for the kids' dinner. "What I really needed," Bea said, "was another me."

She would get mad at him, complain to her friends, and wonder what she had done to deserve such a lump of a husband. She asked him to get a date book and carry it with him at all times so he never forgot where he was supposed to be when, or what he'd promised to pick up for the kids on his way home. "People have been trying to get me to take notes my whole life, and I can never make it happen," Troy told her. "If I tried again, I'd end up disappointing you."

This wasn't what Bea wanted to hear.

She couldn't understand how the things she used to love in Troy— his easygoing, come-what-may attitude, his spontaneity—could now be the source of so much frustration. It was as though she had three kids, only one of them was forty-two years old. With hairy shoulders. And smelly feet.

"I knew marriage was work," Bea told us. "But why didn't my friends warn me exactly how much work?"

The Problem: One Bailout Too Many

Bea thought she was being a good wife by doing everything. She supported Troy, she was patient with him, kind and tolerant. But she was also bailing him out every step of the way. For all intents and purposes, Troy had become a tenant in his own home. And a big problem with tenancy, say economists, is moral hazard. Tenants tend to treat their houses worse than owners do because they don't have a stake, or an investment, in the property.

Here's proof—proof from the other side of the world, where even though their water drains counterclockwise, tenants still behave like tenants and owners act like owners: In Argentina, economists Sebastian Galiani and Ernesto Schargrodsky had the rare chance to test whether property rights can make people a) feel more invested in their homes, and b) behave more responsibly as a result. They looked at a destitute neighborhood on the outskirts of Buenos Aires that had grown into a squatters' wasteland. The plots of land were all owned by people who didn't live there. In the early 1980s, the government started paying those owners to transfer their land to the state. The state then deeded the land to the squatters. Overnight, squatters turned into home owners.

But since some of the original owners didn't comply with the government plan and their cases got tied up in court, some squatters still had no formal rights. This gave the economists a dream scenario: a test sample made up of two groups, living side by side, who started out very similar to each other but whose situations changed suddenly and through outside circumstances.

The Dream Life of an Economist

Other dream scenarios economists envision when they're not design-
ing monetary policy:

- A hot date with the Laffer curve.
- A three-way with Suze Orman and Maria Bartiromo.
- A lifetime subscription to the *American Statistician*.
- Another Great Depression just to see what it'd be like.
- Monetary neutrality.
- Backstage passes at Davos.
- An Adam Smith bobble head.

Galiani and Schargrodsky found property rights had a profound effect on people's lives. For starters, people who were given titles invested more in the construction of their homes: The proportion of
houses with good-quality walls rose by 40 percent, while the proportion with good-quality roofs rose by 47 percent. The newly entitled
also gave their kids a better education. These kids missed fewer days of
school, on average, than other kids, and they stayed in school longer.

Troy may not have been a destitute Argentine squatter, but Bea did
see in his couch-surfing skills a certain squatterlike quality. Either
way, Troy certainly wasn't acting like an investor in his marriage. He
wasn't building roofs (or even patching the old roof when it leaked),
investing in his kids' education ("homework" wasn't part of Troy's vocabulary), or putting in any quality time with his wife, who was feeling more and more like his landlord and less like his business partner.

Not that it was a one-way street. For her part, Bea wasn't giving
Troy much of a chance to invest. Her natural inclination to take care

of people meant that she rarely offered Troy the opportunity to make his own investments in the family. And her nonconfrontational approach to confrontation meant Troy never had to face any repercussions. She asked him only to do menial chores, but that's like the manager at McDonald's asking his drive-through teller to give out the correct change. It's a starting point.

This well-intentioned quality of Bea's, combined with Troy's tendency to let others take care of him, had created a perfect storm of moral hazard. The insurance Bea offered him as his wife and caretaker directly affected his approach to the marriage. Why try any harder if Bea would always be there to bail him out?

The Solution: Get Invested

It might have been true that without Bea, Troy would "be passed out on the side of the road." But in fact, he'd never put that theory to the test. And neither had Bea.

Until she did.

At the breakfast table one sunny spring morning, she announced that she was promoting Troy to co-CEO of their marriage. And no, it wasn't negotiable. And yes, that meant things were going to change. For starters, he was now in charge of managing his stuff: his money, his slippers when one went missing, his special dandruff shampoo, his piles and piles of old LPs that were growing moldy in the basement. Also, if he wanted to spend time with her and the kids, he'd have to take the initiative—she wasn't insisting on family dinners anymore or begging him to come to soccer games and actually pay attention.

She stopped doing his laundry. She moved all her money into her own bank account and cut off his allowance (yes, for years she had given him a spending allowance). She no longer thought so much about his likes and dislikes when she went to the supermarket; if she wanted eggplant, dammit, she was getting eggplant. At night, after dinner, she'd do her dishes and help the kids with their homework before sending them off to bed. Sometimes they'd forget to say good night to their dad, who was either on the couch or sitting on the front porch looking at the stars.

While forcing Troy to invest in his own affairs, Bea also took the step of divesting herself from some of the family duties she'd always handled. She continued handling Little League and homework, but she made Dad the go-to weekend CEO if the kids needed a ride to a birthday party or someone to practice goal kicks with in the yard.

Pretty soon, not only was Troy's dirty underwear piling up, but his kids were waking him up on Sunday mornings demanding he make waffles, watch TV with them, take them to the batting cages, or help them collect garden slugs for dissection. Bea left the house early to do her own thing—getting her nails done, which she hadn't done in ages, or meeting a friend for coffee, or hopping on the treadmill at the gym—so Troy would not even have the opportunity to pass the buck.

Troy, meanwhile, was shocked at how energetic and *needy* his kids could be. Not that he didn't love them, he just didn't really *know* them. "I would take a bullet for those boys," said Troy (we did admire his flair for the dramatic). "But, man, are they a handful."

Bea was cautiously optimistic. She knew she was being extreme, and she didn't know whether Troy would sink or swim. "To be honest, I was terrified he would ignore me and everything would turn to shit," said Bea. "Which isn't what I wanted, but I didn't have a choice at that point." She had friends who stayed in bad marriages and were miserable, and she had friends who walked out the door before they'd even tried to fix what was broken. She didn't want to follow either course, so she'd settled on plan C, sudden as it may have been.

Luckily for her, Troy wasn't as dumb as he'd acted for the past decade or so. He started to notice that what he did—or didn't do—mattered. If he didn't do his laundry, his clothes would be dirty. If he didn't interact with his kids, they sulked; if he did, their faces lit up.

One day, his younger son, seven-year-old Matty, came home from school with a card he'd drawn in art class for his "weird" and "cool" dad, Troy. The "weird" part touched Troy because it meant that Matty understood his quirks and loved him anyway.

Troy was getting out what he put in, which was a novel experience for him.

"As my relationship with my kids changed, I started to appreciate what Bea had been doing all this time," said Troy. "I always felt like a better husband compared to the guys I know. I never complained about my wife like they did. I had no complaints, in fact. But Bea was the one who had legitimate complaints, and I was the clueless one."

Troy didn't become a new Troy altogether. He didn't wake up one day and put on a suit and tie and get a job at a pinwheel factory. He didn't get a job at all. But he did start to invest, slowly taking to the job of co-CEO with an enthusiasm he'd never shown for anything else, at least not since the summer of '87, when he spent a week whittling Bea a turtle out of a bar of soap.

Then one summer weekend, Troy organized a family camping trip to Lake Michigan. He booked the sites three months in advance, bought two tents (on Bea's credit card, but still), planned the campfire menus, and figured out a few kid-friendly day hikes. "I almost started to believe in god," said Bea; that's how miraculous the whole thing seemed to her. Oh, and last time we checked, Troy wasn't lying by the side of a road.

CASE STUDY #2

The Players: Lana and Joe

Lana and Joe met fourteen years ago on a blind date arranged by their *parents*. Lana had sworn off mom-arranged blind dates after the first dud her mom set her up with—a self-made "entrepreneur" who had supposedly started his own hedge fund and who played Ringo in a Beatles cover band on weekends. But since then, she had gone on so many bad dates that in a moment of weakness she agreed to have coffee—just coffee!—with her mom's friend Cheryl's friend Judy's son Joe, a guy she had last seen when she was five years old and they were in the same music class together.

Turned out Joe had grown up to be a real adult. He was mature, funny, asked Lana a lot of questions, didn't lunge at her for a sloppy kiss at the end of the date, and had that one character trait so elusive among single, thirty-something men—he was normal. "I was sure there was a catch," said Lana.

Joe was also relieved to find that Lana was normal. Not normal as in boring or like everyone else, but normal as in sane, with a good head on her shoulders and an independent spirit. They both had wry senses of humor and thick skins, and even on those early dates, they would tease each other and laugh about their own foibles. They wanted a lot out of their lives and expected a lot from themselves, but they also understood that life is lived in the moment. This shared philosophy is what initially drew them together and what kept them going in those first few years.

Well, that and an unexpected pregnancy. Except it wasn't so unexpected, since neither could deny being too lazy to use a condom one drunken night or whispering afterward in the dark about how if worst came to worst, they would move to Costa Rica, open a surf shop, and raise their love child in a tentalow on the beach.

Instead, they tied the knot at city hall.

Over time, their strong-willed personalities caused them to butt heads—a lot. They were one of those couples who seem to thrive on fighting, the kind that pick each other apart one minute and have hot make-up sex the next. Lana pushed Joe's buttons by telling him when he was acting like his manic-depressive mother. Joe pushed Lana's right back by ignoring her phone calls when he thought she was being too needy. Each often faulted the other.

"Joe is extremely moody," Lana told us. "One minute he's Mr. Dad and the next he's curled up in the fetal position talking to himself. It drives me crazy. He's a drama king, and I'm much more calm and levelheaded about things."

"Lana is a live wire," Joe told us (obviously, we didn't interview them at the same time). "If I'm five minutes late, she'll start calling me obsessively. She has no internal monitor in her head telling her to chill out. She says what's on her mind, without thinking first. I love her, but she's nuts."

Joe and Lana were the kind of couple you meet at a party and at first you think, "They'll be divorced within a year," and then, by the end of the night, you're wondering what the secret to their success is.

Whatever their secret, it worked for them for many years . . . until about the time their daughter, Bella, hit puberty. Partly, they started focusing less on each other and more on Bella's increasingly complicated issues—whether going to band camp would annihilate her social life, why it wasn't okay to have her own Facebook page yet, and when, if ever, she would get asked out by a guy now that all her friends seemed to be "dating."

Joe and Lana were not unusual in this regard. Research shows that marital satisfaction plummets after the birth of a first child. Couples are nine times more likely to argue and are at greater risk for depression. They get overwhelmed; conversation and sex fall off a cliff. Couples who make it past the first few years—and also survive the first few years after their second child is born—are often home-free. But even then, there's a catch: Plenty of couples crash and burn again when their kids hit puberty. "It is one of life's great ironies that just as the physical demands placed on parents by young children diminish, the emotional burdens of raising querulous adolescents take over," writes psychiatrist John W. Jacobs, adding that "if, as the burdens of parenthood mount, the spouses fail to devise a reasonable method of taking care of their children and *each other's* desires, serious tensions can develop."

We don't have PhD's, but we're pretty sure Joe and Lana's situation fit the bill of failing "to devise a reasonable method" of looking out for the marriage itself. Lana talked about an "apathy" that had set in when it came to being there for Joe after he'd had a hard day at work. Joe said he didn't have the "bandwidth" to deal with Lana's latest anxiety about the next global pandemic hitting their small town. It was all each of them could do to take care of themselves and Bella. They now argued less (which in their case was a bad thing), cared less, and did less to meet each other's needs.

Lana, whose messiness always irritated Joe, stopped trying to be neater. Joe, whose habit of not calling home when he was planning to be late drove Lana crazy, stopped calling entirely. Lana claimed she didn't have time to exercise, Joe claimed he was too tired to talk. Joe farted more, Lana cooked less.

The Problem: Nothing to Lose

Imagine a line in the sand. On one side of the line is moral hazard. That's a world where you let yourself go completely, you assume your spouse will pick up your socks, will always bail you out, and will never, ever abandon you. You don't bother showing affection, you let those old sweet nothings fall by the wayside, your muffin top expands by the day, and you settle into a comfortable indifference.

On the other side of the line is paranoia. Call it the opposite of moral hazard. You never let down your guard, you clean up after yourself, and you follow your spouse's rules to the letter. You dote, you second-guess, you never provoke. You avoid conflict entirely, out of fear that the minute you bring up tough topics your spouse will shut down the marriage and walk away.

In reality, as you can see in Figure 7, there's a whole spectrum between those two scenarios. You probably wouldn't want a marriage devoid of moral hazard—you need to know you can mess up from time to time and that your spouse won't quit on you. Some moral hazard is key to the functioning of a marriage.

But you also don't want it ruling your life. So wherever you fall on the moral hazard spectrum, your goal should be to inch as close as possible to the middle—to a spot that's a safe harbor, not a safety net.

How do you reach that middle ground? By rewriting the rules of your partnership and bringing back some basic accountability. It's a little-known fact that people tend to work harder when they've got something to lose.

Think of it this way: If Manny Ramirez was up for a contract renewal every year, he might be the greatest hitter in baseball history. But since he gets a few years between every contract, during which time he's got nothing to lose and not much at stake, he can let things

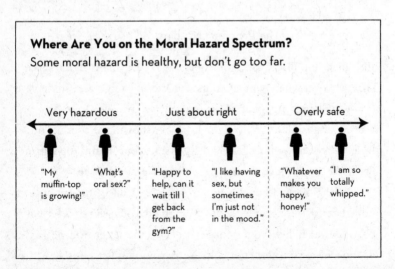

Where Are You on the Moral Hazard Spectrum?
Some moral hazard is healthy, but don't go too far.

Very hazardous   Just about right   Overly safe

"My muffin-top is growing!"   "What's oral sex?"   "Happy to help, can it wait till I get back from the gym?"   "I like having sex, but sometimes I'm just not in the mood."   "Whatever makes you happy, honey!"   "I am so totally whipped."

Figure 7: Finding the Middle Ground

slide. In fact, in 2008 with his eight-year contract with the Red Sox due to expire, "contract-year Manny," as his critics like to call him, put up some of the best numbers of his career: a batting average of .332, a .601 slugging percentage, and 121 RBIs. Come 2009 after he'd signed a two-year, $45-million contract with the Dodgers, all those numbers plummeted. So predictable. Even a whopping salary can't eradicate moral hazard.

You can generally spot moral hazard in a situation where someone who has nothing to lose—or thinks he has nothing to lose—slacks off, thinks only of himself, takes things for granted, or takes too many risks. Moral hazard is one reason 56 percent of the people we talked to in our Exhaustive, Groundbreaking, and Very Expensive Marriage Survey admitted to putting on weight since they got married. And why roughly 46 percent said they are a little less affectionate with their partners than they once were, with the most common excuse being the fact that they're "too busy," and another 20 percent admitting that it no longer even crosses their minds to be affectionate.

The assumption is that the other person will live with a little less—after all, they're married, and that's the way it goes. But people like that have moved all the way to the dark side of the moral hazard spectrum, and they are playing with fire, which is pretty much where Joe and Lana found themselves after fourteen years of marriage.

The Solution: A New Regulatory Framework

Joe and Lana needed a new contract. Rules, regulations, and contracts that have real consequences give us something to lose, and in doing so, they temper the beast of moral hazard.

Joe and Lana could make a regulation akin to a renewal of vows, only of very specific vows, like "I vow to never fart in bed anymore" or "I vow to keep my shoes out of the entryway."

They could, in theory, stipulate penalties for breach of contract—

the silent treatment for six days, for example, or revenge, or, simply, divorce—but more likely, a breach would result in the continued slow atrophy of their marriage, something like what economist Ted Bergstrom calls "harsh words and burnt toast."

Maybe you're thinking it goes against the very nature of love to regulate it. People aren't companies, you say, they're complex, unique souls who respond to each challenge differently.

Okay, fine, but don't forget that marriage is already highly regulated—and we're not even talking about the license from the state or the alternative minimum tax. Couples operate under basic rules, like no cheating, no flying to the Bahamas without telling the other person, no buying a house without mutual consent. So why not add a few more rules to the list if they can improve the state of affairs? Moral hazard arises when there are no consequences, and there are no consequences when there are no rules.

For Joe and Lana, it wouldn't be enough to simply vow never to get complacent. The contract needed to be structured and specific.

Before they hit their era of apathy, they were pretty good about meeting halfway. Maybe Lana didn't love to get on the treadmill, but she did it anyway because she wanted to look her best for Joe. Joe didn't care whether his hands were washed, but he washed them when he came home to keep Lana happy. They needed to get back to that place of tolerance and compromise, and to do so, they needed regulations. The four things Lana told us Joe could do that would help her feel appreciated were to

1. call when he was running late.
2. wash his hands when he came home from work.
3. talk and interact with her and Bella when he came home.
4. go #2 in the upstairs bathroom when she was making breakfast downstairs.

Moral Hazard: It's a Lifesaver!

Rules can do more than save marriages—they can save lives. Economists Michael Conlin, Stacy Dickert-Conlin, and John Pepper looked at whether hunting regulations intended to control deer populations had an unintended effect on safety. They compared hunting accidents in Pennsylvania from 1990 through 2005.

In an effort to thin the deer population, beginning in 2000, Pennsylvania started allowing hunters to shoot both bucks and does on the same day. Prior to that, you could only shoot bucks on certain days and does on other days. In 2002, the state changed the law again, this time to protect younger bucks who were being overharvested (a fancy name for killed). Now you could shoot any size doe, but only bucks whose antlers met the minimum size requirement (bigger antlers = older buck).

During the either/or years, as well as the years when you couldn't shoot young bucks, hunters had to be much more careful deciding whether or not to fire—they wouldn't want to shoot a buck on a doe day, or a buck with small antlers, and risk getting caught. Conversely, if hunters were allowed to shoot either sex, of any size, the economists theorized, they might be less careful in deciding whether to fire. After all, whatever they shot would be fair game.

And that's where the potential for moral hazard lay: When there was no penalty for shooting a deer of a certain sex or size, hunters might be liable to take more risks when shooting.

And take risks they did. The economists found that hunters were more likely to accidentally shoot other people between the years 2000 and 2002.

Moral of the story: Sometimes the solution is simple—scrap the "anything goes" approach and devise an either/or. *Either* you can go to your men's crocheting club tonight, or you can watch football all day Sunday. Pick your pleasure.

Joe told us he would weep for joy if Lana could bring herself to

1. tidy up the house and keep Bella's sports gear out of the hallway.
2. occasionally use the words "please" and "thank you."
3. agree to a little more foreplay when they got around to having sex (if this shocks you, know that it shocked us, too).
4. try to get back on the treadmill—*not* that he didn't love her no matter how she looked, he was just saying that, you know, maybe she'd feel better if she got in shape again.

They wrote their lists down and exchanged them. They decided that agreeing to three out of four requests would be enough—for example, Lana could say she would put her own stuff away, but couldn't always guarantee she'd get around to Bella's stuff, and Joe could say sometimes he needed to come home and have thirty minutes of quiet time to unwind before fully engaging with the family. But three out of four ain't bad. And as for the consequences: The minute one of them slacked off, the other would follow—in other words, no clean hands, no foreplay.

Putting everything on the table removed the mystery of what had happened to the marriage. There it was, the stuff they'd let fall by the wayside, in black and white. It was true that parenthood had taken its toll and that Joe and Lana's "querulous adolescent" sapped a fair share of the couple's combined energies. But as psychiatrist John Jacobs says, "Knowing how vulnerable marriages are today," you'd be helping your kids "if you remembered regularly to focus attention on your couplehood."★

Joe and Lana's new contract exposed the ways they'd let moral hazard get the best of them. By refocusing on each other—in just a few

---

★Or as Homer Simpson put it, "Marriage is like a coffin and each kid is like another nail."

simple ways—they could remember why they fell in love to begin with and how much they stood to lose if they stayed on their current path.

To moral hazard–proof your own marriage, start with a simple contract and a few stipulations. Should you specify how many back rubs you'll give your husband per year? Before saying no, think about it for a second. If you never do it (and we're assuming in this scenario that he likes it), you're sending the message that you know you don't have to and he'll adapt—after all, what husband expects his wife to rub his back every day when she's got a full-time job and 2.5 kids? Maybe the worst that happens is he'll gripe about it once in a while. But you can handle a little griping, right?

Wrong. A little griping leads to a little resentment, which leads to a little withholding, which then leads to you griping and you being resentful and you withholding—and before you know it, something that would've taken five minutes of your time has become a source of tension. The point isn't that back rubs are the key to a happy marriage, but that withholding something your partner would love, no matter how inconsequential, has a ripple effect. In a marriage, nothing happens in a vacuum.

At least for the first few months after you draw up your agreement, periodically track your progress. Go back every week and check off that you've both done what you promised to do. For example: Did you say hello when you walked in the door on Wednesday, or did you make your usual grunting sound instead? How many times did you check in with the other about dinner plans and offer a suggestion? Did you arrange for a babysitter on Saturday night and book movie tickets? Did you have sex every day last week? If you shorted yourself by one night, are you both okay with it? (By the way, if you really specified sex every day in your contract, and you stuck to it, you should probably write the follow-up to this book.)

In essence, what a contract does is reset the status quo—that default we all cling to (see chapter 2 on loss aversion for a refresher on status quo bias). The trick is to not let the new contract become a new status quo. Revisit it occasionally and check that it's still relevant, and that your needs haven't changed recently. If they have, tweak the contract—but don't do a major overhaul. Small changes can have huge payoffs.

CASE STUDY #3

The Players: Carla and Pete

Carla met Pete at a rodeo. She was a fashion writer in New York City, and on a lark, she took an assignment from a men's magazine to cover a rodeo in Wyoming—not that it didn't cross her mind that maybe she'd pick up a cute cowboy along the way.

Pete was a cute cowboy. He was riding bulls at the rodeo, and when he wasn't doing that, he worked on a cattle ranch and trained horses. He planned to spend the rest of the year in Wyoming and then head to Virginia—where he'd gone to a military college—to start up his own business. He was tall, blond, soft-spoken, polite, confident, straight-talking, strong, emotionally intact—in short, he was everything that the guys Carla had spent the past fifteen years dating weren't.

They had a weeklong whirlwind romance that Carla never thought would go anywhere. "It seemed impossible that two such different people could ever make it work," said Carla. "He wore *chaps*."

Fast-forward six months, five cross-country visits, thousands of dollars in long-distance bills, weekly letters (yes, Pete still wrote *letters,* like with a pen and paper, which Carla obliged with letters back to him), and, finally, a marriage proposal, and Carla and Pete were not only *possible,* they were *actual*.

True, it was a romance of opposites from the start: city girl and country boy; atheist and Christian; Manolo Blahniks and Carhartts. But it worked.

"He brought out the best in me," said Carla, who after so much time in Manhattan was ready to get off the treadmill—the literal treadmill at Crunch she spent half her life running on and the figurative one she'd been on ever since she'd moved to the city from Ohio to make it big in magazines.

"No one had ever made me laugh so hard in my life," said Pete, who had never been on any kind of treadmill, spiritual or otherwise, but who knew enough to grab a good thing when he saw it.

The only issue was how to join their disparate lives. Pete trained horses, built fences, and communed with nature. His heart would shrivel if he was forced to live in a walk-up apartment in the West Village with a view of a gas station. Carla didn't want to be the agent of Pete's destruction—she loved that he was a horse whisperer and outdoorsman—and she was also more game to try country living than Pete would ever be to brave the city.

So she loaded her stuff into his truck and they set off for Virginia.

They bought a house on eight acres, and Carla jumped right into her new life. She started a vegetable garden, learning the difference between kale and chard, rutabaga and parsnip. Pete had a dog named Cowboy, and Carla got a second dog at the pound. Wallis sat by her side all day as she wrote freelance pieces from her home office and followed her around the backyard as she inspected her seedlings. With no treadmill for miles, Carla started running through the woods behind their house and scouted out some trails with stunning views of the mountains. She learned to cook, regaling Pete with her ever more adventurous dishes like house-dried venison jerky, peanut-butter crepes, and something called "Coca-Cola ham" when he came home after a long day of building horse fences.

But even as she explored new sides of herself, Carla had days where she thought she'd go nuts from the isolation. Pete didn't have this problem. He could go for weeks without speaking to another human being. He built fences in near total silence, occasionally nodding to Cowboy, his right-hand dog.

Carla, on the other hand, was social. She missed her friends in New York. How many days in a row could she endure in which the only creatures she spoke to were Wallis, Pete, and herself? She would panic and worry about money, about her career, about her lack of close friends. She would obsess over the decisions she'd made in her life that had led her to this place in the literal middle of nowhere. She looked in the mirror and couldn't recognize the person staring back, wearing the same frayed jeans, turtleneck, and L.L.Bean vest day after day after day after day.

It didn't help that Pete worked seven days a week, from before sunrise to after dark. He was committed to growing his business and building their nest egg, and he had an unparalleled capacity for work. He saw that Carla was increasingly moody and not quite the barrel of laughs she was when they'd fallen in love. But he figured she'd adapt. And she did try to adapt, but it wasn't easy when she had a husband who told her to "turn that frown upside down" whenever she said she was depressed. For Pete, depression didn't compute. "We had a great life," said Pete. "We were in love. What was there to be sad about?"

Carla started sleeping until noon. Pete would come home and the kitchen would be dark. He would find Carla lying on the couch, watching *Supernanny* reruns, and eating week-old Coca-Cola ham for dinner, trusty old Wallis at her side.

The Problem: Perverse Incentives

This might be a good time to tell you that Pete was the guy who compared his marriage to the conquering of the Aztecs by Hernán

Cortés, who said when it comes to the holy bonds of matrimony, "failure is not an option."

On the one hand, this philosophy meant he'd never leave his wife and he'd do anything to protect her and their marriage. (Thus the fifteen-hour workdays, the saving money, the undying loyalty. We should all be so lucky to have a guy like Pete.) But on the other hand, it meant he was blind to the warning signs when failure really was creeping in. It didn't occur to him that anything could break up his marriage, so he saw Carla's condition as a temporary blip that would get better with time.

Pete's view of their marriage created what an economist would call a "perverse incentive," an incentive that has the opposite effect of its intent. Here's an example from the corporate world: Companies often encourage managers to cut their departmental budgets. But if a manager does cut his budget by 15 percent, his reward is a 15 percent lower budget the next year—hardly an incentive to make further cuts. Medicaid reimburses doctors more for diagnostic tests than for their time, which means doctors are incentivized to see you quickly, ask few questions, and ship you off for an MRI. Such perverse incentives create moral hazards in that they tempt people to do the opposite of what they ought to be doing.

Or let's take another example, this time from the world of sports. In baseball, there's something called "the designated hitter rule" that lets a team designate a player to bat in place of its pitcher. Pitchers tend to be awful hitters, so the rule is supposed to make for a more action-packed game.

At least, that's the intended effect. The *unintended* effect, according to a pair of researchers who crunched thirty years' worth of data, is that more batters get beaned—meaning hit, intentionally, by the ball—by the opposing pitcher in games with a designated hitter. Why? Because pitchers never have to step up to the plate, they don't have to worry about the retaliation factor—the fear that if they "accidentally" drill a batter in the ribs, they might also get "accidentally" hit in return by the opposing team's pitcher when the teams switch sides. The researchers, an economist and a mathematician, were able to figure this out by comparing the rate of hit batsmen in the American League, which uses the designated hitter rule, with the rate in the National League, which doesn't. The difference? The rate of hit batsmen was 15 percent higher in the AL than in the NL.

Pitchers in the AL have no incentive *not* to bean batters because they're insured against being hit back, whereas NL pitchers have every incentive to watch where the ball goes. In trying to make the game more exciting, baseball's rule makers created a moral hazard by tempting pitchers to throw 95 mph fastballs into the guy standing innocently at the plate.

Perverse, right?

Which brings us back to Pete. One side effect of his monolithic view of marriage was that he didn't allow for the fact that in real life, failure *is* an option and breakdowns *do* occur—so he didn't develop the skills to deal with either of those outcomes. And because he figured the marriage—the insurance that was the marriage—was a guarantee of lifetime coverage, he had no incentive to make any sacrifices or adjustments of his own. Perversely, his otherwise admirable no-fail approach wasn't incentivizing him to be the best husband he could be.

Pete was a good guy who had fallen into a bad moral hazard trap.

One day when Pete came home from work, the house was empty. Carla was gone. There was a note on the fridge saying she was driving to her parents' house and would be back in a few weeks, if at all, and that she wanted to make the marriage work, but it would require serious change. Pete was shocked. He had always assumed the hard part for Carla was making the decision to move to the country—but that once she did, it would all work out. Pete was well-intentioned but ill informed.

The Solution: Smart Incentives

Just as incentives can mess up your life, they can also save it from going off the deep end. Think about that stomachache and the year spent seeing doctors in hopes of a cure. Your insurance was a moral hazard: You had no incentive to worry about costs because you were covered. Similarly, pitchers in the American League have no incentive to refrain from breaking the ribs of opposing batters, insured rental car drivers have no incentive to keep the backseat free of dog hair, and overconfident husbands have no incentive to go the extra mile for their wives.

People with insurance have every incentive to be reckless—not that they'll necessarily *be* reckless, but we shouldn't expect them to be superhuman, either. How do you make it so people can enjoy the benefits of insurance but also have an incentive to act responsibly?

You charge them.

That's where deductibles and co-payments come in. The idea is that by making policyholders share some of the costs, they'll be incentivized to consume less and take more precautions. Living in Virginia, Pete was reaping all the benefits and not sharing any of Carla's costs—isolation, loss of close friends, the screeching halt of her once flourishing career.

We're not endorsing Carla's solution of running away from home—that's a move that could easily backfire for other couples—but in this case, it was the jolt Pete needed. And Carla, too. "The whole time I thought it was my problem, that I needed to stop feeling sorry for myself and live with my decisions instead of bitching all the time," she told us. "But I couldn't turn it off. And I realized that didn't mean I was crazy. I mean, yeah, I'm crazy, but I also could have used some help from my husband, and I wasn't getting any."

The thing is, Carla never asked for help. She tried to feel better on her own, failed, and then retreated. Pete came home, told her to turn that frown around, and she retreated even further. What Carla needed was for Pete to lighten her load—to share her costs and help her enjoy the benefits.

Living where they did would require Pete to make some co-payments.

Not that Carla used the word "co-payment"—she's a fashion writer, not an insurance underwriter—but her solution was exactly what economists would have recommended.

While she was at her parents' house, she came up with a list of things Pete could do to take on more responsibility for her long-term happiness, assuming they stayed in Virginia:

- Pete working six days a week instead of seven, so that they had one full day to spend together, either just the two of them or out with the handful of friends they'd made since moving there. Carla tended to gripe about missing her old friends—her "real" friends—but she admitted she hadn't given anyone in Virginia a real chance. She asked Pete to help her with that project by carving out some leisure time in his otherwise all-work-and-no-play schedule.

- Pete footing the bill for a Web designer to create a blog and website for Carla. One of the problems with Virginia, as she saw it, was that it was the perfect place for Pete to grow his business and a horrific place for Carla to grow hers. She lived in the boonies, too far to meet and network with editors. She worried that pretty soon her contacts in the city would forget her altogether.

- Pete putting his handiness to use at home and installing central heating. He had been promising to do it for a year and hadn't made any progress. Carla was tired of freezing. It was time to pay up.

- Pete helping with dinner. Not every night, but some nights. In the beginning, Carla relished the retro irony that she'd turned into a housewife who served her husband dinner every night. But lately, she felt like, well, a housewife who served her husband dinner every night.

"I felt a little demanding," admitted Carla, "but in reality I'd asked very little of him up until that point, and I think he realized that." And indeed, Pete agreed to all the co-payments, eagerly and without argument. He even made a co-payment on his own, one that Carla hadn't specifically stipulated: He bought her thirty-two chickens and built a McMansion-like coop for them to live in, complete with a roosting loft and a skylight. "I thought you'd think it was fun," he said. "And you can write about it on your new blog!"

And you know what? She did, and she did.

THE BOTTOM LINE

1. **Invest in your relationship.** People tend to pay more attention to quality when they're invested in the final outcome. The more you put in, the more you'll get back.
2. **Regulate.** Nothing wrong with making a few rules, minimum requirements you each need from the other to make your marriage work. You can even write them down. Pull out the rule book when one of you seems to have forgotten your end of the bargain.
3. **Don't count on a bailout.** If you find yourself walking past a pile of dirty socks with the thought "she'll get to that later" passing through your slacker head, reconsider your trajectory. Your marriage doesn't come with a money-back guarantee.
4. **Be affectionate, go to the gym, wear something besides sweatpants.** Getting lazy is normal, but it's also very very bad! Your spouse deserves your best, not your third best.

5

INCENTIVES

Or, Getting Your Spouse to Do What You Want

THE PRINCIPLE

If you can stand it, put yourself in the shoes of Maurice "Hank" Greenberg, the man at the helm of insurance giant American International Group circa 2001. You've got nice shoes. You've got a big office with a nineteenth-century King George III desk and a "lesser" Van Gogh valued at $6 million. Your corporate jet has a StairMaster so not a single moment goes to waste, and your personal driver is on hand to shuttle you to your home on the Upper East Side or your sprawling estate an hour outside of town. You've got a cool $200 billion in company assets at your disposal and the thrilling and unsettling knowledge that if something goes wrong with AIG, you could ruin the lives of many, many hardworking Americans. You've got offices in 130 countries, thousands of employees report to you, and it's your job to figure out how to get them—not to mention the whole lumbering enterprise—performing at maximum efficiency.

So: How do you do that?

Do you channel Mussolini and give rousing two-hour speeches every day in the fourteenth-floor auditorium? Do you take your army of SVPs out for a day of trust exercises, zip-lines, and hot stone massages? Do you line the halls with employee-of-the-month photos?

If you're Hank Greenberg, you offer your best guys the potential to earn lots and lots of money. You offer them a practically unheard-of pay scale. For example, you say to Joe Cassano, son of a Brooklyn cop and an up-and-coming trader you just appointed to run an elite group within AIG: Here's the deal, Joe. If your team works hard and makes me look good and earns tons of money, I will let you pocket, free and clear, 30 to 35 percent of your profits. This is no small gesture: Even on Wall Street, where traders love to brag that they "eat what they kill" (translation: get a cut of the business they bring in), 30 to 35 percent is a whopping slice of the kill.

Joe Cassano really likes the sound of this proposal. He goes back and tells his guys, Check it out, Hank says we can take home *a third* of what we bring in. And now that the brass ring has been offered, Joe's guys reach for it in a big, big way: By 2005, the unit's revenues grow to $3.26 billion from $737 million in 1999. Joe's personal compensation will come to more than $300 million.

Economists generally approve of compensation structures like this. To some extent, bonuses are, and have long been, the lifeblood of Wall Street. At its most basic, this is how the thinking goes: Pay workers an hourly wage and you will get an hourly-wage type of performance; offer workers the promise of a windfall and they will work as if their lives and the lives of their children, their mothers, their accountants, and their pet Chihuahuas depended on it. "A cornerstone of personnel economics is that workers respond to incentives," writes Edward P. Lazear, an economist at Stanford's business school. "Specifically, it is a given that paying on the basis of output will induce workers to supply more output."

This all makes perfect sense, just as it makes perfect sense that incentives would apply not only to "personnel economics" and Wall

Street, but to nearly every aspect of our lives. We told you in the last chapter how good incentives can combat moral hazard. In this chapter, we'll show you how they can accomplish something equally miraculous: getting people to do things you want them to do.

But first, some examples. If you're the U.S. government and you want Americans to stop smoking (because you care deeply about your citizens, of course, but also because smokers are bleeding Medicaid dry), you jack up cigarette taxes until people decide they're better off, financially, quitting. If you own a gym and the treadmills have been empty lately, you offer the first month free to all new members. If you're the city of Longmont, Colorado, and you're tired of drivers running red lights, you install cameras that catch offenders and automatically send tickets in the mail. Credit-card companies offer a year without interest for new balance transfers. Shoe stores advertise the second pair for half price. Self-help books guarantee six-pack abs or a better marriage.

Incentives rule at home, too. When your kids don't eat and you're at the end of your rope, you incentivize: You want ice cream tonight, better eat your broccoli. (We're not saying this is the right thing to do, by the way, or that we're proud of it, but we have a life to live and we don't have all night.) Every time you try to get your spouse to do the dishes or clean the basement or finally hang that picture you had framed six months ago, you use incentives: You offer kindness, you come home with flowers, you issue threats, ultimatums, and promises. When his gut starts spilling over his belt, you buy him a NordicTrack for his birthday as a way of maybe sorta gently suggesting that he exercise once in a while. You book the babysitter and reserve a room at that romantic bed-and-breakfast you went to for your anniversary to increase your chances of getting lucky for the first time in ages. Heck, getting married happens to be one of the most effective incentives around: Swear you won't run off on me, and I'll make an honest woman (or man!) out of you.

THE PEOPLE SPEAK . . .

About Incentives

Many of the people who took our Exhaustive, Groundbreaking, and Very Expensive Marriage Survey—at least the 49 percent who were being honest—admitted to using incentives to get their spouses to do things they couldn't otherwise get them to do. Among the tactics deemed "effective" or "very effective":

- Giving praise (49 percent).
- Offering to do something in exchange (48 percent).
- Explaining how they'll actually *benefit* from doing the thing they don't want to do (43 percent).
- Asking repeatedly (25 percent).
- Pointing out that their friends' spouses do it (15 percent).

Without incentives, Wall Street would atrophy, gyms would die out, your kids would get rickets, and your spouse might forget all about the sex part of marriage. Not to put too fine a point on it, but without incentives, none of us would ever do *anything*. So here's an incentive to keep reading: If you want to be good at incentives, you have to understand the catch.

The Catch

This is what happened to Joe Cassano: By 2008, it was apparent that he and his team of supposedly crack traders were losing money. Big money. For years, they had reaped huge profits writing billions of dollars of insurance on debt—debt owned by other financial institutions—which meant that AIG would have to pay out only if the debt started to lose value. In the meantime, they could sit back and collect the premiums. Cassano and his crew assumed defaults weren't in the cards.

They were wrong.

Starting in 2007, the U.S. housing crisis came knocking at Cassano's door, and soon enough, the bets he thought would be a sure thing started to lose billions. Joe's "elite" unit was about to clobber AIG itself. Luckily for Joe, we (you, us, the American taxpayers) spent $182.5 billion to save the company. In the end, Cassano's financial team played a starring role in fueling the subprime mortgage crisis which brought the U.S. economy to its knees.

The best part: Joe Cassano stayed rich. He didn't have to give back his bonuses. Not only that, but AIG kept him on board—at $1 million a month—to try to clean up the mess he'd created. (Which prompted one irate congressperson to ask Cassano's boss what, exactly, one would have to do to get fired.)*

The lesson here, besides never trust guys named Joe or Hank, is that incentives that seem like no-brainers—pay more money, get better work—can backfire if you don't design them wisely. In Cassano's case, those blowout bonuses didn't actually help AIG because the trader was guaranteed his 30 to 35 percent cut, a cut he would never have to return, even if AIG—or, for that matter, *our country*—went belly-up. The incentive itself became the goal, instead of AIG's long-term health—and that's a surefire way for an incentive to fail.

This isn't a phenomenon specific to Wall Street. Economists have discovered that all sorts of incentives backfire, even the ones long considered fail-safe. For example, money. Not Wall Street bonus–type

---

*Mr. Cassano told a Congressional panel that he made prudent decisions, and would have saved taxpayers billions had he stayed on at AIG to negotiate with the government.

money, but regular amounts of money. It turns out paying people sometimes makes them *not* want to do things, like volunteer or get good grades. That's because the money "crowds out" the innate incentive to do good simply for the sake of doing good. (The fancy term for this kind of incentive, in case you want to sound smart at a cocktail party, is "pro-social motivation.") In one recent experiment by a pair of Swedish economists, only 30 percent of women who were offered compensation for giving blood chose to donate, while 52 percent of women who weren't offered money donated anyway.

Other incentives can be easily gamed. Assess teachers based on their students' test scores, and they'll teach only to the test. Great for test scores, not so great if we want to raise kids who have the occasional original thought. Try to curb a rat outbreak, witness the rat population skyrocket. True story: In colonial Vietnam, the French once tried to deal with Hanoi's rat problem by offering bounties for rattails. It didn't take long for some enterprising Vietnamese to discover a quicker alternative to scouring the streets for rats—farm the damn rodents. Which led to an *increase* in the population of rats.

Punishment can be a great incentive to deter crime or bad behavior: The threat of a speeding ticket deters many people from driving 80 mph in a 30 mph zone; the threat of divorce deters adultery (at least for those of us not in public office); and the threat of losing our jobs is a pretty good incentive to show up for work every day. But the threat of punishment can also motivate people to find new ways to misbehave: Institute a "three strikes law" in California and watch violent crime go up across the border in Nevada; fine people for smoking in the airplane lavatory and risk your smoke detector getting stolen; refuse to have sex with your spouse after he offends you, and catch him surfing the Internet for porn at three in the morning.

Sometimes the incentives that seem the weakest or the least likely to work—like telling people they're doing a great job, acknowledging someone's hard work, and trusting your partner, friend, or employee to *not* let you down—can be the most effective incentives of all. Crazy, but true. We'll show you how true in the stories that follow.

It's hard to overemphasize the importance of getting incentives right. They can be the difference between a profitable AIG and an AIG that bleeds the United States dry, between a fat you and a skinny you, between a stagnant sex life and a thriving one. And if they can do all that, they can certainly get your partner to make the bed once in a while.

CASE STUDY #1

The Players: Jenny and Thorold

If there was one thing Jenny (coauthor of this book) knew about her husband Thorold, it was that he hated being told what to do. "Request" that he change his "weekend shirt" on a semiannual basis . . . and see him throw on the same old T-shirt with the picture of a grinning chicken week after week after week. Insist that he remove the thirteen Buddhas, four unidentifiable pieces of wood, and sad little chipped Rwandan gorilla thing from the mantel . . . and ensure they'll be there for life. Remind him, again, that tax day is now only three days away . . . and watch him file for an extension.

There was a time—early on, in the courtship phase—when Jenny loved Thorold's independent streak. "Such a free thinker," she thought. Here, at last, was a guy who wouldn't follow the herd. Who did as he pleased. Who loved *living* life, not getting caught up in the boring details. His contradictions added character. He had an immaculate, well-tended flower garden in which he enjoyed the occasional Pimm's Cup—Thorold is British—but a bathroom worthy of scientific study, since, hey, it's a *shower,* which should naturally stay clean on its own, right? When Jenny would leap up after dinner to wash the dishes, thinking it would be more relaxing to have them out of the way so they could polish off the wine and settle in for an evening of Alfred Hitchcock, she knew that he had a different approach: Finish the wine, watch *Rebecca,* go for a walk, check the next day's headlines, and *then* do the dishes.

"It's not like the dishes are suffering," he'd point out.

It all seemed so romantic.

Even after they moved in together, Jenny didn't need to nag because there wasn't that much to nag about. They had diametrically opposed approaches to life's annoying little tasks—mopping, taxes, mildew—but who cared?

"I'd found a guy who woke me up to see the sunrise, who'd lived on yak-butter tea for a week, and who made me laugh," said Jenny. "I wasn't worried about his lack of closet organization skills."

Then they got married, and Thorold's charming, antiauthoritarian streak started to feel more like an anti-doing-what-Jenny-wanted streak.

Then their daughter was born, and pretty soon, Thorold's charming, antiauthoritarian, independent streak became . . . well, it became not at all cool. Overwhelmed by a new baby, a book about marriage she had to finish writing, a suddenly-too-small apartment, and a looming return to full-time work, Jenny found that her patience with Thorold's "ways" was wearing thin. She found herself making a lot of demands. These demands sounded a lot like nagging—"nagging" being a term she never imagined would apply to her. Could he take out the recycling, *please*? Or change the Diaper Genie bag *every once in a while*? Or wash his juice glass *for once*? And for chrissakes, what was up with him waking up every morning, all chipper and oblivious, and asking, "How was your night?" as if he had been sleeping on Pluto and not two inches away from her as she got up to feed the baby four times?

Thorold loved this change in his wife about as much as he loved knee surgery. How was it possible that not long ago he could do no wrong, and now he was in trouble literally from the moment he woke up in the morning to the moment he crawled into bed?

"I knew she was under a lot of pressure, but I had no idea why I was the one getting blamed for everything," he said.

He tried to be diplomatic and point out that they were each doing the best they could. Jenny would agree and then sixty seconds later be angry again.

Thorold did what was only natural: He started to withdraw. This made Jenny angry all over again. But also sad. Because deep down, Jenny hated the person she was becoming.

The Problem: Nagging

If you asked Thorold about that period of his marriage, he would say he had a slightly different take on the dynamic that was playing out in the house. Here he was, working his butt off, staying up until one or two a.m. with the baby, often sleeping on the couch to let his wife get some rest, and trying to manage a stressful new job that required him to be at his desk, upright and functioning, at eight a.m. each day while Jenny got to hit the snooze button.

Not only that, but he cooked every night, constantly told her what an amazing job she was doing as a mother, and even brought flowers home from work a few times a week. Yes, he sometimes had to work until nine p.m., but the country was in a severe financial crisis, and he couldn't afford to slack off.

And yet. Here was Jenny, insisting that he wasn't doing enough. When you're always doing twenty things at once, he wondered, how can you do *more*? A vicious cycle started: The more she nagged, the more frustrated he became; the more she attacked, the more he retreated and the more she nagged. Were they going to wait until their child was four years old to send out her birth announcement? she asked. Was it truly her responsibility to write all sixteen hundred baby gift thank-you cards, including the ones to his relatives? And could he deign to replace the toilet paper when it was out?

Jenny was using some of the oldest incentives in the books to get her husband to do more around the house: anger, guilt trips, punishment. And on some level, as the words were coming out of her mouth, she believed these incentives would work. Unfortunately, motherhood had melted her brain. The sane part of her knew Thorold hated being told what to do, that as an incentive it was bound to backfire, with her otherwise loving husband turning to stone. And she knew no one—not dogs, not killer whales, and certainly not men—responded well to punishment. She knew all that, yet she still vocalized every ounce of discontent, often with a side of tears. "It was almost involuntary," Jenny said. "I'd try to refrain from saying everything that entered my brain, but three seconds later, out would come this torrent."

One morning Jenny asked Thorold to throw in a load of laundry before leaving for work. He said he'd do it, but then he got a call from the office, got sucked into his BlackBerry, and dashed out the door. (Lehman Brothers had probably collapsed, but what was that next to a pile of pooped-on baby clothes?)

All day, Jenny stewed.

In her mind, she began listing all the things Thorold had failed to do lately: He still hadn't changed the burned-out bulb on the patio, still hadn't moved the winter baby clothes from the bedroom to the storage area, still hadn't booked their flights to England to see his parents, and still—after three months—*still* hadn't fixed the broken curtain rod in the master bedroom. She sat at the computer and wrote him a few nasty emails and then, remembering she was writing a book about marriage, deleted them.

Jenny felt trapped—justified in her anger but aware that her anger wasn't doing anyone any good.

The Solution: Trusting

In all of our research, we didn't find an abundance of evidence pointing to the efficacy of nagging as an incentive in the domestic realm. What we did find was a lot of research about an incentive that naggers might want to consider the next time they are about to make one more demand of their beleaguered spouses. It's called trust. And it means just that. Trust someone to do the right thing, and odds are, if they aren't psychopaths or serial killers, they'll do it.

We can hear you snickering from here: Trust him and he'll feel inspired to mow the lawn, sort the kids' socks, call his mother on her birthday, and do the two million other things he never does but knows I want him to do?

Sure. Whatever.

The fact is, we are far more likely to give when we feel trusted, and that has huge implications for marriage. In our Exhaustive, Groundbreaking, and Very Expensive Marriage Survey, people said praise was *twice as effective* as nagging in incentivizing their spouses to do something they didn't want to do.

Before we tell you how it worked out for Jenny, let's look at an experiment economists have run in the lab. It's called "the investor game," and it shows how effective trust can be at generating goodwill and cooperation and how ineffective punishment can be at generating either.

In the game, one person is designated the "investor" and the other the "trustee." They each get $10. The investor decides how much of his $10 to give to the trustee, keeping in mind that whatever he hands over will automatically triple in value when it gets to the trustee (if he gives $5, for example, the trustee will get $15). Next, the trustee decides how much to give back to the investor, factoring in that the money will *not* triple on the way back.

On paper, cooperation is the best strategy: If the investor gives all $10, it becomes $30 in the hands of the trustee. If the trustee then sends back $20, they each net $20—or twice what they started out with.

In reality, though, the investor is taking a huge risk handing over $10. What if the trustee decides to pocket all the cash and walk away with $40? What incentive does the trustee have to return even a penny?

When economists Ernst Fehr and Bettina Rockenbach ran the experiment, they found that, on average, investors give away more than 50 percent of their money—$6.50 out of $10—and trustees return about 40 percent of the tripled amount—$7.80. The trustee ends up well ahead, with $21.80 to the investor's $11.30. However, he doesn't totally shake down the investor, either, which is what traditional economics—with its emphasis on humans doing only what is in their best interests—predict would happen.

Fehr and Rockenbach then changed the rules. They gave the investor the option to fine the trustee if he didn't get back the amount that he wanted. A strange thing happened: When investors announced to the trustees that they would exercise their option to impose a fine, trustees returned *less* money than they did in the first game. But when investors said they would not impose a fine, trustees returned *more* money than they did in the first game.

What does this all mean? It means you gotta trust people. Why? Because threatening to impose a fine can send a signal that you don't trust people. And when those people know you don't trust them, they think something along the lines of, "screw you."

Whereas, when you *have the option to punish but you don't use it,* you're telegraphing that you trust others to do the right thing. And for that, your trust will often be rewarded.

Trust doesn't work only in the lab—it's the foundation of the free market. You put money in the bank because you trust the bank not to steal it. You buy a set of vintage martini glasses online because you trust they'll be delivered in one piece. You give to Greenpeace because you trust that your $50 will help curb global warming and not be used toward the executive director's new mountain getaway in Telluride.

Now telescope in to your living room. It's you and your partner sitting on the couch, being married. Unlike those people in the lab playing trust games for a day and then going their separate ways, that guy next to you is going to be there again tomorrow, and the next day, and hopefully every day after that until death really does do you part. The nature of marriage, the everyday closeness of it, the eternal back-and-forth-ness of it, makes trust even more critical to keeping you both open and responsive to each other. Without it, small rifts can turn into gaping chasms.

"With people in a long-term relationship, you get the same forces" as you do in the market, says Colin Camerer, a Carnegie Mellon economist who studies trust. "Only amped up."

This is what Jenny finally learned. (It didn't hurt that as part of her research for this book, she interviewed Colin Camerer, who, unbeknownst to him, was teaching her a lesson about the amped-up forces in her own marriage and how to address them.)

When Thorold got home on the Night the Laundry Was Not Done, Jenny tried to muster some trust. She didn't mention the laundry. Instead, over dinner, she asked him about his day and told him about hers. She told herself to trust him to remember the laundry—if not on her exact timetable, then soon enough—and she channeled her energy into that trust and away from her anger. Staying calm was hard for Jenny, because Jenny is highly impatient and, as we mentioned, was highly hormonal at the time. But she knew her lack of trust in Thorold was only feeding his resentment, which in turn was feeding hers. The best way to break the cycle was to start having a little faith in him—and not letting that faith crumble the instant he let her down.

"Of course he *wanted* to do the right thing and help," Jenny said. "But I wasn't giving him a chance to."

After dinner, Thorold went to throw his socks in the hamper and realized he hadn't done the laundry. He felt terrible. But he didn't feel terrible for the usual reason—that Jenny was making him feel terrible. He felt terrible because he knew he'd left her in the lurch. He apologized and stayed up late to do the job. Jenny told him it was okay. And Thorold's recognition really did make everything okay.

Punishing Thorold for forgetting something—no matter how tired and strung out Jenny might have felt—was a demonstrably ineffective incentive. Trusting that he would get to it worked wonders. In this case, Jenny wasn't the only one who learned a lesson: Nowadays, whenever she gets testy with Thorold, he reminds her of this period in their lives and that she would do much better to trust him and not use "that tone."

Think back to those games where trustees give back more when they know the investor won't fine them. For both people to end up ahead, one has to make the first move—in the experiment, it's the investor who goes first, by giving the trustee a wad of money and announcing he won't impose a fine, no matter what. That first move sets off a chain reaction of goodwill—which is the same kind of chain reaction we're all looking to get out of this whole marriage business, right?

CASE STUDY #2

The Players: Rebecca and Paul

Paul and Rebecca were both Tauruses, both headstrong and obstinate, both longtime subscribers to the doctrine of even steven. "I knew I'd found the right guy when I offered to pay for the second round and he didn't argue," said Rebecca. "Some women might find that a turnoff, but I thought it was reasonable. Why should he pay twice?"

"It seemed only fair that she pay for the second round," Paul said, agreeing with Rebecca 100 percent. "It's not 1950."

They met when they were in their early thirties, both working at a technology-solutions company in Cincinnati. Paul had been married once, briefly, and swore the experience had permanently cured him of marriage. Rebecca had been with the same guy for seven years and still wasn't ready to commit. It took a month-long consulting gig in Buffalo, during which time she and Paul were holed up in a run-down hotel with a handful of personality-free co-workers, for her to figure things out.

That was the month they discovered how eerily similar they were. "After ten solid hours of code work every day, we'd have dinner, get drunk, and close down the hotel bar," Rebecca said. Mornings, Paul would find Rebecca barely holding it together at the hotel gym, as determined as he was to make it through thirty minutes of cardio despite a brain-boiling hangover. "Rebecca was the most competitive person I'd ever met," said Paul. "After me."

By the time they got home from Buffalo, Rebecca had ditched her boyfriend and taken up with Paul.

Except when they played chess, or sang karaoke, or took road trips, or hung out with friends, or flew kites, or did anything else that had even the slightest chance of turning into a competition, Rebecca and Paul's courtship was drama-free.

And for the most part, so was their marriage. By the time we met them, they had been married for eight years. They had one kid, one dog, and two aging hamsters they kind of wished would go quietly into the good night. They lived in a three-bedroom Dutch colonial in a Cincinnati suburb. They had fallen into a division of labor that fit their tit-for-tat philosophy. She did all the finances and managed the kid's schedule. He cooked, coached, and packed school lunches. He did doctors, she did teachers. He helped with science projects, she helped with the day-to-day homework. He did the outdoors (raking, shoveling snow, mowing), and she did the indoors (laundry, recycling, sweeping).

Even when it came to their spending habits, they were regimented: They had a tacit agreement that neither would spend insane amounts of money on things for themselves and that they'd both spend roughly the same amount on personal items. Rebecca might buy a new dress, and Paul would feel justified in buying a new lens for his camera. And because he bought the lens, she knew she could buy something else in the future, which would be followed by another gadget purchase on his part, and so on and so forth. It wasn't always 100 percent seamless, but for the most part, it was a system that worked for them.

Paul and Rebecca had arranged their marriage around an incentive structure actually called "tit for tat." It means the same thing in real life as it does in economics—if you do X, I'll do X. Which was all fine and good until the day one of them stopped doing X.

That person was Paul. One day, Paul drove home on a brand-new Vespa scooter. Price tag: $6,000. He'd been talking about getting one forever and figured the hell with it, time to quit talking and buy one. Rebecca was not happy. "Spending six thousand bucks without checking with me was way, way out of line," she recalled. "I'd never spent close to that much on a whim, and if I had, it wouldn't have been on something that could kill me and leave my child with one fewer parent."

The Problem: Tit for Tat

Of course, Paul and Rebecca didn't call their system "tit for tat," nor did they ever utter the words "incentive structure." But that's exactly what they'd created. Their incentive to contribute, to do their chores, to spend within their means, was the knowledge that as long as one of them did those things, the other one would, too.

And can you blame them? The whole setup of marriage, from the minute you say "I do," is a lifelong exercise in tit for tat. No matter how much you love the guy, let's be honest: You're not going to agree to the whole monogamous, sickness-and-health stuff unless he does, too. And while in your best moments you're happy to give unconditionally, you're also human—you expect that when you give your partner a foot rub, you'll eventually get something foot-rub-like in return. Why should you give her a great birthday present this year when last year she gave you socks? Why should you host his parents again when you haven't seen your parents in months? You made the bed yesterday—you'd think he could do it today.

There's no incentive to give if all the other person does is take.

Maybe Paul and Rebecca were a tad extreme in their approach, but as we said, the system worked beautifully for a number of years. Trouble came when one of them decided to stop giving, or "cooperating," in econ-speak. Tit for tat is what's known as a "mimicking strategy," which means when one player stops cooperating, the other player does, too. Think of the Israelis and Palestinians, trapped in a never-ending game of tit for tat: One side waves a white flag, and the other waves one, too. Then one launches a missile, and the other does, too.

In Paul and Rebecca's marriage, the Vespa was the missile, the thing that turned a cooperative outcome into a noncooperative one and a once functioning incentive structure into a failure.

Paul's purchase may have helped him feel sixteen years old again, but on the downside, it eviscerated any incentive a seething Rebecca might have had to refrain from buying a $250 Diane von Fürstenberg dress she'd been eyeing. As Rebecca put it: "If Paul could break the rules like that, why should I bother following them?"

In tit for tat, say economists Avinash Dixit and Barry Nalebuff, "any mistake 'echoes' back and forth. One side punishes the other for a defection, and this sets off a chain reaction. The rival responds to the punishment by hitting back. The response calls for a second punishment."

And so it was that after the Vespa incident, Rebecca started to think of all the ways she could punish Paul. She could remodel the upstairs bathroom without checking with him first. She could cut up his credit cards. She could find a cop and tip him off that Paul was riding a scooter without a license. Come to think of it, she had no incentive *not* to call the cops (except that Paul was still her husband, and it didn't seem right to turn him in to the authorities, no matter how mad she was).

But Rebecca kept running up against the same problem: Punishment wouldn't help her and Paul get back on the right track. It would do the opposite. It would signal to Paul that he and Rebecca were now even and thus open the door for him to go off the reservation again. After all, what incentive would he have to go back to their initial agreement—you scratch my back, I scratch yours—if he knew he could get away with *not* doing so?

"At a certain point, I realized I was trapped," said Rebecca. "If I didn't take the high road, this would probably keep happening."

The Solution: Get Out of Jail Free Card

This is what Rebecca finally did to return her marriage to a cooperative state and incentivize Paul to not pull another scooter stunt: She forgave him.

"I didn't have a choice," said Rebecca. "I could lord it over him forever, scream, shout, spend a bunch of money, but none of that was going to teach him a lesson."

Rebecca didn't know this, but economists have shown that a little forgiveness can be a great incentive. By forgiving Paul, instead of "mimicking" his behavior, Rebecca was resetting their tit for tat and giving Paul a chance to cooperate on the next round. Call it a "get out of jail free card"—one Paul was fully aware he'd pulled from the deck.

"I was shocked," said Paul. He knew he'd broken the rules and told us that based on her first reaction, he sort of feared Rebecca was going to serve him with divorce papers. "When she told me it was fine, that I should go ahead and keep the scooter, I thought, 'What has this woman done with Rebecca?' "

Paul pretty quickly realized that he owed his wife—big-time. Which is just what Rebecca hoped would happen.

Not that Rebecca was all smiles and hugs. There were some strings attached, namely a new agreement, which essentially put some conditions on her forgiveness. Whereas their *tacit* agreement had been that neither would spend "insane" amounts of cash, Rebecca now suggested they try an *explicit* agreement: No purchases over $200 without checking first. Paul wasn't in love with the idea, but he was so pleased with his get out of jail free card, he didn't want to press his luck.

"Fortunately, a helmet costs less than two hundred dollars," said Paul.

CASE STUDY #3

The Players: Colin and Lily

Colin and Lily met in 1996, on the trading floor of a small investment bank in Chicago. Colin was a quiet type, a math and stats whiz who once dreamed of becoming a rocket scientist. He was a guy who looked as if he couldn't quite figure out how he'd landed here, in finance, surrounded by fratty guys who had tribal tattoos under their

Molly's Revenge

Tim and Molly had a good marriage but a big problem. Every morning after Molly left for work, Tim showered and, without thinking, left his wet towel on her side of the bed. This meant Molly went to sleep every night on damp sheets. "Rude," she told us. "Just plain rude."

Molly asked Tim nicely to hang up the towel. She tried joking about it, getting angry, getting sulky—and, of course, nagging. Nothing worked. Every night was like camping in the rain. Finally, she got even. One night, when Tim was out playing Boggle with the guys, she took a shower and placed a very wet towel under the covers on his side of the bed. Tim didn't say anything when he crawled into bed, but he got the message.

Molly punished Tim, an incentive we don't recommend lightly but one we do recommend sometimes, like when your spouse is being an annoying dipshit. In the cold, logical world of economics, the threat of punishment is known as a "coercive incentive." Like speeding tickets and the electric chair and IRS audits, coercive incentives are designed to keep people on the straight and narrow. They're not carrots, they're sticks. Use them wisely.

Thomas Pink shirts, high-fived constantly, and went out after work to drink Irish Car Bombs and fall asleep in their clothes.

Lily didn't have this problem. Lily looked as though she belonged. She drank premium tequila. She wore expensive glasses. She was a star sales trader—her job was to act as a go-between for clients, like Fidelity and T. Rowe Price, who wanted to buy and sell big chunks of stock, and her bank, which traded these stocks on the global exchange. It was a mile-a-minute job, high-stress, and pretty much all day, every day. Lily had to hustle and work her fickle clients, convincing them to trust her and trade with her. And since almost everyone she dealt with was male and hostile, she always felt they were angling to get the better of her. "My clients assumed I would be nicer since I was a woman," Lily said. "Which made me more aggressive."

She managed her clients with what Colin called a "remarkable fuck-you femininity"—total confidence with a whiff of flirtation. "She never gave an inch on price, but she convinced these guys they were getting an amazing deal."

Colin didn't possess a fuck-you femininity, or a fuck-you masculinity, for that matter. He despised wooing clients. He despised *talking* to clients. He got flustered when more than one person called, and he dreaded picking up the phone. He found the trading floor gratingly loud and the guys immature. Colin was interested in *why* stocks moved and the underlying currents in the market; these guys, as far as he could tell, were interested only in getting rich.

Lily may have been busy trying to prove her toughness, but she was no dummy, either: She could see that Colin was different, in the best sense of the word. There was kindness behind those eyes, something bigger going on. "He stood out," Lily said. "Everyone went to him when their clients wanted to know something substantive about a stock. He studied the market, which the rest of us didn't do."

Colin bided his time. He could see Lily trying to fit in, to be one of the guys, but he figured that if she had a brain, she'd get bored with them eventually. "It was a gut feeling," he said.

His gut was right. Two years into her job, Lily was getting sick of the trading floor. She had stupidly dated/slept with a few of her coworkers. "Good lay, bad brunch company," she told us. Colin, sensing an opening, sent her an email asking if she felt like grabbing some dinner.

She said yes.

They drank beer and talked about their colleagues. They also talked about football. (Turns out she was a Patriots fanatic.) And their families. He learned that she had three sisters in New England, whom she visited every month, and a dad she talked to every day. "How tough can you be if you talk to your *dad* every day?" Colin said.

Colin walked her home. She invited him in. Then, as Colin remembers it, "she basically tackled me, had her way with me, and then told me it was okay if I wanted to leave."

He didn't. And, Lily conceded, the company at brunch the next morning was pretty good.

Around the house, Lily was the boss, the CEO, the Decider, which was fine with Colin. When it was time to plan a vacation, she'd call a travel agent, pick the destination, and a few days later announce to Colin where they were going. When he came downstairs in the morning, he'd have two ties in his hand. "Which one?" he'd ask.

"That one," she'd say, barely looking up.

When they decorated their first apartment, Colin didn't lift a finger. "I don't think we had a single discussion about furniture, tiles, or appliances. She just made it happen."

When Lily got pregnant, she made another executive decision: She had no desire to try to balance a job and a baby. "Some women call it off-ramping," Lily said. "I called it getting the hell out." Lily seemed to take to motherhood in a way that, if Colin was going to be totally honest about it, he never thought possible. She sewed pillowcases, arranged playdates, made her own banana-pear purees. She even stopped saying "fuck."

They moved to the suburbs, had another child, and began to orient their lives around a new group of friends. It was a difficult transition, and it seemed to change Lily and change their marriage in a way Colin didn't expect. He felt . . . well, he felt left out. Lily seemed completely focused on the kids—PTA meetings, get-togethers with the soccer team, hiring tutors—and not so much on Colin. Even after the kids went to bed, she was too wiped out to be much company. Either she wanted to crawl into bed and read or she would sit in front of the TV with a drink. Sex didn't even register.

"She made so little effort when it came to me," said Colin. "She asked how my day was but barely listened to the answer."

Unlike the early days, when Lily was "very physical," now she was more likely to complain about being tired, stressed about some decision she had to make about the kids, or worried about money. This baffled Colin, since he thought she loved to make decisions and he knew that they had plenty of money. "It wasn't just less sex, but less affection in general," said Colin.

Colin tried different things to regain her affection and spice up their sex life. He tried complimenting her in all the ways she liked to be complimented, but that usually resulted in her rolling her eyes. "I don't feel like having sex tonight," she'd reply after he told her she had the "nicest ass in the neighborhood."

Then one day he finally got some traction. He came home from a business trip to London with a gift: a ridiculously expensive cashmere sweater he'd bought on a whim after seeing it in a shop window. "Oh, my god, it's beautiful," said Lily. "This is way too nice." She ran upstairs and put it on.

That night, they had sex.

A few weeks later, he heard Lily on the phone with her friend Alexandra saying how much she loved Alexandra's new handbag. He quietly called Alexandra the next day and asked her what kind of bag it was. He wanted to surprise Lily. "Birkin," Alexandra said. "It's Hermès." So he went to Hermès at lunch and asked to see the bag. When he saw the price tag, he asked the sales lady if it was a typo.

"That's eight hundred dollars, not eight thousand, right?"

It wasn't a typo, but Colin bought the bag anyway. (We mentioned he was doing well in the money department, right?)

Lily loved the bag.

Let's be clear here: Colin knew these gifts were over the top. He grew up in a working-class family where $8,000 was what you spent on two cars, not one handbag. But he was feeling desperate. And the gifts made Lily light up at a time when nothing else seemed to do the trick. "They made her so happy," said Colin. "And that happiness was directed at me for a change—and it felt good."

Those gifts? Incentives. Incentives to get Lily to smile, to be happy, to relax, and, ultimately—let's be honest—to show more affection toward Colin.

The problem with these incentives? They didn't last. They got Lily to respond, but her response was fleeting. By the next day, she was back to exhausted, going-to-bed-with-a-book Lily.

The Problem: Overused Incentives Stop Working

Remember Joe Cassano, the $300 million son of a Brooklyn cop? Offering him a sweet financial incentive to do right by the company backfired big-time. For our friend Colin, offering Lily the marriage equivalent of a financial incentive (handbags, sweaters, orchids) backfired, too.

In Colin's case, the reason for the failure wasn't pure greed, it was the simple fact that his incentives didn't have staying power. Unfortunately, it took him some time to catch on to this fact. For a while, he kept the gifts coming. He bought Lily a Kindle, which she seemed mildly excited about. Then came private yoga classes with some fancy teacher he'd read about in the paper. "Thanks, I'll have to set something up for 2020, when my schedule frees up," said Lily, adding, "Why don't you take the sessions? You could use the exercise."

Not exactly what Colin was hoping for (was he getting fat? he wondered).

The increasing ineffectiveness of Colin's incentives would come as no shock to economists, who understand that even the strongest incentives can wear off over time. Uri Gneezy, an economist at the University of California at San Diego, and John A. List, an economist at the University of Chicago, have studied how and why incentives fail. In one experiment looking specifically at whether financial incentives dull over time, they tested how people hired for a simple, onetime task responded when they were spontaneously given massive raises. Would the money make them more productive or not?

Students were recruited to computerize the library holdings of a small midwestern university. Posters advertising the job said the pay was $12 an hour and that the job would last six hours. When the students arrived, not knowing they were being observed, half of them got the $12 wage and got to work. The other half were told—surprise!—they'd be earning $20 an hour.

At first, the $20 students worked harder, logging books more quickly. But after a while, they slowed down and were eventually working at the same pace as the $12-an-hour workers. Like Colin's gifts, the financial incentive—a raise—was a huge success at first. But then the workers' motivation wore off, making the money less effective over the long term.

Marriage happens to be a very long-term proposition. And yet quick and dirty financial-type incentives are all too common. If I buy her a dozen roses, maybe she will forgive me for forgetting her birthday. If I buy him season tickets to the Mets, maybe he'll let me off the hook for Thanksgiving at his cousin Ronny's. If incentives like these do work, chances are it's because they're rarities, one-off little extras. Bring home flowers every day, and eventually she won't even bother to stick them in a vase.

One Friday afternoon at work, not long after the yoga disappointment, Colin found himself wondering what he should get his wife, what would make her happy for the weekend, and . . . it suddenly depressed him. He stopped to analyze the situation. Was Lily responding to the gifts or to him? He knew she loved him (didn't she?), but it felt as though she showed that love more when he came home with nice gifts. What was him and what was Hermès? Would she notice him if he came home empty-handed?

The Solution: Keep It Fresh

Here's some advice you undoubtedly know but frequently forget: In marriage, thoughtful gestures can be far more powerful incentives than material ones.

That's what Colin discovered, by accident. Somewhere between buying Lily absurdly nice gifts and panicking that he had turned his marriage into a tradable commodity, he called home to check on Lily's day. Not great, she said. It was pouring outside, which meant no soccer, which meant their son was bouncing off the walls, which meant their daughter was bouncing off the walls, which meant Lily had a raging headache on top of her seasonal affective disorder. Kyle, their son's friend, came over for a playdate but left crying after an hour because their ungrateful children thought it would be hysterical to play monster for an hour without him.

"Our kids are terrorists," she said. "And I don't have anything to feed them for dinner."

"I'll pick up dinner on my way home," Colin said.

"At eight o'clock? Way too late for them," Lily said.

"I'll come home early," he said.

"Right," said Lily.

"Lily," Colin said, "I said I'll take care of it."

And he did.

He left work at five, picked up a dozen eggs and some vegetables, poured Lily a glass of wine, and cooked the kids omelets, even accommodating their preferences (tomatoes for one, no tomatoes for the other; spinach for one, cheese for the other). He managed to get them to eat almost every bite without complaining, something that stunned Lily into silent admiration.

After dinner, Colin bathed the kids while Lily took her wine and went off to reply to some emails. She read a funny article from a friend about a Paris fashion show ruined by anti-fur protesters. She laughed, something Lily rarely did between the hours of five p.m. and eight p.m., when her children sucked up every last ounce of positive energy in her body. "For two straight hours I didn't have to make any decisions, coax anyone into bathing, threaten anyone's TV time, or plead with anyone to stop hitting," said Lily. "My only responsibility was deciding how drunk to get."

When Colin came downstairs after finally getting the kids to bed, Lily braced for complaints about how exhausted he was. They didn't materialize. Instead, Colin poured himself an enormous glass of wine and sat with Lily. They talked about their day.

Lily was relieved. Relaxed, even. She hadn't realized how a little extra help from Colin would help her mood, and she couldn't believe how rarely she asked him for it. "I was used to doing things myself," she told us.

Colin was relieved, too. And relaxed. Lily hadn't listened to him talk about his day, much less anything going on in his life, for a long time. He couldn't remember the last time he'd seen her so undistracted and available. Though he didn't want to push his luck he even attempted to put the moves on—as subtly as was possible for Colin, a man who had been known to take off his clothes and jump on his wife's side of the bed while she was brushing her teeth—and Lily put the moves on him right back.

The next day, on his way to work, Colin had the following genius thought: "I have *got* to do more around the house. I have *got* to take the pressure off that woman." He resolved to take over the din-ner/bath/bed routine once a week. He resolved to learn to cook something other than omelets. He resolved to pay attention to Lily so that she would in turn pay attention to him.

It should come as no surprise at this point that economists have put the incentive of attention to the test. One experiment we thought was pretty cool subjected volunteers (once again, students) to the mindless task of counting the number of times "ss" appeared on a page of random letters. Subjects were put into three groups and paid for each page they completed. One group was asked to write their names on the pages they completed and hand them over to monitors, who would then carefully file the pages. A second group was told not to write down their names, and when they handed in their pages, the monitors put them on top of a pile of other papers. The third group didn't write their names down, either, and as soon as they finished, the monitors shredded the papers before their hardworking eyes.

THE PEOPLE SPEAK . . .
About Gifts That Worked

In our nationwide listening tour, we asked, "What was the nicest gift your spouse gave you recently?" Among the more memorable responses:

- "He started leaving Post-it notes around the house with sweet messages. We don't spend a lot of time together. I go to school in the evenings, he works all day. This was his way of saying he hadn't forgotten about me."
- "She let me watch the play-offs. I never forgot it."
- "He admitted he was wrong about an argument we'd had a month earlier. He *never* says he's wrong, so it meant a lot."
- "She noticed my haircut."

Guess who finished the most pages? That's correct, the people in the first group, for whom attention and acknowledgment appeared to be a powerful motivator.

It worked for Colin.

Before signing off on incentives, we feel obliged to point out a subtlety lurking in the story of these two lovebirds. Colin was initially trying to incentivize Lily to pay attention to him, right? But in the end, it was Lily who pulled out a pretty fierce incentive: Help around the house and you just might get lucky.

THE BOTTOM LINE

1. **Trust = good incentive.** People tend to do the right thing when they feel trusted by others. If you assume your spouse is going to let you down again, the odds are pretty high he will. If you let him know you're confident he *won't* let you down, the odds are way higher he'll come through.

2. **Nagging = bad incentive.** Do you really need us to tell you that?

3. **Know your audience.** Different incentives motivate different people. Some people respond to flowers, others to a night off from the dishes, and still others to silence (especially when there are kids around *all the time*).

4. **Mix it up.** That said, even flowers lose their power. Throw your partner for a loop by surprising him with a new incentive, like a weekend away with his friends. Talk about long-lasting good will.

5. **One get-out-of-jail-free card per person.** The most common incentive, tit for tat, means you give your all knowing the other person will, too. It's a beautiful thing—until one person defects and comes home with a $6,000 Airstream. Give that guy a free pass just this once. Forgiveness can be a great incentive.

6

TRADE-OFFS

Or, The Art of Getting Over It

THE PRINCIPLE

Every business wants a bite of the Big Apple. But when mega–discount retailer Costco tried to open its first Manhattan store in East Harlem in late 2009, it ran into a problem: An ornery band of old-school New York politicos was demanding the company change its ways.

The issue was food stamps. Unlike virtually every one of its competitors, including Wal-Mart and BJ's, Costco didn't accept food stamps. Since more than thirty thousand East Harlem residents used food stamps, and since Costco had already received $55 million in sweetheart government subsidies and special permission to let its blaring delivery trucks drive through residential neighborhoods from twelve p.m. to five a.m., this was a problem. The city's politicos put the squeeze on Costco: If it wanted to cash in on New York's $564 billion economy, it better start taking food stamps.

Costco faced a trade-off, a choice between two options, each less than perfect: Take the food stamps and reduce profits, or refuse the stamps but risk an anti-Costco frenzy.

In a world with limited resources, trade-offs are inevitable. Mick Jagger, amateur economist, knew it when he reminded us that you can't always get what you want. Your husband, unwitting economist, knew it when you told him to put a ring on your finger or enjoy a long, lonely trip to hell without you. And Greg Mankiw, Harvard economist, surely knew it when he broke down the entire complicated world of economics into ten simple principles.

Mankiw's first principle: People face trade-offs.

The classic example of a trade-off, the one offered up in every Econ 101 textbook in every Introduction to Economics class at every college in America, is the choice between guns and butter. The more a country spends on guns, or the national security needed to protect itself, the less it has to spend on butter, or the household goods that make domestic life better. (Actually, most governments throughout history have opted to not make the choice at all and instead spend recklessly on both guns *and* butter. But this, too, is a trade-off: By consuming a lot today, they fleece future generations who are left footing the mother of all bills.)

Unless you're the government and you've figured out a way to have it all right now, weighing trade-offs is no easy feat. Consider the limitations: There are only twenty-four hours in a day, a finite number of dollars in the bank, and way too many people crying out for our attention. Do we live in a cramped apartment in the city and get home fast or enjoy the comforts of suburbia and commute an hour each way? Do we work fifteen hours a day and stash away some cash or work part-time and make it to every one of Margot's ballet recitals? SUV or Prius? Public school or private? Save money or go on vacation? GE or Míele? Sex or sleep? Every day, we face a barrage of decisions about how to allocate our time and money most efficiently, which means weighing boatloads of trade-offs in the process.

The basic problem is, we want it all, but we can't have it all.

Luckily for us, in 1890, an economist named Alfred Marshall came up with a way to make smart trade-offs by using something called a "cost-benefit analysis."

Marshall was king of the economics castle in England in the early twentieth century. He's known for many things, including being one of the fathers of neoclassical economics and broadening the discipline from a study of markets to an examination of human behavior, which naturally we think is pretty interesting (being interested ourselves in human relationships). But one particularly big contribution he made was pointing out that consumers will buy a good if the marginal benefit is greater than the marginal cost.

The cost-benefit analysis wasn't just a game changer for professors of economics. Companies use the cost-benefit analysis to decide whether to spend billions of dollars on research for an erectile dysfunction drug to knock Viagra off its perch or to push ahead with a flashy new headquarters. Small businesses use it to choose to subsidize parking for their customers rather than offer health benefits to their employees. Governments use it to raise or lower taxes and to choose diplomacy or war (unless you're George W. Bush and want to invade

Alfred Marshall, Player of the Century

Marshall's coauthor on his most famous textbook was his wife, whom he met at Cambridge when he was her professor and she was his student. He got booted out of Cambridge for the affair—something about celibacy rules—married the girl, became an even bigger deal than he was, and then got hired back. In other words, he faced a trade-off—job or girl. He picked the girl and got the job back anyway. Oh, to be an early-twentieth-century British economist named Alfred!

Iraq, in which case you merely consult the dark, tiny heart of Donald Rumsfeld and send in the tanks).

But calculating costs and benefits is harder than it looks. Some costs—most costs—aren't self-evident. For example, let's say you're an actuarial consultant to pension funds and you're debating whether to stay put or go to graduate school for a PhD in Early Netherlandish painting. The cost-benefit analysis of that decision might look like this:

Costs	Benefits
$45,000 tuition	Bigger brain
	Ability to sleep late on Fridays
	A job you like, if you get a job

Pretty straightforward, right?

Wrong. There are other costs to factor in, what economists call "opportunity costs." Opportunity costs are what you have to give up to get something else—and you can't make a smart trade-off without thinking about them. (On Greg Mankiw's list of ten principles, opportunity costs are number two.) Opportunity costs force us to go beyond the obvious. Going to graduate school isn't merely flushing $45,000 in tuition down the toilet, it's flushing all the things you have to give up to follow that dream of being an expert in Early Netherlandish painting, too—like an income and exiting the workforce at a moment when you were set to get a big promotion. Once you start accounting for opportunity costs, that cost-benefit analysis starts to look a whole lot more complicated:

Costs	Benefits
$45,000 tuition	Bigger brain
Income, including potential raise	Ability to sleep late on Fridays

A relatively carefree, debt-free life	A job you like, if you get a job
Career advancement	
Free weekends	
401(k)	
Motorcycle	
Motorcycle gear	

Suddenly the cost of that fancy new degree isn't just $45,000, it's all the opportunities lost by not staying in your mind-numbing job.

We're not saying stay. Hell, we're all for following your dreams (we followed ours, writing this book, but that inspired another set of trade-offs that you probably don't want to hear about). We're saying that when you weigh trade-offs, you have to weigh *all* the costs and *all* the benefits, which means figuring out your opportunity costs and factoring them into your decision.

Like we said, this can be complicated. It can look like this:

$$C'(s; \theta) = \frac{(1 - \mu)\widetilde{g}_N(s) + \mu g_M(s)}{f_P[F_P^{-1}((1 - \mu)\widetilde{G}N(s|) + \mu GM(s))]}$$

The good news is, you don't have to know any math to decide whether takeout or delivery is the best option for tonight's dinner. The bad news is there's a complication.

The complication: When we're identifying costs and measuring benefits, we easily get sidetracked by things like our feelings, the direction of the wind, and the number of times our spouses told us we looked smokin' hot this month. Or in econ-speak, we have "decision-making biases," stuff that clouds our ability to think rationally. At the very moment we most need to engage in a reasoned, calm cost-

IN PLAIN ENGLISH:

Decision-Making Biases

When you should know better ... but you do it anyway.

benefit analysis, we're blinded by emotion, impatient for solutions, and incapable of seeing the total costs or appreciating the total benefits.

In this chapter, we'll introduce you to three couples who suffered from three of the most common decision-making biases. These biases include underestimating the impact of small changes, or not "thinking at the margin"; obsessing over sunk costs, or decisions we've already made and can't undo; and fixating on fairness, that very human impulse to think we're getting the short end of the stick even when we've got it pretty darn good.

CASE STUDY #1

The Players: Claire and Shawn

When we met them in the kitchen of their Wisconsin home on a cool, bright September day, Claire and Shawn seemed like your typical functioning couple. Our plan was to spend the morning interviewing Shawn and a bunch of his friends and then, in the afternoon, take on the wives.

As Shawn wandered outside to referee a fight over which kid had the right to play with the plastic picnic basket, Claire looked appreciative that she wasn't the one playing mediator.

As Claire reminded Shawn on her way out to pick up some Capri Suns later for the kids' soccer games, he looked grateful for the reminder.

As Shawn grabbed a beer at five minutes past noon, Claire commented that she wished *she* were the one talking first so she could start drinking already.

"No talking about our sex life," Claire said.

"I wouldn't dream of making the guys that jealous," Shawn said.

But as soon as we moved out to the patio to start the interviews, the mood changed. Shawn sat down, cracked open his beer, and took a scary-long drink. He looked as though he would rather eat glass than talk about his marriage.

So, we said to the group, What kinds of issues are you dealing with in your marriage?

The guys all fiddled with the labels on their beer. "Things are good," volunteered Shawn. "But money is tight and we fight about it sometimes." We got some other tidbits, too, like the fact that Claire had an annoying habit of hovering over the kids at the playground.

"Kids are meant to get dirty, fall down, and get hurt," he said. A few months earlier, he had ended up at the emergency room with their oldest daughter after she fell off the monkey bars and split open her lip. He'd gotten an earful from Claire, which he said went something like this: *"How about watching your kids at the playground for a change?"*

Shawn also noted that the current ratio of back rubs to blow jobs in their house—ten to one, give or take—was a little too weighted toward back rubs for his taste. But in general, he sounded content. "We're lucky," he said. "We don't really have any big issues."

A few hours later, we sat down with the wives. The mood was more relaxed with the women, most of whom couldn't wait to drink wine and talk about their relationships. Claire jumped right in: She thought Shawn was as sexy as the day she met him and considered him her best friend. Their issue was money, something that had always been a source of tension between them, starting with the fact that Claire worried about it and Shawn didn't.

Claire kept track of every dollar coming in and out, looking over all the bills and receipts. When Shawn did the food shopping, she'd grill him about choosing the organic avocados and the fancy frozen chicken nuggets. "He's thinking of the kids' health and I totally appreciate that, but they don't *need* organic everything. Pesticides can't get inside an avocado!" She, of course, paid all the bills, since Shawn's typical reaction to a bill was to either ignore it or accidentally throw it out with the recycling.

It hadn't always been like this. When they met in their twenties, money was the last thing on their minds. Shawn was a pitcher on the local minor league baseball team, and Claire was a waitress saving up to go to cooking school. He came into the restaurant where she worked, noticed her, and asked her out. Within a month they were living together, and in less than a year they were married. The entire team came to the wedding. They were like family, Claire said, and she felt lucky to be part of a close-knit group of guys "who supported each other through anything."

Claire went to cooking school. Shawn retired from baseball after a shoulder injury made it clear he'd never get to the majors. He got a good union job at a small industrial company. They had a baby.

With only one of them working, money was tight, and not long after the baby arrived, they were staring at $10,000 in credit card debt. "Baby formula is expensive," Claire said. "And so's all the other stuff— car seats, carriers, bouncy chairs. It never ends."

But they were young and creative and found ways to bring in extra cash. Shawn took a coaching job a few nights a week, and Claire went back to waitressing on Shawn's off nights. Gradually, they chipped away at their debt.

Shawn's old baseball team also came through. "A few of the guys got together to paint our house when it looked like it was going to fall down," she said. "The wives helped out with babysitting on the nights that Shawn and I both had to work."

It was hard, but they managed.

Then came the wrench.

When Claire was pregnant with their second child, Shawn got an offer to be the pitching coach for the same minor league team he'd once played for. Ever since retiring, he'd been looking for a way back in. Here it was. The problem: It came with no health care, a salary that barely topped minimum wage, and a punishing travel schedule.

"We always said we would support each other's dreams, and I believed that was important," Claire told us. But when Shawn came home and told her about the offer, her initial response was, "No way." Her first pregnancy had been complicated, and the second one was already high-risk because of her age, and there was no way, she told Shawn, she was going to take a pass on health care. The hospital bills alone could push them back into debt, only this time with two kids to support. And what would happen if one of them or one of the kids, God forbid, got *sick*?

In spite of her fears—and after much pleading on Shawn's part—Claire finally decided she couldn't in good conscience deny him his dream job. But they agreed that he wouldn't start until after the baby came. He would hold on to his office job and its health benefits in case anything went wrong with the delivery.

We said that sounded like a good compromise.

"As if," Claire said, taking another swig of wine.

The Problem: Fixating on the Big Issue

Soon after the baby was born, Shawn hit the road with the team for six days, leaving Claire at home with a newborn and a toddler. Like their first daughter, their second girl had no inclination to sleep. "Sleep like a baby? Who came up with *that* expression?" she said.

Even though she'd given Shawn her blessing, Claire was angry. And her anger intensified with each trip. "Shawn would call from the road and I would be too mad to talk. I wanted him to be happy and do what he loved, but it was hard on me," she said. "He knew what babies were like. Those first months. No sleep, lots of crying, and total exhaustion. And I was doing it with a toddler and no husband."

Things went from bad to worse when the economy face-planted in 2008 and Shawn took a major pay cut.

Suddenly, every night was a replay of the same high-decibel conversation.

Claire: "Did you talk to them about your salary?"

Shawn: "No, I did not. Stop asking. It's bad enough without you harassing me."

Claire: "You need to get a new job. You need to get money from your parents. We need to get a loan. We need to do something. Have you seen our credit card statements?"

Yes, Shawn had seen them and he knew they were higher than they had been the previous month. He wasn't a moron.

During these arguments, one or both of them would throw out ideas, usually suggestions for what the other person could do to fix the family's financial problems. Claire said Shawn could do construction work during the off-season, but Shawn said he was away from the kids too much already. He suggested Claire take care of some of the kids in the neighborhood, like an informal day care center. Claire loved that idea, countering that she was *not a babysitter, thank you very much.*

Claire would wake up in the middle of the night, struck with new ideas that could fix everything, like how Shawn could maybe "take up" medicine and bring in a doctor's salary (she could handle him being at work all the time, she told herself, if he was raking in the

THE PEOPLE SPEAK . . .
About Thinking Big

To be fair, this is the way most of us would approach Claire and Shawn's problem. When faced with difficult trade-offs, like whether to make more money and have less time with the family, we tend to think about radical changes, like how winning the $250 million Powerball will let us work less—or not at all—and have more time at home. Before you know it, all the money's gone anyway, blown on weekly lotto tickets. Among the other *big* changes couples we interviewed said they'd thought of to solve their woes:

- Hit up a wealthy in-law estranged from the rest of the family.
- Borrow against 401(k).
- Sell sperm.
- Sell eggs.
- Start side gig selling coke (not the beverage).
- Put ten-year-old to work babysitting neighborhood two-year-olds.
- Vacation in backyard.

cash), or that she needed to figure out a way to get on Mario Batali's radar screen so he would offer her a job as his sous chef for half a million a year.

But guess what? Shawn hated needles, school, and being nice to people he didn't like, so medicine was never going to be in the cards. And Mario Batali had yet to call Claire, even though her number was listed and she'd bought all his cookbooks at full price.

The Solution: Thinking at the Margin

From an economist's perspective, the problem wasn't that Shawn wasn't getting paid enough (okay, that was a problem, but it wasn't *the* problem), it was that Claire and Shawn were focusing only on giant solutions. Hitting up the parents, getting a new job, and borrowing money were big deals. They couldn't be done in a day or without a lot of blood and sweat. They might not even be doable solutions in the first place.

Economists would suggest a different tack. They would recommend thinking at the margin, meaning weighing the costs and benefits of smaller, incremental changes.

Here's how thinking at the margin works: Imagine you're deciding between taking out a $10,000 loan at a 5 percent interest rate or an $11,000 loan at a 6 percent interest rate. The two loans sound sort of similar. Six percent is a little higher than 5 percent, but it's a small price to pay for having more cash in hand, right?

Not really. Five percent interest on a $10,000 loan is $500. Six percent interest on an $11,000 loan is $660. The marginal benefit of the bigger loan is an additional $1,000 in your pocket. But the marginal cost is $160 a year in interest (the difference between $660 and $500), which is in fact a whopping 16 percent of the $1,000 marginal benefit.

Evaluating the costs and benefits of that extra $1,000 is thinking at the margin.

Businesses boost returns by thinking at the margin. Airlines sell cheap, last-minute seats when flights aren't full because a little money is better than none at all (how's that for sophisticated economics?). Hotels post bargain rates on Priceline for unsold rooms for the same reason. They're not getting the same profits they would have by selling the seats and rooms at full price, but whatever they get is more than zero. In other words, small stuff can have a big impact on the bottom line.

Which is something that Shawn—who would die before asking his parents for money and wasn't about to walk out on his dream job—started to think more about the more Claire yelled at him.

One night after a particularly brutal argument about money, Shawn lay in bed staring at the ceiling, trying to avoid the toenail shards flying at his face from Claire's clippers, and wondering what would happen if his beloved wife tried dipping one of those freshly trimmed toes back into the working world. She loved to cook, she made amazing food, and there were plenty of people right there in Madison who were willing to pay for amazing food. Shawn kept going: And maybe if he could stay home a few hours every day and watch the kids, Claire might have the time to cook—even better, she could bake muffins, something she could do blindfolded. Who didn't love muffins? The opportunity cost would be team workouts that he'd have to skip, but on the other hand, he'd get to spend more time with his family and give Claire the extra time in the kitchen.

Finally, someone was thinking at the margin, weighing the costs and benefits of incremental change. Someone was making Alfred Marshall proud!

Claire saw a few problems with this plan.

"Who's gonna take care of the kids while I do all this baking?"

"*I* will," he said, pointing out that if he wasn't getting his full salary, he didn't have to be at work at the crack of dawn. "I'll go to work at eleven every day and you do your baking in the morning."

"Who's going to buy my muffins?"

"Anyone with good taste," he said.

"No, I mean where am I going to sell them?" she said. "Are we also going to open a store? Am I supposed to sell them on the side of the road?"

"Slow down," Shawn said. "We'll give a few boxes to some coffee shops in town and see what happens."

"No way," she said. "I don't like talking to strangers."

"We have no money," Shawn said.

He had a point.

They gave it a shot.

Claire and Shawn labored over a detailed script she would present to the coffee shop's owners when she went in and made her pitch. She whipped up a batch of blueberry muffins and a few wacky variations—walnut and strawberry, pear and pumpkin, cream cheese and banana—and took them to the place around the corner. The owner looked puzzled by the woman standing in his doorway with a tray of muffins and two kids tugging on her windbreaker. Claire was so nervous, she wanted to vomit.

But the owner must have been charmed by her pitch (or had nothing to lose), because he agreed to put a dozen muffins on the counter the next morning. They sold out by ten a.m. He offered to take two dozen off her hands daily. Soon, Claire was getting a good cut on each muffin the shop sold as well as access to its kitchen. While she was there, she'd wander out of the kitchen and mingle with the customers, meeting a whole new group of people and getting ideas about what people wanted (scones, minimuffins, the occasional crumpet). The owner suggested they think beyond muffins. They talked tarts.

When last we checked in, Shawn and Claire were still in debt, and they still argued plenty. But they had a cool new technique for fixing things when they felt broken: thinking small. In at least one case, thinking small turned into something big—a little more money, a little more time with the kids, and a way for Claire to pursue her culinary dreams, as she put it, "one muffin at a time."

CASE STUDY #2

The Players: Caroline and Tom

Explaining to your kids that Mom and Dad met at a frat party when Mom was doing a keg stand isn't exactly the fairy-tale scenario most couples dream of. But it was Caroline and Tom's fairy tale, dammit, and they weren't apologizing.

Caroline was inverted, all five feet ten inches of her, when Tom first saw her. Three beers without a breath. "How many girls do you know who can do that?" he asked us. Once she was right side up again, they struck up a conversation.

"About what?" we asked.

Blank stares from both of them.

"I can't remember a thing about what we said to each other," said Tom. "I just remember thinking she was too cool to give me a chance."

"I thought he was way too Alex P. Keaton," Caroline said.

But she did give him a chance. And they did go out. And five years later, they got married.

Their keg-stand days behind them, they pursued advanced degrees: Caroline in law and Tom in clinical neuropsychology. They'd heard stories about how tough grad school could be on couples, but they didn't put much stock in them. They were solid. "We'd be in the library a lot, big deal," Caroline recalled thinking.

After law school, Caroline landed a job at a major firm and pretty soon was clocking eighty- and ninety-hour weeks, flying to Düsseldorf at the whim of the partners, and keeping a toothbrush and three pairs of fresh underwear locked in her office desk for frequent all-nighters. The inhuman schedule wasn't hurting her marriage, she told herself, since Tom was writing his dissertation and working brutal hours in the lab. Besides, it wasn't like they had any kids.

All true. But there was one problem she'd overlooked: She and Tom never saw each other. Slowly but surely they were growing apart, becoming more connected to the people in their respective worlds—her colleagues at the firm, his fellow academics—than to each other. They rarely had dinner together, never hung out and read the paper together on weekends the way they used to, and communicated mostly by email.

When they did spend time together, they had a lot less to talk about. "I didn't know the people she worked with, so none of her stories were very interesting," Tom said. Caroline had met a few of Tom's lab partners and thought they were geeks. "Of course they're geeks," Tom told her. "They're neuropsychologists! But if you gave them a chance, you'd see they're way funnier than the lawyers you hang out with."

Caroline and Tom started to see faults in each other they'd never noticed before. Tom saw a combative and self-important side of Caroline, and Caroline thought Tom could be passive-aggressive and moody.

One night, Tom came down with the flu and was laid up in bed. Caroline, who had made plans that night, decided to pick him up some pizza, drop it off at home, then meet her friends at the bar. When she mentioned her plan to a friend at work, he looked surprised. "He said if he was sick and his wife handed him a pizza and went back out, he'd be hurt," Caroline told us. That struck a chord. "I saw myself from the outside, and I didn't like what I saw."

The pizza incident inspired Caroline to talk to Tom.

"What's going on with our marriage?" she asked, expecting that at worst, this would lead to a garden-variety fight. What ensued was not garden variety. The floodgates opened. Tom said he felt as if Caroline had traded their dreams of a family life for a soulless corporate job. She was shocked that someone who rarely looked up from his computer, who spent fifty hours a week in a lab studying endless iterations of brain wave activity, could be so hypocritical.

"We both felt neglected, and we blamed each other," Caroline told us. But that was only half of it. "During that conversation we both realized we didn't know each other anymore and maybe we didn't want to."

A few months later, Caroline moved out.

The Problem: Sunk Costs

Being apart was harder than they expected.

"I would come home and want to hear about Caroline's day," said Tom, admitting that he missed her law firm stories. "They were actually pretty funny in retrospect."

Caroline started to wonder if she'd moved out too soon and if she hadn't given the marriage enough of a chance. "I never saw myself as a quitter, but with Tom, I bailed at the first sign of trouble. It didn't feel right."

They decided to try again. But how? The time sinks in their marriage—their jobs—were still there. Caroline was on track to be partner, and Tom was interviewing for jobs at top-ranked universities. They barely had time to shower, much less piece their marriage back together. Yet they couldn't slow down now and throw away all the time and money they'd invested in being superstars. "We'd sacrificed years of our lives, more than $100,000 in tuition bills and our marriage, basically," Tom said.

Economists would argue that fixating on past investments—or what's known as "sunk costs"—when weighing what to do in the future is a waste of time. Sunk costs are just what they sound like: sunk, buried, kaput, *finito*. Let them go, a wise economist would say, focus on future costs and benefits, not money you've spent and can't get back.

The French and British governments learned this the hard way when they kept the money-sucking Concorde flying for so many years because grounding it would be too embarrassing and they'd already spent billions trying to prove their aeroengineering prowess to the world. NASA is often accused of throwing good money after bad. In 2008, the agency tossed an extra $100 million at the already over-budget and long-delayed Mars Science Lab, in part because it had already sunk $1.8 billion into it, according to Alan Stern, an astrophysicist and former NASA administrator.

Remember Greg Mankiw, the Harvard guy with the list of ten economic principles? Prior to becoming a famous economist, he grappled with his own sunk costs. Before getting a PhD in economics, he was accepted into Harvard Law School. He deferred law school, started his PhD, and a year later switched to law school. But in his second year studying law, he realized he was a far better economist than lawyer, so he quit law school and finished his PhD. "Remembering the irrelevance of sunk costs, I moved across the parking lot from the Harvard Law School to the Harvard Economics Department, where I have now been on the faculty for over twenty years," he said.

Think about all the sunk costs that have sucked you dry over the years. The bad movies you suffered through because you paid $10 for the tickets. The $20 sea urchin sashimi you ate even though it tasted like rancid algae. The daylong shopping trip that ended with you buying a crocodile-skin belt you neither wanted nor needed (nor liked) but felt compelled to buy to justify the day you spent trying to spend money.

Or picture this: You buy a house in a town with the highest property taxes in the stratosphere just so your kids, who are still in diapers, can one day attend the town's award-winning public school. A few years have passed and you've sunk untold amounts of money into the house. Now your kids are old enough to start elementary school. Only you recently met some people whose kids go to a nearby private school, and those kids are so well behaved and intelligent that you're leaning toward sending your kids there, at a cost of $25,000 per kid per year. You're stumped. You keep calculating the buckets of money you invested in the house, but you're also increasingly certain that little Sophie needs the "enrichment" programs at the private school and little Toby might be a bully unless someone sings "Kook-

Gut Check on Your Marriage

The next time you start to wonder how your marriage is doing, try an experiment. Take a pen and a piece of paper and draw a chart like the one below. The y-axis is how much time you spend on things, and the x-axis is how important each of those things are. Then start plotting.

For example, cuddling. Maybe you consider this an extremely worthy activity, yet you spend negative two minutes on it each day. Plot it on the graph at the lower right. Or let's say you believe that making assumptions about what your spouse is thinking is counterproductive, yet you do it 14 times a day. That should go in the upper left. Existential dread? Maybe you're right where you want to be.

Pretty soon a picture of your marriage will emerge that might surprise you. You'll see how much time you spend on the important things—and how much you waste on the trivial. If your chart looks like this one, you might think about making some changes. You might, for example, work with your spouse to move the stuff in the top-left quadrant down to the bottom left, and start investing more energy and time into the things that matter. An economist might say that's better resource allocation; we just think it might make you a little happier.

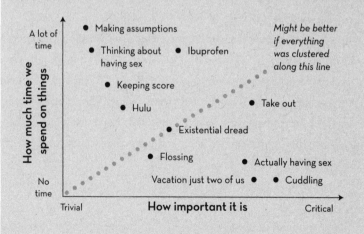

aburra" in Mandarin to him twice a day. Your choice: Stick to the public school plan or jump ship and ensure your kids have a shot at being president someday.

The Solution: Ignoring Sunk Costs

Caroline and Tom were facing a trade-off: Scale back on work and make more time for each other or stick to the same schedules and risk a permanent split. It might have been an easy decision, but their sunk costs were clouding the view.

They decided to try to have their cake and eat it, too. Caroline moved back in, and she and Tom planned to spend every Saturday together, riding bikes, reading the paper, going to the movies. They said they'd go to church on Sundays and committed to leaving work at a reasonable hour once a week so they could have a civilized, no-interruption dinner together. But they were lucky if they managed one nice dinner a month, and Saturday bike rides invariably got put off when one or the other had work that, for whatever reason, couldn't wait until Monday. "We weren't in as deep a black hole as before, but we were still stretched thin," Tom said.

Everything changed when they tried to have a baby and couldn't. Month after month, they did the dumb tests with the smiley faces ("You're ovulating!") and confusing pink lines ("Wait, is it two lines for pregnant or one?"), but no baby came. When they went to a fertility specialist, the doctor suggested they slow down for a few months before starting treatment to see if reducing their stress levels might have an effect.

"She also said that with all my travel we probably weren't having enough sex," said Caroline. "She was right."

They took a few weeks off together and went camping in the Pacific Northwest. They hiked and read and slept and had a lot of sex.

And somewhere between the bottom of the Cascades and one of the peaks, they decided to let sunk costs be sunk. They realized that they'd pursued their careers with blinders on, losing sight of what was important to them: family, friendship, and an occasionally BlackBerry-free day.

Oh, and when they weren't busy having deep realizations, Caroline got pregnant.

A few months later, Caroline took a less stressful job at a less prestigious law firm and Tom started working in a research lab, also a less prestigious job but one that paid along the lines of a university position and had regular hours. "It hurt, but I'm glad we went through it," said Caroline. "If we kept going on the same path, we'd be rich, successful, and divorced."

CASE STUDY #3

The Players: Abby and Gus

Abby and Gus met the year after college, at an investment firm in Japan that was stacked with recent graduates looking for international experience. Gus was South African, Abby was American, and they hit it off right away, debating world politics, arguing about South Africa's progress with the legacy of apartheid, and pondering the significance of Bill Clinton's libido.

They read to each other—he sold her on Carl Hiassen, she introduced him to Milan Kundera, climbed Mount Hotaka, and spent many nights getting drunk on silly amounts of sake. During Japan's weeklong nationwide vacation, they flew to Bali, where they passed the first two days playing Frisbee on the beach and swimming and the last five battling a nasty parasite that hammered them with fevers, nausea, and the nagging fear that they'd been stricken with Dengue fever.

"I thought I was going to die," said Gus.

"He was fine," said Abby.

They loved their high-octane work environment, but they also knew they couldn't take the cutthroat nature of banking indefinitely. They talked about the future, and it sounded—to Abby, at least—as if they wanted the same things: a big family, freedom to travel, fulfilling work.

A year passed, and Abby announced she was done working until the wee hours helping rich people get richer. She was ready for another adventure.

She suggested to Gus that they move to Hong Kong. Or maybe London, or Mozambique. With their degrees and their experience, she said, they could find jobs no problem. "I was interested in relief work then," she said.

Gus said he wasn't ready to commit to living somewhere else yet. If he left Japan, he wanted to first travel the world. Abby, he said, was "welcome to come."

Welcome to come? "That's what you say to your drinking buddies or your mom," Abby told him. "Not your *girlfriend*, who you led to believe you wanted to spend the rest of your life with."

It was unfair, she said, for Gus to have let her think that their relationship was something more than some postcollege fling. Gus saw it differently. He'd had a blast with Abby. He wouldn't trade a day of it. It's not like he wanted to break up, he just wasn't ready to settle down yet. He wanted to explore. To *experience* things. Why did that make him a jerk? Who made Abby queen of the relationship train schedule? It was unfair of Abby to expect him to settle down before he was thirty.

"I thought Gus was it," Abby said. "I had no doubts. He was confident in a way that was sexy—not arrogant, just sure of himself. He picked up some Japanese and acted like he'd been speaking it for years. He convinced people in the bank to give him work that he had no idea how to do, and then he'd find someone to explain it to him."

She'd assumed he was equally confident about her. But not one to play the victim, Abby packed up and moved to London, where she found a job at an anti-nukes nongovernmental organization and eventually started dating someone else.

When Gus, who had been dating girls who couldn't hold a candle to Abby, heard through a friend that Abby was seeing someone else, he was extremely jealous. He flew to London and told Abby he wanted her back—but, he added, he still wasn't ready for marriage.

Abby's reaction: "No deal." She wanted a commitment or nothing at all. "Was I bluffing? A bit. But I wasn't going to set myself up for disappointment again."

Gus took a few days to weigh the costs and benefits, and finally promised to make an honest woman out of her within the year. Abby dumped the interim boyfriend.

"It's not like there was anyone else," said Gus. "I just wasn't ready as soon as she was."

The early years of marriage were fun. They had a child and discovered they were compatible parents, with similar views of everything from calming a baby down to going out on their own at least once a week. They split the child care equally and pursued their careers. Things were moving along swimmingly when one night, a year after the baby arrived, Abby took Gus out for Thai—his favorite—and said she had something she needed to discuss with him. At thirty-two, she wanted to go to medical school.

"To be a doctor? That's insane," Gus said, supportively. They were old. They were happy. They were debt-free. Why rock the boat? But the idea had been planted, and they discussed it on and off for more than a year. By the time Abby decided to take the plunge, Gus was encouraging; he'd found a career he loved and he wanted the same for her. Gus said he'd have her back—emotionally and, of course, financially.

The next decade was a drag, pure and simple. Abby struggled through a year of pre-med classes, endured a heavy course load once she got into medical school, and in the meantime had another baby. "The clock was ticking," she said.

As soon as the baby was born, she embarked on an unforgiving eighty-hour-a-week residency. "I was spending about twice as much time at the hospital as I was at home," she said. "No exaggeration."

Gus supported the family, as the chief financial officer of a web-design company in Los Angeles, and did the bulk of the parenting, too. He took the kids to their doctors' appointments, found babysitters when he had to go on business trips, and met with school guidance counselors. As for Abby, she would often slip into bed long after Gus went to sleep and slip out of bed before he woke up.

Gus knew in his gut that all this sweat would pay off down the road, and that Abby was working hard both for herself and for her family's future. Still, he found himself feeling increasingly put-upon. He would pick fights with Abby—when he was lucky enough to get an audience with her—and then manage to be out of the house on the rare weekend mornings she was home. "I didn't trust myself to be nice," he told us. "I was resentful. All the time."

The Problem: Inequity Aversion

Economists recently uncovered a shocking truth: No one likes getting the short end of the stick. And further, our "inequity aversion," a desire for fair outcomes, leads us to make decisions that aren't always in our own best interest.

This was a radical departure for economists, who for a long time based their work on the assumption that people acted in their own best interest. Fairness was irrelevant in a free market. For example: I will gladly collate for $2 an hour even if everyone else in this copy shop is collating for $5 an hour because $2 is better than zero, which is what I was making before I got this asinine job.

Not so fast. Once my inequity aversion kicks in, which is pretty much at the end of day one, I'll quit this job because it's totally unfair that I'm making less than the other boneheads here. I'll go home, grab a Bud Light, switch on the basketball game, and think about finding a new job tomorrow.

"If you worry excessively about 'does someone have more than me,' you'll be miserable," Cornell economist Robert Frank told us. "But you can't help it—life is graded on a curve."

What does this have to do with trade-offs, you ask?

Well, in considering this one simple trade-off—a) keep a job that pays very little money, or b) quit that job, have the freedom to drink beer in the middle of the day, and make no money—I've let my sense of what's fair and not fair guide me to option B. And now I'm broke.

About thirty years ago, a group of three German economists named Werner Güth, Rolf Schmittberger, and Bernd Schwarze invented a game to see for themselves how fairness influences economic decisions. They called it "the Ultimatum Game," and it became something of a sensation—in the eggheady world of economics, at least. Here's how it's played:

You have $100. Your task is to decide how to split that money with another player, whom you don't know. Let's call her Judy.

There are rules. You can't talk to Judy, and you're in a separate room from her. There is no negotiating, haggling, or bargaining. You will play only once, meaning if you cheat Judy, no worries, you'll never have to see her again. But there's a hitch. If Judy doesn't like your offer, she can reject it and then neither of you gets to keep a cent.

Naturally, you want to offer Judy as little as possible so you can keep as much as possible. But if you offer her too little—say, $5—she might view the offer as unfair and reject it, leaving you both worse off.

From a purely economic standpoint, Judy's desire for a "fair" offer is silly. If you give her only $1, that's still $1 more than she had before the game started. She should be happy with what she gets. But when economists run this game, more than half of the players reject offers of less than $20. And probably because they know the other person will reject an "unfair" offer, two-thirds of people paying make offers between $40 and $50. Only four in one hundred people offer less than $20.

It's in Our Nature

A group of particularly ambitious economists and anthropologists took the Ultimatum Game one step further. They set out to see how several small-scale societies played the game, from the Khazax in Mongolia to the Quichua in Ecuador. They discovered that some tribes gave away more money, some less, but in general, fairness appeared to be a pretty universal motivator.

Of course, there were some outliers. The Lamalera in Indonesia, for example, proved to be unusually generous, offering on average 58 percent of their money (as whale hunters who whale hunt together in canoes, they are accustomed to sharing, the economists concluded). On the opposite end of the spectrum were the Machiguenga in Peru, whose members offered only 26 percent of their money—emblematic, said the economists, of a society that works more in family units than in community ones. Some groups, including the Gnau of Papua New Guinea, offered up a relatively large amount of money but faced high levels of rejection. The authors chalked this up to cultures in which accepting gifts is a sign of weakness and subordination.

As the economist Richard Thaler says: "Most people prefer more money to less, like to be treated fairly, and like to treat others fairly. To the extent that these objectives are contradictory, subjects make trade-offs."

Thaler is, of course, pointing out what any couple who has been married for more than ten minutes knows: Fairness matters. The only difference between the Ultimatum Game and a real marriage is that the stakes in marriage are a lot higher than $100.

But as any couple will also tell you, seeing fairness as black or white—and the choice as stay or walk out—isn't a winning strategy. Unless you're in a truly failing marriage, fairness is a moving target. Some days may not feel fair, but over many years together, things tend to even out. Overweighing fairness in the short run may well come back to bite you in the long run—and lead to some god-awful fighting along the way.

Which is precisely where Gus and Abby found themselves midway through Abby's residency.

Gus had started to dislike Abby's ambition, a quality he had once admired in her. His own career was stuck in neutral. Sure, she made some contributions, including hiring the nannies, researching the kids' schools, and organizing a few playdates. But the bulk of the work fell on Gus. When the kids were sick, he was the one taking them out of day care, and he was the one taking his own sick days to do it. Abby didn't get sick days.

"I can't do everything all the time," he would tell Abby, and, "I didn't sign up to be a single parent," and, "When are you going to start pulling your weight around here?" and, of course, "This isn't fair."

Abby accused Gus of being selfish. She was doing the best she could, she thought, often leaving the hospital after a long shift to pick up the kids from school, even though she hadn't slept for twenty hours. "Is it *fair* that you get to hang out with the kids and I don't? Is it *fair* that other moms actually get to see their kids every morning? Is it *fair* that this job is turning me into the world's worst mother?"

Abby was angry at her husband for having agreed to back her and then complaining about it. She was mad at her kids for seeming to prefer Gus's company. She was mad at herself for putting everyone through such an ordeal. "I wanted to give up," she said. "I wanted to give up on my residency. I wanted to crawl into bed and sleep for two months."

The Solution: Get Over It

Economists say that in a market economy, people inevitably face trade-offs between equity—or what's fair—and efficiency, or the optimal allocation of resources. Not everyone gets to be rich, even though that's unfair. Some people have to own the businesses and other people have to work in the mailrooms. Some people get to finish their residencies and others get stuck watching the kids.

The problem with fixating on life's unfairness is that it precludes our ability to think clearly about trade-offs, which can lead to very inefficient outcomes.

The solution: Get over it.

Not exactly a high-concept solution, but the only way to tackle inequity aversion is to will it away—to recognize that the more time you spend in an it's-not-fair mentality, the less time you have for calculating the long-term benefits of a trade-off, for tallying up the short-term costs, and, ultimately, for finding solutions.

For a long time, there was nothing fair about life in Abby and Gus's house. But Abby didn't quit her residency and Gus didn't walk out the door. Before things got too out of hand, they found ways to muscle through the final stretch—to stick to the trade-off they'd agreed to in the first place.

The key was finding things that benefited each of them a little bit and the overall situation a lot. First, they banned taking the fairness temperature every day. Then, they found small things to improve their daily routines (they were thinking at the margin!). For example, Abby started doing more cooking, which she enjoyed. On her rare days off, she'd try to cook a few big meals—a lasagna, some beef stew, a few quiches—and freeze them so that Gus wouldn't have to do all the cooking (or order pizza every night). "I wanted him and the kids to have healthy food," she said. "I wanted not to see a Domino's pizza box at four a.m. when I came home. It also made me feel like more of a mom."

Abby convinced Gus, a frustrated former marathoner, to jog home from work three days a week. "For Gus, exercise is sanity," Abby told us. "If it means asking the sitter to stay for an extra half an hour, fine." While there were no direct benefits to Abby on this front, there was a huge one for Gus: He was happier and more relaxed. And that was an indirect benefit to Abby *and* the kids.

They went away every few months for a night, leaving after the kids went to bed and coming home by lunch the next day. Cheap motels were the venue of choice. "Close by and not too pricey," said Gus.

And they tried not to let their sex life slip. It had gotten to the point where two months would pass and they wouldn't have so much as touched toes in bed. They resolved to have sex at least once a week. At first, Abby thought it felt too mechanical to force herself to have sex when she could hardly keep her eyes open. But she told herself that if she could stay up for her patients, she could do the same for her marriage. "It was weird," she told us. "I thought that I didn't have an ounce of energy left in me and definitely no energy for sex. But I agreed to try it, and it made me feel better. I felt more connected to Gus at a time when our lives were otherwise disconnected."

They weren't perfect, of course, and they still had spats about who was doing more day to day. When Abby would come home after a twenty-four-hour shift and need to sleep, Gus was still sometimes irritated rather than sympathetic. When Gus was hard on the kids, Abby would sometimes regret that she didn't feel she could interfere: He was the one doing more of the work; what right did she have to tell him how to do it?

But they mucked through nine years, and came out in one piece. Abby still couldn't believe she had a "Dr." in front of her name, and Gus bragged about how hot his wife looked in scrubs. He said he couldn't wait until the day they could move to Small Town, USA, and she could be the local doctor and he could grow lettuce. "It wasn't *my* achievement," Abby said. "It was ours. There's no way I could have done this without him."

These days, Abby does more parenting and Gus has more freedom. He travels a lot, something he rarely got to do when Abby was a resident. She works nine to five as a radiologist, is on the PTA, and has taken up boxing, a sport she said is good for "aggression release." And while Abby doesn't work in a hospital anymore, let's just say Gus likes her to keep a few extra pairs of scrubs around.

THE BOTTOM LINE

1. **Calculate costs and benefits.** When it comes to Big Decisions, trusting your gut is a valid approach. But facts help, too. A well-thought-out cost-benefit analysis is a a great way to understand what's really at stake. (We recommend using a giant whiteboard—très romantique.)

2. **Think at the margin.** Winning the lottery, going on *The Price Is Right,* selling drugs. Sure, those might solve some of your problems. But small changes can have big impacts, too—and they're much easier to pull off.

3. **Let sunk costs be sunk.** You're never going to get back what you've spent, whether it's time, money, or energy, so don't let any of that drive your decision making. If you sweated blood to get to the corner office, but you can't remember the name of your first-born child, you might want to reconsider the path you're on.

4. **Life's not fair.** And neither is marriage. Some years, your spouse might get to pursue his dream of upholstering furniture, but other years, it'll be your turn to quit your job and do yoga every day.

7

ASYMMETRIC INFORMATION

Or, Why You Should Tell Your Partner Stuff

THE PRINCIPLE

The date was going so well. Aaron was cute. He was smart, with a PhD in Russian history and a tenured position at a good university. And he was Jewish. And he paid for dinner. And he laughed at Leah's jokes. He walked her home, gave her a kiss, didn't try to weasel his way upstairs, and emailed her the next day to ask her out again.

So why was Leah hesitating to say yes?

Because of the same nagging question she asked herself after every other good date she'd been on: If he's that great, why is he still single?

Her friends wanted to wring her neck every time she started down this road. *You're your own worst enemy,* they said. *Stop second-guessing. Do you want to be single forever?*

We don't know Leah that well, but we disagree with her friends: We think she was on to something.

We'll tell you why in a minute. But first, let's try a little thought experiment: Imagine you're in the market for a used car. You see an ad for a ten-year-old Toyota Corolla DX in the *Penny Saver* and it sounds perfect: Manual Trans. 56K Miles. Rides Like New. Spent Life in Grandma's Driveway in Boca. Must See to Believe. Only $500!

You head out first thing Saturday morning to meet the seller, a guy with a mustache and a pinky ring who tells you you're never going to find another deal like this. "I'll be honest," says Pinky Ring. "It's not even about the money for me. I'm just doing my grandmother a favor. She's ninety. She shouldn't be driving."

"When was it last serviced?"

"Oh, uh, a few months ago."

"Do you have the paperwork?"

"Not on me. I'll have to look for it."

"When did your grandmother buy it? Do you know who owned it before? Has it been in any accidents?"

"Accidents? No, no way. Look at it! I think she bought it new . . . yeah, that's right, she bought it new."

"You have the receipt?"

"I can ask her, but I doubt she's got it. She's a little out of it these days."

That once-in-a-lifetime deal is starting to sound more like a too-good-to-be-true deal.

Economists have a name for the too-good-to-be-true scenario: "the lemon problem." The term was coined by the economist George Akerlof in 1970 (who, thirty-one years later, won the Nobel Prize for it) and refers, in part, to markets in which one person has more information than the other—when there's an "asymmetry" of information—and to all the bad stuff that can happen as a result.

Your Corolla situation is asymmetrical because Pinky Ring knows the car has actually been in three accidents and had the transmission replaced and the odometer reset after one hundred thousand miles—but you don't know any of that. So you're at a disadvantage. And when you write him a check, then drive that Corolla home and it doesn't start the next day, you're going to be kind of angry.

Same goes for Aaron and Leah. Aaron knows he has a habit of losing interest in a girl immediately after sleeping with her, is a Class-A commitment-phobe, and doesn't want kids—but Leah knows none of this. So she's at a disadvantage. And when she goes out with Aaron again because, why not, such a nice Jewish boy, and then goes home with him and never hears from him again, she's going to be kind of angry. She'll probably feel like an S-L-U-T and vow to never have sex again until there's a ring on her finger.

That's why we don't blame Leah for proceeding with caution, no matter how great Aaron seemed on that first date.

Without information, we can't make informed decisions. And when we can't make informed decisions, we either make uninformed decisions, which can lead to disaster (slut, lemon), or we opt out entirely, which means we could be missing out on a great guy or a truly mint car.

It seems abundantly clear, doesn't it? Only back when Akerlof identified the problem of asymmetric information, it wasn't at all clear to economists. When they came up with their theories about consumption and the market, they started with the assumption that buyers and sellers both knew all the relevant information about the goods and services on the market. This was called the theory of "complete" information, and it was how the invisible hand of the market was thought to work.

Akerlof thought complete information left too many important questions unanswered—namely, Why would anyone buy a used car? Shouldn't the fact that someone wants to sell their car in the first place suggest there's something wrong with it?

Akerlof's questions underscored a flaw in the theory of complete information, which is that sometimes sellers have *more* information about what they're selling than buyers do. Only the seller knows if he's got a lemon on his hands.

Take this to its logical conclusion and the entire used-car market collapses. Knowing that the seller is likely to keep information to himself, the buyer can't trust him from the get-go. If the seller insists the car is awesome, the buyer wonders why he's selling it to begin with. If the seller offers to drop the price, the buyer senses desperation

IN PLAIN ENGLISH:

The Invisible Hand

From Adam Smith's *The Wealth of Nations*: A business owner is "led by an invisible hand to promote an end which was no part of his intention. Nor is it always the worse for the society that it was no part of it. By pursuing his own interest he frequently promotes that of the society more effectually than when he really intends to promote it."

Translation: Even when we're out for our own self-interest (say, making money), we're guided, as if by an invisible hand, to do good for the world.

Translation: Everyone wins in a capitalist society.

More than two hundred years since *The Wealth of Nations* was published, the invisible hand is still an economic fundamental. Unfortunately, there are plenty of situations—including the used-car market—in which the invisible hand isn't just invisible, it actually doesn't exist:

- You should be in line for a promotion, but instead it goes to your narcoleptic co-worker because the boss is too busy playing golf to pay attention to what his staff is up to.
- You should be watching the best show on TV tonight, but instead you watch reruns of *The Jeffersons* because your partner has the remote and so has all the power.
- We should be able to power our homes with wind energy by now, but instead we're burning through the world's oil resources because it's more convenient.

and suspects there's something *really* wrong with the car. Since the buyer doesn't know what she's getting, she offers to pay a price that won't make her feel like a total idiot if the car turns out to be a lemon. That price, said Akerlof, is about halfway between the cost of the car in mint condition and the cost of a clunker.

Problem is, that price also means sellers of mint cars will take their cars off the market, figuring they'll never get a fair price. All that's left: lemons. Asymmetric markets are problematic for everyone, sellers included.

And not just in the used-car market. How can health insurers figure out what premiums to charge if they don't know which of their customers are overweight smokers and which are teetotaling triathletes?

How can mortgage lenders settle on an interest rate without knowing which borrowers can be relied on to pay their bills on time and which are destined to default?

How can a company hire a new employee without knowing whether he burned down the cafeteria at his old job?

How can a woman—or a guy—decide to go home with someone when they don't know if they're looking for a soul mate—or just a fling?

But before you start crying a river for used-car sellers, insurance companies, mortgage lenders, corporate bloodsuckers, and slimy single guys, remember that there are ways to even out the information. Used-car sellers can stick to certified pre-owned models that have the makers' stamp of approval. Insurers look at every detail of your medical history to see if you so much as touched a cigarette in the last thirty years. Mortgage lenders do credit checks. Employers ask for references. And single men and women, well, for them it's a little murkier, but some judicious Googling can go a long way toward sussing out the psychopaths.

To economists, information is typically a good thing: The more we know, the more equipped we are to make smart decisions and the more efficiently markets function.

The same holds true in your marriage. A constant exchange of information is vital to keep your little economy humming. That's why you always call when you're running late, so your spouse knows to hold off on dinner. And that's why you never fail to speak up when your feelings are hurt, so your spouse knows to apologize. And that's also why you explain you have a headache, so your spouse knows it's not that you don't *want* to have sex, it's just that, you know, you *can't* right now. For medical reasons.

Wait, what?

You're not always that transparent with each other? You don't always call? You sometimes don't feel like talking? You tend to keep things to yourself until you explode? You think he should know what you're thinking without you having to tell him?

Could there be some asymmetry in your marriage?

Ours, too. In fact, we'll wager that many of the problems in the category of "communication" stem from asymmetric information. When you filter certain details because you don't want your spouse to know the full story, or because you're worried about how she'll react, there's asymmetry. When you assume he'll know what you want or what you think or what you'd like him to do, and therefore you don't tell him directly, there's asymmetry. When something's bothering you but you keep it to yourself—asymmetry.

In this chapter, we're going to talk you through some of the ways to balance out the information, including sending your partner signals, saying what you mean and doing what you say, and recognizing when too much information is causing imbalances of another kind. It's not really that hard, it's just economics.

CASE STUDY #1

The Players: Bill and Angela

Bill and Angela claim they "surfed the entire Internet" before they found each other. Both had been married before and were initially reluctant to use online dating sites.

"I'm not *that* desperate," Angela thought.

"Don't only desperate women look for a date on the Internet?" Bill thought.

But enough of their friends had found first, second, or third husbands and wives online that they finally sucked up their pride and posted their profiles.

For Bill—"Restaurateur seeks table for two"—the online dating world was like another wondrous planet, filled with women who asked for nothing more than walks on the beach and candlelit dinners. He could do both. He'd been bereft and he'd been burned, by a first wife who died in a car accident when he was in his late twenties and a second who left him after two years for one of his friends. Perusing the profiles, he was "like a kid in a candy store." He went on dozens of dates, many of them fun and many of them duds, like the woman who waited until he was in the bathroom to order the most expensive wine on the menu. "She didn't last long," said Bill.

Angela—"Hey, stranger. Need a lift?"—wasn't ready to jump into another marriage right away. She had been with her first husband for twenty-two years, ever since high school, and wanted to sow the oats she'd never had a chance to sow before. She estimated she went on a hundred dates that first year and, like Bill, met plenty of ding-dongs along the way. One of her more memorable losers: the guy who claimed to be a six-foot-tall math whiz and Fulbright scholar but was in fact barely over five feet, couldn't figure out how much to leave the waiter for a tip—and then asked to borrow cab fare home. "Back then, I didn't care when I had a lame date," she said. "I would find an excuse to leave early, go home, and get back online."

But eventually, Angela said, she'd sown enough oats. She'd had her fill of meaningless sex, conversations about exes, and two-for-one appletinis. She yearned for the real thing. She started being more discerning. She ruled out people who included only head shots, who had gone to colleges she'd never heard of, and who used more than one exclamation point in a single paragraph. She also kept an eye out for inflated language, anyone who was trying too hard to impress. Stuff like, "I get totally stoked when I'm with a woman I care about, and will do anything to make her happy," was too over the top to be trusted. *Anything?* Please.

She was surprised by how few people fit the bill. After several weeks of searching the profiles, she had found only four serious contenders.

Bill was one of them.

On their first date, they went to a lake and Bill rented a paddleboat. "Cheesy," said Angela, "but cute." As they paddled around and made small talk about the fish and the perils of online dating, Angela asked how Bill got along with his two teenage kids from his first marriage. "I think they hate me," said Bill. "They still haven't forgiven me for remarrying. After their mom died, all we had was each other. It wasn't easy for them being raised by a single dad, but as long as I *stayed* single, they managed. When I finally got serious with someone, they flipped out."

Angela had been on a lot of dates with men who had kids—she herself had a daughter in high school—and to a man, each one claimed to have a "great relationship" with them, no hard feelings post-divorce. Considering that her daughter had plenty of hard feelings since the divorce, and considering no kid likes to see his or her parents split, she had a hard time believing these guys. "I guess they were telling me what they thought I wanted to hear," said Angela. "But what I wanted was honesty."

Bill was equally relieved to meet a woman who was real, who didn't beat around the bush: "Within the first hour, I knew she had a daughter who was flunking out of school, her husband sent her a hefty alimony check every month, and she'd dated half the Internet."

Bill and Angela got married six months later.

When we met them a couple of years into their marriage, they told us they almost didn't make it past year one. The problem had a lot to do with the way they communicated—ironic, considering how open they'd been with each other on that first date. According to Bill, Angela never told him when she was upset with him. "She expected me to read her mind," he told us. "But I'm not a mind reader. I don't have X-ray vision, either."

Angela said it was hard for her to tell Bill when she was angry: "I've never been very good at handling conflict. I'm much better at bottling things up." She'd get short-tempered or whiny, thinking he'd eventually notice something was off and apologize. She told us about the time their dishwasher wasn't draining and Bill said he would fix it and it took him two weeks just to get around to going to the hardware store to find the part he needed. "No follow-through. That kind of thing was standard behavior for him."

Standard behavior, said Bill, was telling your husband what's on your mind. Instead, he said, Angela would be snippy or pouty and Bill would assume she was having a bad day. "I once asked her if she was getting her period," said Bill. "I never made that mistake again." Angela could be in a funk for days or weeks, and then, said Bill, she'd explode out of nowhere. Like with the dishwasher. Bill said he had no clue Angela was stewing in a cauldron of rage until one night, after dinner, she opened the dishwasher, slammed it shut, and told Bill she was going to shoot herself if she had to hand-wash another goddamn dish.

The Problem: Pooling Equilibrium

Bill wasn't an imbecile. He knew the dishwasher was still broken. It was right there on his list of things to deal with—a running list he kept in his head. He didn't worry about *when* these things got done, as long as they got done eventually. Which they did.

What he didn't know was that Angela also kept a running list in her head—of all the things Bill hadn't gotten around to finishing. Topping her list: the dishwasher.

Now you might say that since Bill *knew* the dishwasher was still broken, he should have also known, on some semiconscious level, that Angela would be unhappy about it. Fair enough. But economists would argue that he couldn't possibly have known that—or at least not known the depth of her rage—because she never told him.

In the absence of information from Angela, Bill continued to do what he had always done: kiss her when he came home from work, tease her about how her Caesar salad needed salt . . . and put off fixing the dishwasher.

Some people, most people, have a very special name for the stewing wife/clueless husband paradigm: "marriage." But we prefer a term from economics called a "pooling equilibrium." This is when someone can't distinguish between two different things because he doesn't have the necessary information. Think of it as the "how can I make you happy when you act the same whether you're unhappy or happy" equilibrium.

In the real world, an employer might face a pooling equilibrium if the two résumés on his desk are from candidates who both went to Harvard. One candidate might be smart, but the other might just be an Ivy League blowhard. The employer can't know for sure which is which. To be safe, he settles on a high salary befitting a smart Harvard grad. It's his loss if he inadvertently hired the blowhard.

A mortgage lender might face a pooling equilibrium if it can't tell which borrowers are reliable and which are serial defaulters. In which case it has to charge the same high interest rate to everyone—not good for business, since that will likely drive away all the reliable, yet cost conscious, customers.

Most people prefer a "separating equilibrium," in which the good guys can be discerned from the bad. But for that you need information, information only the other person can provide. *If* he or she chooses to do so. And in Angela's case, she was opting for door number two.

The Solution: Signaling

Behind door number one, however, was a fairly painless solution for fixing Bill and Angela's problem: signaling.

You might remember this concept from chapter 3, and the woman who started using signals to tip off her husband to the fact that she was in the mood for sex. In that case, signals helped two people coordinate better when all their previous attempts failed.

Signals are one of the most often used tools for evening out information imbalances. Good signals are sent by the informed party to the uninformed. They are chock-full of facts. And the more they cost the sender in terms of time, money, or effort, the more credible they tend to be.

A guy selling his Chevette who produces a vehicle inspection report and accident history without being asked is signaling to a potential buyer that the car won't break down on the way home.

In spending millions on a thirty-second Super Bowl ad, companies are signaling to viewers that their products are worth their weight in gold.

Infomercials for exercise balls used by astronauts on the space station are signaling durability. In fact, the makers are so confident, they'll refund all your money if you're not 100 percent satisfied. Those balls must be amazing!

Banks often set up shop in old buildings with grand architecture as a way of conveying a sense of longevity and letting the world know that thieves will have a tough time breaking down the doors.

Fortunately for Angela, she didn't have to devise all sorts of creative signals like money-back guarantees or proofs of purchase. She could simply signal using words or those so-called nice gestures that we hear spouses sometimes offer each other. Whichever signals she used would require effort, and the effort itself would help boost her credibility.

"All I need is one word," Bill finally told her. "Something so I know what you want from me. I promise not to turn it into a big thing."

Angela's first husband had never made a promise like that. He was as bad at handling conflict as she was, only instead of bottling and then exploding, his approach was yelling and slamming car doors. "I

Watch What You Say

A recent study out of California State University, Dominguez Hills, looked at how word choice can signal all kinds of information to potential dates.

Subjects were asked to read two emails, one from "JimJ789" and one from "FrankXYZ." Both emails were written to "Jenny123." The content of each email was virtually the same. Only the tenor was different. Both guys said they managed a small retail store, liked to travel and spend time with friends, and were looking for a woman to share their lives. But Jim expressed more "emotionality," meaning his adjectives tended to convey stronger feelings than Frank's. Jim said he "loved" his job. Frank said he was "satisfied" with it. Jim said travel "excites" him. Frank said he feels more "content" when he returns from a trip. Jim said he had a "fantastic" life. Frank said he "likes" his life.

By a wide majority—72 percent—subjects recommended Jenny date Jim, in part because he seemed "more confident, happy, enthusiastic, cheerful, energetic."

counted myself lucky to have found a guy in Bill who responded to me with his heart, not his ego."

The next time Angela added something to her list of things Bill hadn't done, she swore she'd confront him head-on. One Friday, a few days after the door to the patio fell off its hinge, she decided to surprise Bill with a home-cooked meal instead of their usual takeout. She whipped up a chicken Marengo and set the table with the awful place mats Bill's sister had given them for Christmas. With their images of Santa flying over a gingerbread house in sunny Florida, the place mats were a constant source of comic relief. Only this night she wrote on his mat in indelible marker—where he would see it when he picked up his plate to serve himself seconds—"I am turned on by a man with a hammer and a new hinge in his hands . . . especially if that man is you."

Bill fixed the door the very next day. Or maybe it was the day after. But the point is, it immediately rose to the top of his list and was checked off posthaste.

CASE STUDY #2

The Players: Kate and Dave

Kate and Dave have been married fifteen years. They met in law school, in a constitutional law study group. One thing they had in common from the start: their ages. They were practically the only two people over thirty among hundreds of classmates fresh out of college.

"When Dave first asked me out, he said something like, 'I'm an adult, you're an adult, let's hang out,' " Kate told us. "Not exactly a great sales pitch, but I had no social life to speak of, so I said what the hell."

On that first date, Kate and Dave discovered they had a second thing in common: They had both been teachers. Kate spent a few years in Central America with the Peace Corps, teaching elementary school in a small town in Costa Rica. Dave taught history at a charter school in the Bronx and tended bar.

They went on a second date, and a third, and before they knew it they were officially dating. After graduation, they landed plum jobs as litigators at big firms in Philadelphia. "Not exactly the 'good' work we planned to do with our lives, but definitely interesting work," said Dave. "And we had massive debts to pay off."

Over the years, Kate and Dave excelled at their jobs. They were textbook professionals, with their own offices that had doors that locked and windows that looked out onto the city. Each had a secretary. They carried briefcases, were respected by their peers, and could talk a jury into believing almost anything. If you were lucky enough to be invited to a dinner party at their house and were seated between, say, a circuit court judge and a top editor at the *Inquirer,* you would have been impressed and maybe even intimidated.

But if you knew the truth—if you were a fly on their wall on any given weeknight, you would be relieved to see that when it came to their jobs as husband and wife, they weren't nearly so intimidating or impressive.

That's because they argued a lot. They let little tiffs and misunderstandings escalate into full-blown fights. Dave admitted it was partly his fault: He clammed up when he got upset, and that tended to make things worse. But, he said, he was only like that because in the past, whenever he tried to talk to Kate, she either got defensive or denied culpability or shot back that Dave was the problem, not her. "Welcome to living with a lawyer," said Dave.

Kate admitted she was quick to hear criticism in Dave's voice, even if it wasn't his intention. But she also said the littlest thing would set him off, and if she was defensive, it was only because he was always on the offensive. (How's that for defensive?) "He organizes his life with military efficiency. I'm more laid-back," said Kate, adding that in this way they tended to defy traditional gender stereotypes. "I'm always like, 'What did I do now?' "

For example, they told us, one night Kate came home late from work—not an everyday occurrence, but not all that unusual, either. As she walked up the front steps, she was still on her BlackBerry. Dave opened the door, wearing an apron and a big grin. Kate thought he looked adorable but had to finish sending an email, so she held up a wait-a-second finger and returned to her typing.

"Guess what," said Dave, "I—"

"Hold on," said Kate. "I just have to finish . . . ugh, this is so annoying . . . one sec . . . this guy won't leave me alone . . . Christ. . ."

As Kate walked past her husband, she didn't notice his grin curdle into a grimace. Dave had gotten home early, cracked open a bottle of Malbec, and started cooking Aunt Judy's porky meatballs. He wanted to celebrate the fact that he'd won a motion in a lawsuit he'd been working on for more than a year.

Good plan, wrong night.

Kate was late and frazzled. She didn't seem to have the time for him or even care that he'd been slaving over a hot stove. When she finally hit send on that *super*-important email she'd been writing and went to say hello, it was too late. Dave's mood had changed.

"What. A. Day," Kate said, plopping onto a stool and helping herself to a glass of wine.

"Oh yeah?" Dave said, trying not to let on that there was a lit stack of dynamite in his head. "Must've been."

"You don't know the *half* of it," said Kate, who simultaneously checked her email again and launched into a long story about how her lunch with the judge she clerked for one summer lasted *three hours* and by the time she got back to the office she had no time to prep for a deposition she was taking and had to wing it but thank *god* they had been discussing *Palsgraf v. Long Island Rail Road* over lunch because at least it was fresh in her mind when she sat down to grill a woman who was suing the city for damages after tripping on a sidewalk and breaking her collarbone.

Dave said nothing. He just slammed the oven door shut on his roasting asparagus and threw his oven mitts on the counter.

"Everything okay?" Kate asked.

"Yup," said Dave as he chopped an onion to within an inch of its life. "Everything's fine."

"You seem stressed out. You sure everything's okay?" Kate asked again, beginning to think she'd once again failed him without knowing how or why. She wished he'd spill it already, but at the same time she was scared to hear the truth, scared it would ruin an already unpleasant night.

Not that the truth was forthcoming: "Mmm-hmm," replied Dave.

Kate asked if she could help in the kitchen. Dave said he had it under control.

Kate asked how Dave's day was. Dave said good.

Kate repeated that Dave seemed stressed. Dave said not to worry. Everything was hunky-dory.

Kate asked if he wanted to watch *Terms of Endearment* on cable while they had dinner. Dave said yessiree, that would be fantastic.

The Problem: Revealed vs. Stated Preferences

Dave *said* he was fine, but the way he *acted* indicated he wasn't fine. He said he wanted to watch a movie, but he spent the whole movie cleaning up and working on his Amazon wish list. He told Kate he didn't mind that she'd kept him waiting and couldn't bear to part with her BlackBerry, but he was out of sorts enough to burn the meatballs and liquefy the asparagus.

An economist would point out that Dave's "stated preferences" grossly contradicted his "revealed preferences"—and, further, that stated preferences are the less reliable indicators of how we really feel and what we really want. One of the classic examples of this discrepancy is known as "the Bradley effect," named for Los Angeles mayor Tom Bradley, an African American who lost the 1982 California governor's race even after being significantly ahead in both the opinion polls and the election day exit polls. Prior to the election, voters said they wouldn't have a problem electing an African American for governor, but when the day came, in the privacy of the voting booth, a majority checked off the white guy.

Or consider ice cream. If anyone believed that Americans wanted to lose weight, as 55 percent said they did in the latest Gallup poll, no one would go into the ice-cream business. Yet the freezer at your local Piggly Wiggly is packed with pints of rocky road and butter pecan that have to be restocked daily because Americans can't get enough of that icy, creamy goodness. Indeed, only 27 percent of Americans said they're *actually* trying to lose weight, found Gallup. Actions speak louder than words. Thank you, economics.

But while ice-cream makers can apparently tell the difference between what people say they want and what they really want, it's not that easy for married people. We put a lot of stake in what our partners say, and we get confused, frustrated, or angry when what they do doesn't follow what they say.

Note some of the stated preferences couples told us their spouses had made compared to what they later revealed via their actions:

What They Said	What They Did
"I don't care what we eat."	Refuse to go for sushi.
"I'll clean up."	Watch TV.
"We need a vacation."	Forget to ask for time off work.

"We should be having more sex."	Fall asleep on the couch.
"I'll watch the kids tonight."	Come home late.
"I'll never move to the suburbs."	Spend weekends at open houses.
"We need to stick to our budget."	Buy a home theater.
"I'll plant the impatiens this year."	Watch the weeds grow.

In Dave's case, aligning what he said ("I'm fine") with what he did (mope, seethe, ruin dinner) might have gone a long way toward keeping Kate informed. We know *why* he didn't say anything—he was scared of her response—but keeping silent wasn't a productive choice, either.

The Solution: Truth-Telling Mechanism

The more Dave said he was okay but didn't act okay, the more Kate searched in vain to figure out what on earth his problem was. And can you blame her?

The obvious solution—obvious to anyone except, of course, Dave—was for Dave to come out and say what was on his mind. He could stick to the facts, the way he did every day in his job, as in, "Kate, it upsets me"—maybe he doesn't tell the intern it "upsets" him when the copies he asked for never materialize, but you get the idea—"when you don't call to say you'll be running late, and when you're using your BlackBerry to, in effect, be with someone else instead of me. I was excited to enjoy a nice dinner together tonight, because something great happened at work, but now I'm in a bad mood."

See how good that feels?

Had Dave said those words, then Kate might have responded: "First, tell me the great thing that happened at work! Right after you do that, I'll apologize and admit I should put my BlackBerry down and think of you first when I walk in the door. But now I'm impatient to hear your good news. So while you tell me, I'll finish dinner. And when we're done, I'll clean up, take off your clothes, and have sex with you repeatedly."

But let's say Kate and Dave never received these scripts. Let's say Dave continued to keep his emotions to himself. In that case, an economist might have put the ball in Kate's court, saying she could try imposing a "truth-telling mechanism" that would persuade Dave to speak up.

A truth-telling mechanism is something a "principal" (a person trying to get someone else to do something) imposes on an "agent" (a person who is expected to do that thing). Examples of principals and agents include bosses and employees, insurers and insured, professors and students, diners and waiters. The "principal-agent problem," as it's known in economics, crops up any time agents aren't inclined to do what principals want them to do. To sway them, principals have to make it worth the agents' while. Bosses promise raises. Insurers offer lower rates to safe drivers. Professors write letters of recommendation for stellar students. The better the diner's experience, the bigger the waiter's tip.

When principals want agents to tell the truth, they can impose a truth-telling mechanism. For example, the IRS (principal) threatens to audit taxpayers (agents) to increase the odds that people will truthfully report their income. Dating websites (principals) do background checks so that online daters (agents) will choose to be up front about their checkered pasts. (One site, True.com, has even put its truth-telling mechanism—"We Screen for Felons"—on its home page.)

As for our principal (Kate), she needed to assure Dave (her agent) that it was safe to speak his mind. One way she could do that was to build her reputation for *not* lashing out when he came clean with stuff he was angry about. It wouldn't happen overnight, but she could start by, for instance, vowing to nod and say "Gotcha" or "No problem" or "Sorry" when he told her to get her nose out of her BlackBerry for five stinking minutes.

We're not saying she had to bend to every one of Dave's demands. She didn't have to say, "You're right, I'm a horrible wife," every time Dave was mad—she just had to listen and avoid getting defensive.

You might not think it's very romantic to apply the roles of "principal" and "agent" to you and your beloved. Then again, who died and made "husband" and "wife" such amorous words? At least principal and agent are adaptable, since either of you can play either role depending on the situation. That means it's never on one person to fix every problem.

Unfortunately, neither Kate nor Dave was reading this book at the time, and that's why it didn't dawn on Kate to devise a truth-telling mechanism to get Dave to open up. Thus, Dave didn't tell Kate about his day, and they didn't have sex repeatedly that night after all.

CASE STUDY #3

The Players: Scott and Maddie

Scott really liked Maddie. He hadn't met a woman he liked as much as Maddie since the woman whose name could not be uttered. He thought Maddie might be the One. But . . . but . . . What if she wasn't? He didn't have a very good track record with this kind of thing. After he had broken off his engagement to the woman whose name could not be uttered, his friends and family had all whispered some version of, "Yeah, we never liked her that much." That drove Scott crazy. If they didn't like her, he asked, why didn't they say anything *for the five years he dated her*? You seemed so in love, they said, we figured she was a different person with you than she was with the rest of the world.

This time, Scott was going to get it right. He decided to do something a little drastic. He would introduce Maddie to his best friend, Liz, and if Liz approved, he would move forward. If Liz had any hesitation whatsoever, he would have to consider dumping Maddie. Liz was clearheaded, had a great marriage herself, had known Scott forever, and had Scott's best interests in mind. Also: She never, ever candy-coated the truth (except when it came to that other woman, but no one's perfect).

He was straight up with Maddie. "I like you a lot, and I feel like this could be the real thing," he said. "But first, we need to go to D.C."

"D.C.?" Maddie asked. "Why D.C.?"

"I want you to meet my friend Liz," said Scott.

"And why do you want me to meet your friend Liz?"

"Because I trust Liz, and I want to see what Liz thinks," said Scott, "of you."

"Interesting," said Maddie. "I thought it only mattered what *you* think of me."

"It does matter! And I think . . . I think . . . a *lot* of you, but I told you what happened last time, and now I don't trust myself," said Scott.

Maddie had to admit—she was offended. Couldn't they figure out if they were right for each other without an outside judge? Why was some chick named Liz deciding the fate of her relationship? It was absurd.

But after much pleading from Scott, she gave in. As Maddie told us, "I figured if Scott dumped me because some friend told him to, he wasn't the right person for me to begin with. It was a test for him, too."

The three of them went out to dinner—Liz left her husband at home so she wouldn't be distracted—and it turned into a long, drunken evening that ended with Liz announcing that Maddie had her stamp of approval and Maddie announcing that she liked Scott even more for having a friend like Liz. "I felt like we had just gotten married," said Maddie. "That's how ridiculously official the whole thing was."

Scott and Maddie eventually did get married, and they even appeared to be living happily ever after. They laughed at each other's jokes when no one else did, they had flexible jobs that allowed them to spend plenty of time with their two daughters, they took bread-baking classes together, and they played in the same coed softball league. It was what you might call a well-balanced relationship.

On the outside.

On the inside, Scott and Maddie had their share of conflict like every other couple. In their case, conflict itself was the problem.

Scott gave the example of a recent argument they'd had about money: Maddie wanted to create a budget and force them to stick to it. Scott didn't want to have anything to do with budgets. Maddie said that they were living paycheck to paycheck and that if they didn't start budgeting, they'd never save any money, never build up a college fund for their kids, never be able to retire comfortably, and certainly never be able to afford a bigger house so each kid could have her own room and stop living, as she put it, "like the Joads."

Scott understood all that, but he didn't see why they couldn't save money by being more aware of what they were buying and buying less of it. Making a budget, he said, would make him feel like a kid with an allowance.

At this point in the argument, said Scott, Maddie took it up a notch. Suddenly it wasn't about the budget, it was about him not being sensitive to her "needs." She said he was stubborn and asked why he couldn't at least agree to give her way a *chance*. She said he wasn't thinking about the children—*the children*. She added that she had been stressed lately because she wasn't getting a ton of free-lance work. She said their grocery bills had been unusually high the past few weeks and maybe it was because of the new $13.99-a-pound salami they'd been buying. She noted that she hadn't bought a pair of shoes in three months. She concluded that Scott didn't do enough cleaning around the house, which was a "toxic-waste site," and if it continued, they'd have to hire a cleaning person and that would to-tally break their budget wide open.

Scott vaguely recalls a part of his brain registering some of what Maddie said as factual. He knew he was being stubborn, and he knew he could have humored his wife by agreeing to a budget. She'd prob-ably do all the work of making the spreadsheet anyway. But last he checked, he did too care about her needs and those of their kids, and their house was hardly a toxic-waste site. Was he wrong or was he right? Was he good or was he bad? Was it time for Letterman?

The Problem: High Information-Processing Costs

Maddie's words had turned to static. Scott couldn't process what she was saying anymore, so he shut down and heard nothing. This had be-come a pattern.

"We would be talking about one issue and then she'd be pacing back and forth telling me everything that was wrong as if I either had to fix it all or just be her punching bag," he told us.

"One thing would remind me of another and I wanted to get it all out," Maddie said.

But to her endless frustration, Scott never replied, "Thank you, Maddie, you're totally right. I've seen the error of my ways and I now understand we should do things your way." Instead, he went into a conversation coma.

Maddie was making things *too* symmetric—Scott had to know

everything that was wrong, rather than just what needed fixing at the moment.

Other couples we interviewed also said that in their efforts to communicate openly and honestly—to eliminate information asymmetries, as it were—they sometimes went overboard. Call it TMI, or too much information.

In economics, there's also such a thing as TMI, and it can lead to high "information-processing costs." These are the costs of digesting

THE PEOPLE SPEAK . . .
About Honesty

In our Exhaustive, Groundbreaking, and Very Expensive Marriage Survey, we asked people to tell us how their communication had changed over the years and when and why they chose to keep information to themselves. Here's what we found:

- More people regretted being *too* honest with their spouses (42 percent) than not being honest (35 percent).
- 42 percent said they'd withheld important information from their spouses.
- Among the likely or very likely reasons for withholding information:

    89 percent said they didn't want to upset their spouses.

    72 percent said they thought their spouses would make too big a deal out of it.

    67 percent said they didn't want to get into a lengthy discussion.

    48 percent said they were embarrassed.

    43 percent said they didn't want to have to compromise.

all the information we need to make a decision. Picture the cereal aisle at the grocery store. The sheer volume of choices can lead to hours of indecision. Imagine all the time we'd save if there were only two cereals to choose from: sugar or no sugar.

Research shows that too much information can paralyze us. In one study, the psychologist Sheena Iyengar set up a stall at a grocery store where she sold fancy jams. She put out a selection of either six or twenty-four jams, depending on the time of day. While more people stopped by to browse when she had more choices, many more people bought jam when there were fewer flavors to choose from. Only 3 percent of the people who stopped in made a purchase when faced with twenty-four varieties, vs. 30 percent who bought a jar when there were just six varieties.

In a marriage economy, the person receiving a torrent of unfiltered information from their partners can become inundated, too. That's annoying if the information relates to all the chores you haven't finished or all the ways your son will fall behind in math if he doesn't get a special tutor. But TMI can be particularly unpleasant when it happens during the course of an escalating argument or a heated discussion. In these cases, what economists call high information-processing costs, psychologist John Gottman calls "flooding." Gottman says when a spouse feels inundated by his or her partner's arguments and complaints, his heart rate shoots up, making him unable to participate in the conversation in any productive way; he's flooded.

That's what leads to the kind of coma Scott found himself in.

The Solution: Optimal Reporting

One of the ways the market tackles high information-processing costs is through optimal reporting, where someone (or some computer) whittles down a huge amount of information into just what consumers need to make decisions. That's what college rankings do. If your kid's a sophomore in high school, you can either spend the next two years visiting every college in America to find the one that's right for her, or you can spend an hour reading through the rankings and pick a few schools that look as though they'll do the trick.

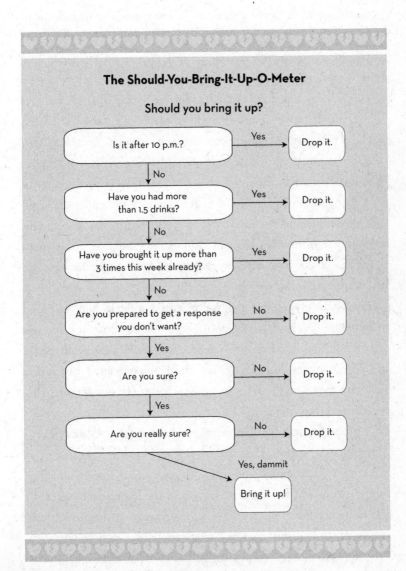

If you're in search of the best meatball parmesan in New York City, you can either spend your savings tasting every meatball parmesan in Manhattan, or you can go to the Internet and see what people recommend.

And if Maddie wants Scott to agree to a budget and to sweep the kitchen floor once every two weeks, she can bury those requests in an onslaught of twenty-seven other "requests," or she can take those two items and isolate them—leaving all the other minutiae in her own head, where they belong.

It took a day at a spa for Maddie to come to this conclusion.

She was lying on a table, enjoying something called a "cocoa scrub" (a gift certificate from Scott from the previous Valentine's Day), and all she could smell was chocolate. She was so wrapped up in chocolate that for the first time in her life, she didn't actually want to eat a piece of chocolate. She thought about all the chocolate she'd eaten in her life, and how she'd always felt she was about eight pounds too heavy, and how her life would have been different if she could control those cravings, and why did she have to be so extreme, what was wrong with a little moderation?

Then suddenly she had a vision of Scott and she laughed out loud imagining what Scott would do if he was in the room and she was saying all this stuff to him. She saw his face—listless, distracted, wanting to be anywhere but here—a face she'd seen so many times during their arguments, and it occurred to her that maybe less *is* more. That was the first step.

"I probably spent the first five years of my marriage doing what I now call 'information dumping' on Scott," Maddie told us. "Part of me knew I wasn't getting anywhere, but part of me couldn't help it."

Her spa revelation was only half the battle. Not a week later she found herself dumping on Scott all over again. Scott got up midstream, walked out the door, and didn't come back until the next day. "At that point, I knew something had to change," said Maddie.

While Scott was gone, Maddie spent a lot of time in the car, clearing her head. "I've always loved going for long drives," she told us. "Being in the car by myself, listening to the radio." It occurred to her that this—driving with no destination in mind, clearing her head—was something she could do *before* all hell broke loose, instead of after. "Now, when I feel myself becoming overwrought, I will literally drive around until I figure out what's bothering me. Or I'll write it all down in a letter and isolate what's important and what I can leave out."

That's what we call optimal reporting.

By the time Maddie's ready to talk to Scott, she's whittled her words down to a few crisp sentences. The upshot: He's able to hear what Maddie says. "I'm not terrified to have a discussion with my wife anymore," said Scott. His coma days are over.

THE BOTTOM LINE

1. **Be transparent.** Transparency is the grease that keeps economies functioning. It's also what your spouse needs in order to know what's going on with you.

2. **But not too transparent!** Marriage isn't an excuse for an information dump, and your spouse doesn't need a detailed list of everything he's done wrong today, or every person who mistreated you at the office. Save that for your blog.

3. **Send clear signals.** A signal can be a word, a gesture, a joke, or a home-cooked meal. Whatever it is, it ought to communicate information in a thoughtful and clear way. Here's one: Taking off your clothes when you get into bed—we hear that sends a certain signal very clearly.

4. **Say what you mean.** Saying one thing and doing another—that's only human. But it can be very confusing for the person you live with. So rather than "I'm fine, really," try a version that's closer to the truth, i.e., "I had a rough day and can't handle anything more complicated than *Law and Order* and tacos right now."

8

INTERTEMPORAL CHOICE

Or, Being a Good Person... When You Get Around to It

THE PRINCIPLE

We plan on being good. We plan on socking a little away each month for the tuition bills that loom over us like an anvil. We plan, upon waking each morning, to eat every one of our recommended daily servings of fruits, vegetables, and whole grains. We fully intend to keep ourselves in presentable physical shape, to wear clean underwear, to stop losing our tempers when our kids spill their milk (again) just as we're finally sitting down to dinner, and to care for, nurture, and honor our dear, dear spouses.

And then life gets in the way.

We rack up credit card bills buying stuff we'll never wear, make peace with another five pounds of flab, lose our tempers with our kids, and generally treat our dear, dear spouses like sexless errand boys we happen to share a life with.

What gives?

Our ability to make sound intertemporal choices is what gives.

Intertemporal choice is a fancy name economists have for a decision we make today that has consequences in the future. It's a hot field of study in recent years because such decisions not only affect individ-

uals like you and me, they also have huge—and hugely expensive—
public policy repercussions. Gorge on pepperoni pizza pockets and Dr
Pepper today, and before you know it, you'll be contributing to
America's skyrocketing health care costs tomorrow. Wait yet another
year to start contributing to your 401(k), and chances are you'll be
looking to Uncle Sam for a handout when it comes time to hang up
the spikes. Ring up thousands of dollars of credit card debt today, and
you could be one of roughly sixty-four hundred people declaring
personal bankruptcy tomorrow.

The man credited with putting the concept of intertemporal
choice on the economic map, back in the early nineteenth century,
wasn't a trained economist and didn't win any big awards for his insight. His name was John Rae, and he was a slight, mutton-chopped
Scottish schoolmaster-turned-medical-inspector who ended up living in Hawaii. His interests included geology, farming, ice-skating,
and, like Adam Smith before him, the wealth of nations. Specifically,
why some nations become rich while others remain stuck in the
poorhouse.

Rae posited—because that's what Scottish schoolmasters do, they
posit—that rich countries get rich in part because the people in those
countries are good at exercising self-restraint, at taking the long view.
They can delay gratification. "Such pleasures as may now be enjoyed
generally awaken a passion strongly prompting to the partaking of
them," wrote Rae in his 1834 treatise, *The Sociological Theory of Capital.* "The actual presence of the immediate object of desire in the
mind by exciting the attention, seems to rouse all the faculties, as it
were to fix their view on it, and leads them to a very lively concep-
tion of the enjoyments which it offers to their instant possession."

In other words: There's no time like the present.

Rae didn't go on to achieve nearly the fame and fortune Adam
Smith did—he spent his later years administering smallpox vaccines,

not quite equivalent to inventing economics, but nothing to be ashamed of, either. And anyway, among the hordes of economists studying intertemporal choice today, he's become something of a legend. While Smith made the case that countries become rich by saving, Rae pointed out that countries can save only if they're able to exercise self-restraint. Anyone who's tried to become richer, happier, or skinnier knows that self-restraint is kind of critical to the whole enterprise.

So why are we so bad at it? A couple of reasons.

The first is something called "hyperbolic discounting." Never mind the complicated terminology. The basic explanation is that we don't value having things in the future nearly as much as we value having those things today. That makes it very tempting to go for what's immediately gratifying, even when we sense it's a bad idea.

Let's say your friend has $10 in his wallet. He's pretty psyched, because that's $10 he can spend on a bottle of wine or a movie ticket. That $10 feels real, immediate, and useful. But, he tells you, someone's offered to give him $20 in a few months if he hands over his $10 today. What should he do? You tell him it's a no-brainer—he should say yes, that's double the money!

Now imagine that's *your* $10 and someone comes along to offer you the same deal: $10 today for $20 in the future. Suddenly, it's not such a no-brainer. Give your money away when you can use it to go

IN PLAIN ENGLISH:

Hyperbolic Discounting

It's always Miller Time.

to the movies tonight? No can do. That's essentially how hyperbolic discounting works. It underscores how the temptation to keep the $10 you have now is far more powerful than your ability to hold out for more money down the road. It takes patience, generally speaking, to get to the future, and patience is something we don't have in spades.

Or take exercise, one of the classic examples of hyperbolic discounting. Exercise is something only crazy people actually enjoy, yet you know you need to exercise anyway because it's good for you—that is, it *will* be good for you at some point in the future.

Here's one way to think about it: Motivating to get on the Stair-Master will cost you six units of value (your time and energy). But the benefits (abs of steel, pecs of titanium) will be worth eight units of value. Net gain for you? Two units! StairMaster, here you come.

But wait. There's a problem. Those eight units come later, somewhere off in the distant, hazy future when your abs finally become steel, while those six units have to be invested immediately. Still with us? Now, because you value future units far less than today's units, you convince yourself that those eight units are worth only, say, four units (meaning you "discount" them, a lot). Once you discount those eight, you're looking at spending six units today in order to get four units tomorrow. Just like that, you're suddenly *down* two units. Bag the gym, it's time for happy hour, bitchezzzzzzzzz!

	Cost Today	Benefit Tomorrow	Net Gain/Loss
Actual value of embarking on exercise regime	6 units	8 units	+2 units
Perceived value of embarking on exercise regime	6 units	4 units	-2 units

Go ahead and say it—you would never be a hyperbolic discounter. You're no idiot. You make room for what's important. You know the value of exercise, and that's why you belong to a gym and get on the treadmill after work every day. Or, rather, every other day. Well, sometimes once a week. Anyway. Let's move on.

What about money? You're probably good at that, too, right? You're aware that Social Security is a nonstarter and it's all on you to cover the cost of retirement. You know condos in Sun City don't come cheap, and you know you're unwilling to work a day past the age of fifty-nine. That's why you set aside a chunk of cash every month and why you contribute the maximum allowed to your 401(k). Or, rather, you plan to set the money aside, only last month you couldn't because you had to buy new speakers since the old ones had a scratch on them. And yes, you've attended your company's information session on setting up a 401(k)—you'll be signing up just as soon as you find a pen.

The thing is, you're not alone. We all say we're going to save, but even people with 401(k) plans don't use them: 58 percent of people eligible for 401(k)'s in 2007 didn't bother putting in a dime, according to the Center for Retirement Research at Boston College. This is sort of pathetic. It's not as if retirement plans are difficult to master: Specify a percentage of pre-tax pay to have deducted, decide what funds to invest it in, then sit back and watch our nest eggs grow. Sun City here we come.

Yet many of us apparently do find it difficult. For one thing, we haven't the foggiest idea how to invest. Unless we went to business school, understanding portfolio theory and researching asset allocation is about as intuitive as removing a spleen. But the bigger problem is that most of us don't like to save. We want to save. We plan to save. But when it comes time to save, we spend our last dime on raw denim jeans and cosmetic dentistry.

The Old-School View

Neoclassical economists can't offer a whole lot of insight into why we don't save. They don't spend a lot of time psychoanalyzing the human mind. What's the point? They believe people are rational and do rational things, like balance their checkbooks and eat lima beans and hug their loved ones. By their reckoning, we should figure out how much money we'll need to retire comfortably and then start saving exactly the right amount today, factoring in the 20.6 working years we have left, 2 percent inflation, and Treasury yields of roughly 4 percent. Neoclassical economists look at graphs like the one below, which illustrates the power of compound interest, and think: "Come on, people, how can you *not* save?"

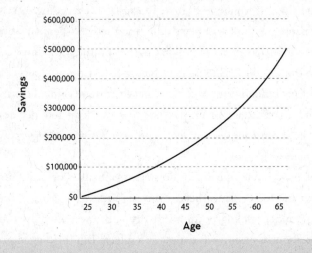

The Power of Compound Interest

Recall we said there are a couple of reasons we're bad at making smart intertemporal choices. The first reason was hyperbolic discounting. The second is known as "the hot-cold empathy gap." We like the name. We also like what it means: When we're in a "cold" emotional state—meaning calm, sane, and levelheaded—we are 100 percent confident that our future self will also be calm, sane, and levelheaded. Any of these thoughts sound familiar?

- *When I get to the movie theater, I'm going to walk right past the popcorn stand and eat my healthy bag of trail mix instead.*
- *I need to get up early tomorrow for my kickboxing class, so I'm only going to have one drink at Jim's party and be in bed by ten p.m.*
- *Sure, I'll go to the mall with you—I'll just window-shop.*
- *Will. Use. Condoms.*

Too bad when the time comes for us to act on these decisions, we've moved out of that cold state and into a hot one, when we're liable to do the exact opposite of what our cold self planned to do.

"When one is not hungry, afraid, or in pain, for example, it is very difficult to imagine what it would feel like to experience one of those states, or to fully appreciate the motivational power such states could

---

IN PLAIN ENGLISH:

Hot-Cold Empathy Gap

Today: I'm never going to shut the bar down again.
Tomorrow: Come on, just one more drink!

have over one's behavior," writes George Loewenstein, an economist at Carnegie Mellon and the man who coined the term "hot-cold empathy gap."

When we're in a hot state, we shut the bar down and go home with the bartender, because who's going to find out anyway?! Instead of buying the twenty-six-inch tube TV we planned to, we throw down $3,500 on a fifty-five-inch 3D LED HDTV so we can watch all ten discs of the *Neil Young Archives* (Volume 1) on Blu-ray. We buy the schnauzer in the window, bad-mouth our best friend, and yell at our spouse for failing to include a bag of baby carrots in the kids' lunch bags.

When we're in a hot state, we say things we don't mean, act in ways we're later embarrassed by, and inflict pain that we spend years trying to repair. When we're in a cold state, we can't imagine being the hot people we sometimes become.

One recent study illustrated the hot-cold differential in a particularly icky way. A group of male students at University of California at Berkeley were recruited to participate in a study on "decision making and arousal." The questions had to do with sex, including their sexual preferences and the likelihood that they would engage in unsafe sex or immoral sexual behaviors. But here was the catch: One time they answered the questions, they were asked just to imagine that they were sexually aroused (this was meant to represent a "cold" state); another time, they were asked to masturbate before answering the questions (this was meant to represent, you guessed it, a "hot" state).

You can probably figure out for yourself the difference between the two sets of answers, but we'll give you a taste. When the men were asked if they could imagine being sexually attracted to a twelve-year-old girl, the average answer when they were in a cold state was 23, on a scale of 0 (essentially, could not imagine it at all) to 100 (essentially, could totally imagine it). When they were in a hot state, the average was 46. When they were asked whether they would slip a drug to a woman to increase the likelihood that she'd consent to sex, the average answer in a cold state was 5; in a hot state, 26. Creepy.

Clearly, we're perverted, weak, lazy, gluttonous spendthrifts destined to have thick thighs, indigent retirements, resentful spouses, and, in some extreme cases, rap sheets. What are we going to do about it? Do we need locks on the refrigerators and live-in personal trainers? Do we need accountants who Taser us every time we overspend? Do we need heart-rate monitors to tell us when we're in a hot state and not capable of making a rational decision?

Actually, yes.

The good news is there's a proven way to make better intertemporal choices—and to stick to them. It's called a "commitment device," and it can be anything that forces us to do things we don't want to do but that we know will pay off down the road. While locks, Tasers, and heart-rate monitors might appear extreme, all three are pretty effective at getting us to stick to our guns.

Not that you have to go to such extremes.

There are plenty of less painful commitment devices. Taking added deductions on your taxes, for example, won't hurt as much as being Tasered, but it will force you to commit to saving: You give the government more than you have to in the form of an interest-free loan and you'll have less money to waste on stuff you don't need. When tax time comes around, you'll get a fat refund check that you can deposit straight into your savings account.

That 401(k) you're still mulling over? Also a commitment device (once you actually sign up). By deducting 6 percent of your pay, you're forced to set aside money you might have otherwise blown on a wine fridge and mountain bike.

All this fascinating talk of taxes and retirement savings and we nearly forgot to mention the mother of all commitment devices: mar-

It's All in the Follow-Through

StickK.com, a website created by Yale economist Dean Karlan, together with a colleague and a student of his, is one of the first cyber-commitment devices on the market. The site lets you bet either money or your reputation that you can stick to a resolution. You choose the stakes, setting the amount of money you'll automatically donate to your most hated charity if you fail to follow through and/or agreeing to let your friends and family receive weekly email updates on your progress. Among the commitments people have posted:

"Ask a random attractive girl to coffee."
"Save money for wedding/financial stability."
"Eliminate swearing in front of the kids."
"Call Nana at least once a week."
"Ignore Jamie the Slut."

riage! In case you haven't realized it yet, marriage is a great tool for committing. To not having sex with anyone else. To thinking of someone other than numero uno. To holding down a job. To sharing the joys and burdens of mortgages, kids, and in-laws. To commit, fully and fervently, to the long view.

Yes, we can walk out the door at any time. Half of all married couples do just that. But for the most part, we got married because we wanted to commit to the person we loved, not just date him or her indefinitely.

Unfortunately, the daily work of *being* married doesn't appear to be as motivating as the act of *getting* married. Once we're hitched, it can be tough to take the long view. We therefore postpone tough conversations. We swear we'll be nice . . . tomorrow. We put off sex, we snap, we fail to save enough for our kids to have braces *and* go to college. Despite having made a commitment for life, we can't bring ourselves to commit from one day to the next.

Now, if you can commit to reading this chapter, we promise you'll learn a few easy ways to improve your intertemporal decision making or minimize your hyperbolic discounting and help you steer clear of hot-cold empathy gaps. Which is all a geeky way of saying we're going to show you how to curb your selfish, lazy impulses and bring out the enlightened, loving spouse that we know is in there somewhere, dying to be set free.

CASE STUDY #1

The Players: Alice and Mark

Mark was having a terrible month, and Alice knew it. First, their two sons had gotten sick, one right after the other, and since Alice was away on a business trip, Mark had been the one to get up with them, clean up after them, and change their sheets four times as they puked their guts out through the night. Then, as soon as the stomach bugs passed, Mark had to rush off on a six a.m. flight to Arizona for a business trip of his own. Arizona was two time zones away, and he was gone for three days—enough to mess up his already screwy internal clock—and for good measure, he got the kids' bug while he was there. Then, his eighty-seven-year-old mother fell down again and ended up in the hospital. When Mark got back, he was inundated with insurance claims and hip X-rays and figuring out why none of his mother's doctors ever talked to one another. He was thinking of putting his mother in a home, which left him racked with guilt.

"I wouldn't call it the best month of my life," he said.

Mark shouldering the bulk of the load had become standard in his marriage to Alice. When he and Alice met eight years ago, he was a once divorced, not terribly ambitious, midlevel marketing executive from Chicago and she was a type-A, take-no-prisoners content strategy director for an online ad agency who, by some miracle Mark could not grasp, was still single at age forty. Mark immediately saw in Alice all the things his ex-wife lacked: She was successful, self-assured, and sexy.

His ex-wife never had many friends, was clinically depressed, and suffered from an array of chronic ailments Mark was never sure were real. He wanted kids, but she couldn't handle the stress. He wanted to travel, but she didn't like the hassle. He'd felt trapped and unwilling to divorce someone that needy . . . until she announced that she wanted to move in with her mother. "She claimed her mother was the only one who knew how to deal with her," Mark said. "I said go ahead, but I'm not going with you."

When a friend set him up with Alice, he didn't expect much. Forty and single in New York? He'd been on enough dates to know what this probably meant: scary-skinny gym rat, neurotic, three cats. Alice showed up in knee-high purple suede boots and a fitted black dress. First impression: intense, smart, not anorexic, a bit cold. Mark wasn't convinced he *liked* Alice, but he was pretty sure he wouldn't mind sleeping with her.

After a second bottle of wine, Alice warmed up. The force field came down. She smiled more and started showing him pictures of her nieces and nephews, explaining how one—her favorite—loved to read *Fancy Nancy* books in bed at night wearing plastic high heels and Mardi Gras necklaces. Alice said she wanted to take her to New Orleans for her sixteenth birthday.

Alice wanted kids. But her love life had been one train wreck after another. There was the guy who was okay having sex with her but not holding her hand in public. The real-estate agent/booty caller who never asked her out before ten p.m. the same day. The French guy who had the French thing going for him but not the English language. Oh, and the supposedly commitment-phobic banker who was now posting Facebook updates about how great his new fiancée is.

Mark seemed different. He wanted commitment. He was looking for a monogamous relationship that would one day, maybe, possibly, lead to a marriage that was healthy and fun. He was nice in the way she imagined midwesterners to be nice but also had a sardonic sense of humor that kept him human. "He was genuine, which is not a quality in great abundance among New York City guys," Alice said.

After ten months of intense dating, they married, went to a fertility specialist, and had twins within a year. Alice hated the idea of a nanny ("Why would we pay someone to do what we're perfectly capable of doing ourselves?"), but she also liked her job and knew that if they wanted to stay in the city, they needed her paycheck. They decided that Mark would work part-time and take care of the kids the rest of the time. Alice would stick to full-time work and continue to make a lot of money.

Alice was aware that Mark's job was hard. "Selling online ad space is a joke compared to managing two boys," Alice said. "I had no illusions about that." So when Mark endured the forty-eight-hour barf-a-thon, the trip to Arizona, and his mother's fall, some part of Alice knew she needed to step up and help more.

She resolved to get up earlier a few times a week to make breakfast for the kids and get them off to school—things Mark usually did since he was the early riser. She'd try to get home early from the office to make dinner and give him the downtime he needed. She'd carve out a day soon to let him unwind—to sleep in, or just sit in a coffee shop for a few hours and read the sports section in peace.

These were all intertemporal choices—decisions that would reverberate into the future. They would affect Mark's happiness, the marriage's health, her career (should a co-worker call her out on leaving the office early too often, it wouldn't be pretty).

But following through on those decisions was a different story. Every morning, there was something more pressing than making breakfast: a meeting she couldn't miss, an hour she needed to prep for a presentation, a conference call that had already been rescheduled twice. She'd get home late and Mark would be cleaning up after dinner again. "I'll clear my calendar tomorrow," she'd tell herself as she wolfed down a plate of his leftover linguine. And she meant it. Until tomorrow came and another important meeting materialized.

"That's okay," Alice told herself. "I'll give him a day off soon and that will make up for it."

The problem was, she could never find the day. At one point, she remembered the kids had hockey games in some far-flung corner of Connecticut on an upcoming weekend. She circled the date in her calendar and promised herself she'd get up early—the coach started warm-ups at inhuman hours—and take the kids herself, letting Mark stay home and watch the Bears lose again. She would have to cancel a trip she'd planned with some girlfriends, but her husband was worth it. She made a note to herself to tell Mark she'd go to the games. "Must call girls and tell them I can't come," she told herself. Maybe she'd even book a sitter and plan something special for the two of them when she got back from Connecticut, like dinner at that Turkish restaurant they liked. Hey, they could have sex!

But she kept forgetting to cancel the plane tickets or email the girls to tell them she was bailing. And she never told Mark about her plan to take the boys. It was hard to find time to do everything.

"I'll get to it tomorrow," Alice said to herself. "As soon as I get through all this other stuff."

By the time the hockey weekend arrived, Alice was deep into the latest issue of *Us Weekly*, en route to Florida with her friends. Work had been brutal, and the tickets were nonrefundable. Plus, she needed the break. "It'll help me be a better wife when I come back," she told herself.

The Problem: Hyperbolic Discounting

Remember the exercise example earlier in the chapter—going to the gym today costs six units, with the future benefits worth eight units? And how the reason we don't go to the gym is that we discount those future benefits by half?

That's pretty much the calculation Alice was making—however subconsciously—every time she put off helping out Mark. It would cost her a weekend away with friends to shuttle the boys to their hockey game, but it was totally worth it for the joy and gratitude it would ultimately bring her husband. Net gain.

Yet that net gain was somewhere off in the future. It was abstract, and who knew if it would even register with her frazzled husband? Compared to today's net gain—a weekend of piña coladas and pedicures on the beach—Mark's future joy and gratitude didn't seem worth as much.

	Cost Today	Benefit Tomorrow	Net Gain/Loss
Actual value of taking kids to hockey	Fun weekend with gal pals	Happy husband	Healthy marriage
Perceived value of taking kids to hockey	Fun weekend with gal pals	Happy husband (probably, maybe)	Lost weekend

The classic move of a hyperbolic discounter.

Before we tell you how Mark reacted to Alice's weekend away (it's called building suspense), we'll give you another example of hyperbolic discounting you can probably relate to. This one has to do with movies. Inspired by their own experience renting videos, a team of researchers did an experiment to see whether people can follow through with something as simple as the movie they plan to watch.

Using volunteers at the University of Illinois at Urbana-Champaign, they handed out a list of movies and asked the volunteers to pick three they wanted to watch. One group was told to select all three movies immediately but that they'd watch them only in the future, while the other group was told they'd be picking each movie the day they watched it. What neither group knew was that the list comprised two kinds of movies: highbrow movies that either had won Oscars or had subtitles—think *Schindler's List*—and lowbrow movies like *Sleepless in Seattle*.

Lo and behold, the group that was picking movies to watch in the future had the noblest of intentions, with 71 percent going highbrow for their third film. In contrast, the group picking the movies they would watch right away was more likely to choose the easy, lowbrow route for their third, with only 44 percent opting for highbrow. The lesson? Deep down, we know *The Piano* will enrich our minds, but we can always enrich our minds tomorrow—tonight, let's tuck in to *Mrs. Doubtfire*.

As for Mark, he didn't have to be up on the latest research to know Alice was taking the lowbrow route. He was getting increasingly frustrated as the month dragged on. What happened to his wife? Where was she when he needed her most?

When she got back from Florida, he finally boiled over. "You went to Florida while my mother was in the hospital, our kids were running in twenty directions, and I was slammed at work," he said. "Is that what you call support?" Oh, and another thing: It was fairly embarrassing that his whole family was pitching in to take care of his mom, making meals and visiting her at the nursing home, while Alice had only deigned to stop by briefly once or twice. "I'm sick of making excuses for you," he said.

Alice's first reaction was to fight back: "Your mother doesn't even like me!" But as soon as the words came out of her mouth, she knew she'd blown it. Mark shook his head and walked out of the room. This was a very bad sign.

The truth was, Alice had no defense. She certainly wasn't going to tell Mark that she had planned to come home earlier (for real!), cancel her weekend away (what a martyr!), and generally be a better wife (seriously!). She couldn't admit that she had seen the stress on Mark's face but hadn't done a thing about it. She considered mentioning that bonuses were being decided at work, which was why things had been crazy lately, but she could hear how that would sound and wisely decided to keep it to herself. During the height of her self-pity, she started listing all the things she never got to do for herself anymore, all

The Commitment Device Cure

On our listening tour, couples told us about some pretty creative commitment devices they'd come up with—though none had any idea they were borrowing a page from economics:

- Train for a marathon to raise money for leukemia research in order to commit to getting in shape. Hard to back out when you've raised $3,000 for the cause.
- Leave town for three days while he (the husband) trains the baby to sleep by "crying it out." Can't exactly run in to comfort the kid if you're not in the same city.
- Sign up for a program that alerts each other every time there's a credit card charge of more than $50. Can't splurge on shoes or expensive wine without the other person finding out.

the sacrifices *she'd* made to be a wife and mother—no Pilates, no girls' nights out, no sleeping in.

She kept that to herself, too.

We feel a little bad singling out Alice since a lot of us are just like her. We get overtaken by events. We intend to help our spouses, then conveniently forget the plan. But think back to your kindergarten teacher's words of wisdom: Just because everyone else is doing it doesn't make it okay.

"I really did want to be there for Mark," Alice told us. "But I kept getting distracted by other things."

The Solution: Commitment Devices

After the fight with Mark, Alice had a crisis of conscience. She knew she'd become the kind of checked-out spouse she wouldn't want to be married to herself, and she knew she had to make some changes. But where to start, and how to commit? She began by making a list of problem areas, hot spots that led to tension between her and Mark. Then she tackled each one with a commitment device (she didn't use that term, of course, but coincidentally, that's what they were):

- **Problem**: Alice's late-night dinners with clients three times a week meant Mark was in charge of giving the kids dinner and getting them to bed.
  Solution: Breakfast meetings instead. No excuse to stay late at the office.
- **Problem**: Being totally uninvolved in the kids' extracurricular activities.
  Solution: Sign up to be an assistant on her sons' ice hockey team. Since all the other parents would know she was an assistant, she'd be most hated mom if she didn't show.

- **Problem:** The mother-in-law.

  Solution: Promise to bring her dinner every other Monday. To do this, Alice, who hates to cook, called a catering company and prepaid for one month's worth of Monday menus.

- **Problem:** Not enough time with Mark.

  Solution: Prepay a babysitter to come one Saturday night a month. As with the catering arrangement, the money up front made it harder to cancel date night when the time came.

It was a great plan, but like all plans, it wasn't foolproof. Inevitably, things came up that got in the way. Alice still had to travel occasionally for work, and some nights she'd be legitimately trapped in the office until late. But Mark wasn't complaining. "I could tell she finally heard me," he said. "And that went a long way."

CASE STUDY #2

The Players: Howard and Jen

Howard would be the first to admit that he had a domineering personality. "He's a bully," Jen told us matter-of-factly, in a group setting that did not include Howard. But it wasn't entirely his fault, she added, since he came from a family of five boys and had had to scratch and claw for every ounce of his parents' attention. We thought that was very generous of her.

After college, Howard went to an ultracompetitive law school and, from there, became a trial litigator—hardly the refuge of shrinking violets. He spent his days defending murderers and thieves. His hobbies included football, extreme barbecuing, and stock car racing. "Some guys play golf. Mine drives cars a hundred miles an hour," said Jen.

Though Howard had softened a bit with age, at forty-four he still had a temper he couldn't totally control. Among the many things that set him off: clutter. Did he hate clutter! He dreamed every day that he would be lucky enough to come home to a calm and orderly house, not a living room littered with dog toys, plastic crap, broken pretzel sticks, and a pileup of Matchbox cars.

Jen was also a hard-driving lawyer from a large family, and she, too dreamed of an orderly house. She also worked in a stressful environment and also arrived home tired and in need of peace, quiet, and a strong martini. But unlike Howard, she was somehow able to put aside the chaos when she got home after a long day and focus on the kids. "A cocktail helps," she said.

When Howard got all wound up about the clutter, Jen would explain to him that kids don't *do* order. Which never seemed to register with Howard.

Howard had never been one to register things. Back in college, he asked Jen out over and over again even though she constantly said no. First, he asked her out in the cafeteria line. Then he tried again at a party. That failed, too. "Howard was after me for six years before I gave him a chance," Jen said. "I listened to the Smiths and dated poets. I don't think Howard even listened to music. He was a frat boy."

After college, Jen moved to Washington, D.C., to work in fundraising at an aid group for Palestinian refugees. Howard enrolled in law school at Georgetown, and though he mellowed out some, he still had a reckless streak. He once turned up at a party at Jen's house with his leg in a cast, the result of trying to do a helicopter while skiing in Tahoe. "I'm from Long Island," he told us. "I don't really ski."

One Christmas two years after college, Jen and Howard were both stuck in Washington. He was working because Howard always worked; she couldn't get a flight home because of snow. She was recently single, depressed, and alone. He offered to come over and cook for her. "A culinary pity party," he said.

Howard brought two bottles of red wine, whipped up his grandma's linguine with clam sauce, and capped it off with a pint of Häagen-Dazs.

Then he slept over.

Suddenly, Howard didn't seem like such a meathead. "He was amazing," said Jen. "Completely focused on me and what turned me on, not at all what I was expecting." For two days, they left the apartment once—to get a Christmas tree, which they decorated naked.

Before they had kids, Howard's temper wasn't much of an issue for Jen. She came to expect that he'd blow up at a waiter if his order came out wrong. And she found it kind of funny when he rolled down the car window and screamed profanities at anyone who cut him off. She would wink in sympathy at the waiter or place her hand on Howard's in the car, saying, "Howard. Chill." And often, Howard *would* chill.

Once they had kids, Howard's temper started to flare more easily. He was working more and sleeping less. Their sex life dwindled to once every couple of weeks, with Jen usually claiming exhaustion. And he seemed to lack any understanding about the essential nature of children—namely, that children weren't born knowing how to anticipate and react to Howard's moods. "Howard's a great dad," Jen told us. "He loves his kids. He taught the boys how to swim. He taught them how to say 'please' and 'thank you' and call their grandmother once a week. In some ways, he has more patience with them than I do. But he also has this crazy dark side, and he couldn't get it under control."

At least once a week, Howard would come home from work and completely lose it. He'd walk in the door, frazzled from the traffic, fried from lack of sleep, hungry for dinner, worried about some case at work, and he'd wonder, loudly, why the trash hadn't been taken out, the driveway cleared of tricycles, and why, once again, there were so many *goddamned toys* on the floor.

"Is it really that hard to keep the toys in one room?" he'd ask, addressing the question to anyone within earshot—which was usually his wife, children, and two cats—all of whom were recoiling—"Why did we buy all these bins if we're not going to use them?"

The Problem: The Hot-Cold Empathy Gap

Every time Howard had a chance to calm down, down a glass of wine, and see that he'd ruined everyone's night, he would make a decision: Tomorrow, I'm not going to lose my cool.

And every time tomorrow came, he'd lose his cool.

Like anyone else making intertemporal choices, Howard *knew* that decisions regarding his temper had consequences into the future. He *knew* that being a nice guy today was in the long-term interests of his wife and kids, not to mention himself. (Didn't stressed-out adult males die younger than their cohorts? He thought he'd read that somewhere.) Anyway, the equations were fairly simple:

- Nice dad today = Kids who like me and grow up to be productive members of society.
  Mean dad today = Kids who hate me and grow up to be serial killers.
- Nice husband today = Happy wife, maybe a good sex life.
  Mean husband today = Divorce, weird bachelor guy on park bench leering at women in tank tops.

The problem was that Howard always made the decision to control his temper after he had calmed down—after he'd had some food and a glass of wine. In other words, while he was in a "cold" state. Recall that we said cold states allow us to make calm, reasoned decisions. They also have an uncanny ability to make us forget all about our "hot" states. Cold Howard assumed he would be cold the next day, too, and that Hot Howard was a thing of the past.

Jen would tell him his temper was affecting the whole family. She'd remind him that when he came home all irate and irritable, it "freaked the kids out."

He would promise to keep a lid on his temper, and they would discuss specific ways he could do that successfully.

"What if you left work early and went to the gym?" Jen suggested. "Burn off some of that negative energy?"

"Then I'll never be home for dinner," said Cold Howard.

"Meditation CDs for the car?" she suggested.

"Did you just meet me?" said Cold Howard.

"How about counting to twenty before walking in?" Jen said.

"How about I count to twenty and then we have sex?" asked Cold Howard, who could always be counted on to find an excuse to get it on.

"Ugh, I'm exhausted," she said, pushing him away. "It took a lot of energy to calm the kids down after you went all Unabomber on them."

"I know, I'm sorry, it won't happen again."

This is the way it generally played out. Once Howard had exited his hot state and entered his cold state, he was confident he could be the Howard he wanted to be the next time he came home cranky. He knew he had a temper, but he also knew he could control it. Look how calm he was now!

But time and time again, something would happen somewhere between the office and home, and Howard would lose it. Hot Howard would storm into the house, and all those plans made by calm, cool, and collected Howard would be out the window. Like Alice the hyperbolic discounter, Howard couldn't stick to his plan. He needed a lot more than meditation CDs.

The Solution: Commitment Devices

Howard and Jen spent years trying to find ways to keep Howard's anger in check. He tried the counting to twenty thing (no go) and even gave deep breathing a shot (not even close to a go). "Breathing doesn't work if you can't stop swearing long enough to breathe," Jen told us.

So Howard and Jen finally tried something different.

They devised a commitment device that would get them both more of what they wanted in their marriage. For Howard this meant more sex, and for Jen it meant a calmer, nicer Howard. They called it the Red Flag game. Whenever Howard appeared on the verge of losing his temper, Jen would call out, "Red Flag." If Howard went three days without a red flag, she'd have sex with him. If he went a week without one, she'd have sex with him two days in a row (assuming he didn't get another red flag in the interim). A month, and she would do whatever his perverted heart desired.

It worked the other way, too. Every time Howard blew up and got a red flag, there would be no sex for a week. Two red flags and he had to rub Jen's feet every night for a week. Three flags, and Jen got a day at the spa while Howard got to take the kids to music class and soccer practice.

"He needed something to motivate him," said Jen, and sex, she added, "seemed logical."

Jen assumed the Red Flag game would fail just like all the other ideas they'd had about how to deal with Howard's temper. Best-case scenario: It would work for two weeks and then he'd go right back to crazy mode. "I had read enough self-help books to know that Howard was not going to change," she said. "I married a bully and I got a bully."

But she was wrong. As disturbing as the Red Flag game might

The Economist in the Bedroom

During the writing of this book, we interviewed a lot of economists. Some of them had even won Nobel Prizes. Their combined IQ was probably in the neighborhood of 3,600. But that didn't stop us from asking them for tips on how to have a better sex life—don't geniuses have sex, too?

"I get a lot of requests for advice," said Gary Becker, who won the Nobel in 1992 and the Presidential Medal of Freedom in 2007 and was one of the first in his field to study the economics of marriage. "And I've often thought, 'Gee, marriage counseling would be a lucrative field.' "

Another, who wished to remain anonymous, told us he and his wife have showered together every day for forty years. He said it's all about good habits.

George Loewenstein, the guy who came up with the whole concept of hot-cold empathy, said that after a while, married couples no longer get aroused, or "hot," just from being in the same room. That means when they think about having sex with each other, they're usually in a "cold" state, maybe doing the dishes after dinner or brushing their teeth. And *that* means they're less likely to follow through.

Loewenstein has two suggestions for how to keep the flame alive. First, there should be a rule that if one person wants to have sex, the other complies. No one gets veto power. Second, decide on a frequency and stick to it. "Sex has health benefits and relationship benefits," Loewenstein told us, and we said, Yes, Dr. Loewenstein, we couldn't agree more.

sound to some of you—using sex to reward good behavior?—it was a success for Howard and Jen. For one thing, it kept the anger issue focused. It didn't become a larger issue about Howard's messed-up childhood, it didn't drive them into years of couples counseling, and it didn't involve all-night arguments.

Howard and Jen just wanted a solution to this one problem—they didn't want to talk it to death. And since they knew they each wanted something from the other, they figured out a way to satisfy both their needs. It was a very economic approach, if we did say so ourselves.

There was nothing complicated about it: Howard would walk in the door and take one look at the Matchbox cars littering the floor, and Jen could see the storm starting to gather in his eyes. But then he would look at her and she would see that flash of recognition: A red flag was about to be thrown. He'd then hang up his coat or take off his shoes and try to channel Cold Howard. "I don't know what he told himself," she said, "but he'd tell the boys he needed a minute and a minute later he would stroll into the living room in a much better mood."

Jen and Howard had a lot more sex thanks to the Red Flag game. In fact, Howard got so good at controlling his temper that Jen told us she couldn't handle the amount of sex they were having. "Once or twice a week is fine, but Howard was going weeks without any temper tantrums," she said. "Be careful what you wish for, I guess."

THE BOTTOM LINE

1. **The time is now.** Don't put off for tomorrow the nice things you can do for your spouse today. In the same vein, don't put off the tough conversations. They're not going to be any easier to have tomorrow.

2. **Get in touch with your "cold" self.** That's the you who makes calm, wise, and rational decisions about how to treat your spouse and your marriage. It's also the you who flies out the window when you're tired, grumpy, had a long day, or feel like you need a whole box of wine just to get through dinner.

3. **Commit.** Commitment devices that force you to do something you don't want or feel like doing but know will pay off down the road. Like putting a lock on the fridge so you don't snack on chocolate pudding all day. Or scheduling only morning meetings so you don't get stuck late at the office. Or prepaying a babysitter so you *have* to go out to dinner with you-know-who.

4. **Schedule sex.** This is worth reiterating: Your "cold" self, the one that told yourself you'd put the moves on tonight, might be missing in action by the time you actually get into bed. Put it in both your calendars for an agreed-upon time and just do it.

9

BUBBLES

Or, Making the Good Times Last

THE PRINCIPLE

There's a well-known story in the world of business. Every first-year MBA student learns it. Maybe you've heard it before, too. It's the story of a tulip craze, and here, in slightly embellished form, is how it goes:

In the late 1500s, in the town of Augsburg, Germany, a man is strolling through a stately garden when he spots a flower: a long green stalk, reaching skyward, capped by perfectly formed, silky red petals in the shape of a turban. He's never seen anything like it before. What *is* that? he asks the estate owner. Oh, that? That's a tulip. It came all the way from Constantinople.

"That is one good-looking flower," says the man. "I'd like to buy one for my wife."

"I'm sure we can work something out," says the estate owner.

The man goes home with a tulip.

A few days later, one of the man's friends drops in for a cold Beck's on his way home from work. He sees the tulip on the dining room table and does a spit take. "Jesus H.," he says. "What is that delicate beauty?"

"It's a tulip. My wife is over the moon for it."

The Beck's guy seeks out a tulip for his wife, who also loves it and who tells a few of her friends about it. Those friends tell their husbands, who in turn go out and buy them tulips. At the pub, one guy tells a group of his buddies, sotto voce: "Check this out: My wife liked her tulip so much, she slept with me." These friends tell more friends, who would also like their wives to sleep with them, and . . . just like that, a tulip craze takes hold.

It spreads to Holland, where the Dutch take things to a whole other level. Before long, exchanges form to handle tulip transactions. Tulip farms sprout up all over Holland. Investing clubs are formed where buyers meet to compare different flower-buying strategies. Futures contracts, which allow traders to buy tulips in the future at a price set today, flourish. By 1634, a single tulip bulb is selling for the price of three hundred sheep. A Semper Augustus—a particularly fancy and delicate variety, magenta with white tiger stripes—sells for 5,500 florins, or the equivalent of forty-six oxen. Industry throughout the country screeches to a halt. Why mend shoes when one tulip bulb can make you rich? Why build ships when you can trade flowers? Public notaries ditch their day jobs and become tulip notaries. Holland has officially gone mad.

Then one day in 1637, some unlucky chump arrives at his flower stand, flings open the doors, and kicks back, waiting for someone to offer him a castle-share for a couple of tulip bulbs. He sits there all day, and no one comes. What's the problem? He looks at the sky, wonders if the pending rain is keeping people inside. He walks over to his friend Jan's stall and says, Is it me? And Jan says, No, same story here. Not a single sale today. I don't know what it is. The next day, same thing.

The town starts buzzing with rumors that maybe tulips aren't worth what people have been paying for them.

Panic ensues. Tulip merchants lower their prices: to 2,000 florins . . . 1,000 florins . . . 500 florins. Nobody is buying. Futures contracts become worthless, and overnight, merchants start going belly-up. Thousands of workers involved in the tulip trade, from farmers to traders, from importers to bankers, lose their jobs. A lot of people lose a lot of money.

The tulip bubble has burst.

In the aftermath, everyone looks silly: the farmers who grew too many tulips, the merchants who charged too much for them, the buyers who spent their life savings on them, the media who never questioned the mania.★ Then comes the finger-pointing and the witch hunt: Evict the guy in the forty-five-room castle who sold the most tulips! Ban tulips, this symbol of destruction and greed, from the public gardens where our children play! A long, dark recession settles over a once vibrant country.

Hold on a second, you say. Something about this story, something about the crazy prices and collective mania and lack of oversight sounds familiar . . . where have I heard . . . Oh, right! We just lived through one of those manias, didn't we? The great housing bubble that burst in 2006 and led the stock market to tank starting in 2007. And come to think of it, we lost most of our 401(k)'s in the tech bubble of the late 1990s. And before that, there was the 1920s U.S. stock bubble, and before that the South Sea bubble, and so on and so on.

Bubbles aren't a Dutch thing. They're a human thing. And they're as predictable as rain.

In technical terms, a bubble forms when prices for something rise way beyond its actual worth. They rise because people believe those

---

★We're not sure there was a media, but if there had been, they would have been blamed because trust us, everyone always blames the media.

prices will only keep rising, no matter how absurd they get. And these believers encourage others to believe. They seek confirmation that they're right and disregard any and all evidence that perhaps they're insane.

Then the bubble bursts. And a nasty, prolonged bust follows. The fancy term for this whole process is "the economic cycle."

Figure 8 represents the S&P 500, an index of five hundred large, heavily traded U.S. stocks. The recent peaks and troughs appear dramatic. From 1995 to 2000, the S&P 500 rose 200 percent. In the crash that followed, it fell 49 percent. During the housing bubble, which began in 2002, the market leapt 102 percent. When house prices did finally fall, investors panicked and the market sank 57 percent.

The good news is, as painful as this sounds (and as painful as it felt to watch your savings evaporate), over the long run, the stock market

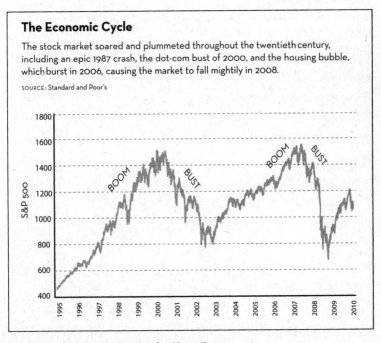

The Economic Cycle

The stock market soared and plummeted throughout the twentieth century, including an epic 1987 crash, the dot-com bust of 2000, and the housing bubble, which burst in 2006, causing the market to fall mightily in 2008.

SOURCE: Standard and Poor's

Figure 8: Things Look Grim in the Short Term . . .

tends to go up. If you look at Figure 9, you see even the "crash" of 1987, which saw a 34 percent dip, looks like a mere blip.

The question that has deviled economists for almost one hundred years is *why* these boom-and-bust cycles occur. Why do we let ourselves become possessed by something as nutty as an overpriced tulip when we should know better?

According to legendary British economist John Maynard Keynes, the reason is simple: We're human. "If we speak frankly," he wrote in 1935, "we have to admit that our basis of knowledge for estimating the yield 10 years hence of a railway, a copper mine, a textile factory, the goodwill of a patent medicine, an Atlantic liner, a building in the City of London amounts to little and sometimes amounts to nothing." Since we can't predict the future, he concluded, we rely on our

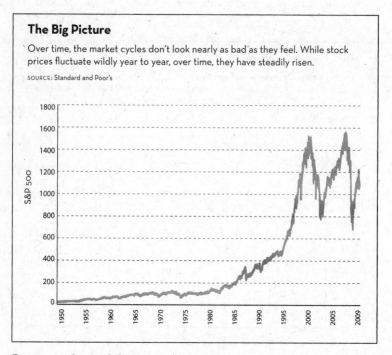

The Big Picture

Over time, the market cycles don't look nearly as bad as they feel. While stock prices fluctuate wildly year to year, over time, they have steadily risen.

SOURCE: Standard and Poor's

Figure 9: . . . But Look Sunnier in the Long Run

The Keynesian Fix

 The next time you watch a new highway go up in your backyard courtesy of the U.S. government, you might have John Maynard Keynes to thank. That's because his prescription for getting out of a bust was massive government spending, even if it meant running deficits.

Governments, including that of the U.S., initially resisted Keynes's idea, believing that balanced budgets were sacrosanct. But in the late 1930s, as the Depression wore on and unemployment skyrocketed, President Franklin Delano Roosevelt decided to give the idea a whirl. In 1938, during one of his fireside chats, FDR explained that the government would start pumping money into the economy. After that, the U.S. joined the war and started spending like crazy, and unemployment plummeted.

At this point, Keynes had become something of a rock star among economic policy makers. And like any rock star worth his chaps, Keynes was a player: He was openly bisexual and an active member of the literary and intellectual circle known as the Bloomsbury Group. As a younger man, he was romantically involved with painter Duncan Grant and writer Lytton Strachey. Later, he married a hot Russian ballerina.

In 1999, *Time* magazine included Keynes in its list of the one hundred most important and influential people of the twentieth century, crediting him with the not insignificant feat of rescuing the global economy: "His radical idea that governments should spend money they don't have may have saved capitalism."

gut. While this might seem straightforward to anyone who has ever gone on a second date or walked down the aisle, it was a fairly radical departure from early-twentieth-century economic thinking, which pegged us as purely rational creatures seeking to maximize our own benefits.

What does any of this have to do with me, you ask? You hate tulips, you stayed diversified through the tech craze, and your house hasn't been foreclosed on. You bought this book to make your marriage work better, not to read about oversexed economists.

Fact is, bubbles are as endemic to relationships as they are to the economy—and making your marriage work better means figuring out how to avoid bubbles when you can, and when you can't, how to make your way out of the inevitable bust.

Here's how a marriage bubble works: Life seems glorious, you're crazy simpatico together, and you feel sorry for all the other poor, miserable married couples out there who don't have what you have. You can feel them watching you—so affectionate, so attractive, so in love. Nothing can touch you, and thus you don't think twice about piling on potential stressors, like having a third kid or stretching to buy a nicer house or agreeing to move next door to your mother-in-law because your husband is *so* attached to her.

Here's how a marriage bubble bursts: Those stressors begin to take their toll. One of you loses your job or quits to start your own vaudeville theater, and your great new house is suddenly bleeding you dry. You fight about money. You fight about fighting about money. Your mother-in-law gets Alzheimer's, requiring your husband to shuttle her to and from doctors' appointments. Then she breaks her ankle. You never see each other except for a few minutes as you're rushing your kids off to school. All three of them.

What do you do? Do you borrow a page from Keynes and spend your way out of recession, splurging on romantic weekends, therapy, and sex clinics? Do you invest in infrastructure, hoping that fixing something—even if it's the basement bathroom—will have a ripple effect on your domestic economy? Or do you take the nuclear option and have yet another child? Kids always bring couples closer together, right?

This is where we come in. First, don't have another kid. Second, we're going to help you out by telling you three things that cause bubbles, how to identify a bubble before it gets out of hand, and, if necessary, how to recover when it bursts.

The first cause is "confirmation bias," our tendency to seek out information that confirms what we already believe and ignore the stuff that doesn't. As Francis Bacon put it: "The human understanding when any proposition has been once laid down . . . forces everything else to add fresh support and confirmation; and although most cogent and abundant instances may exist to the contrary, yet either does not observe or despises them." Meaning, don't believe everything you hear.

The second cause is what's known as "herd behavior," or following the crowd. In some instances, like packing away our pleated Dockers, herd behavior is a good thing; in many other instances, like buying shares in Thiscompanywillmakeyourich.com, it's insane.

The third cause is overconfidence, thinking we're smarter and more talented and better-looking than everybody else and nothing bad can ever happen to us or to our tulips. Why bother doing routine maintenance or the day-to-day work that marriage requires when nothing can possibly come between us?

CASE STUDY # 1

The Players: Kim and Daniel

Kim was well aware that sleeping with professors wasn't looked upon kindly, but she didn't care. She was a free spirit. From age five to six, she wore a shark costume to school every day. In college, she dabbled in lesbianism before settling on boys, mostly. She'd lived in three countries by the time she was twenty-five and experimented with a rich variety of drugs. She liked going to bars alone.

Daniel was a forty-two-year-old professor of international development. He met—or taught—Kim in his Microfinance in the Developing World class during her last year of graduate school. "By the end of his first lecture, I had a monster crush," she said.

Kim's crush wasn't a secret to Daniel. Mostly because during an office hours conference to "discuss" a final research paper, she asked him out.

Figuring she had only a few more weeks of being a student, and he wasn't her adviser or anything, Daniel said yes. He was handsome, but shy. He hadn't had a girlfriend since his mid-thirties, and that relationship ended with her screaming at him on a plane back from New Delhi, moving out of their apartment a few hours after landing, and never speaking to him again. Since then, getting hit on by attractive women was hardly an everyday occurrence.

"If Kim hadn't come along when she did, I'd be a bachelor until the day I died," Daniel told us.

No doubt Kim brought Daniel back to life. They had sex in his office, in the bathroom of a bowling alley, and on the soccer field behind the university gym. One night, after too many dark and stormies, Daniel proposed.

The first few years of marriage were fantastic. She loved his smart friends; he loved her whimsy. Kim went to Bolivia to make a documentary about a rigged election, took social work courses at the college, thinking she might change careers, and for a few months worked on a friend's political campaign. When she'd get discouraged about one project falling apart, Daniel would help her find something else. "Daniel had a lot of friends involved in a lot of different areas," she said. "Politics, economic development, human rights. He would throw a hundred ideas at me and there was usually something I could run with."

For Daniel's sabbatical they went to Kerala, India, for three months, where Kim took photographs and did yoga and he worked on research for a book about matriarchal societies. They rented a house on the water and kept cows in their backyard. "Daniel immersed himself in village life. He knew how to get complete strangers from a completely different culture to open up to him," said Kim.

They extended their stay another three months.

But not long after they got back to their two-room apartment in faculty housing, the bubble burst.

Frustrated that her husband had a career he felt passionate about while she was still bouncing aimlessly from one thing to the next, Kim started picking on Daniel. "Professors can be so self-important," she said. "They all sit around talking about their research as if anyone cared what the Zapotec women of Oaxaca wear, or how they prepare food." She blamed herself for falling for a professor to begin with, a guy, she now believed, who was arrogant about his work and obsessed with getting tenure. And his fixation with finding something for Kim to do with her life was beginning to feel condescending.

"Maybe I don't *want* to do anything for a while," she said one night after he'd suggested she get involved in a friend's study of Galápagos sea turtles. "Maybe I don't need you to manage my career."

Daniel had no idea what had gotten into Kim. He said he knew she loved animals and figured that love would extend to sea turtles: "Sorry for caring."

Kim was going out more often with her friends, not always telling Daniel where she was or when she'd be home, and she was drinking more. Daniel thought Kim was being self-indulgent. "At some point, you have to accept that there is no perfect job and just do something," he told her one day. "You're not a kid anymore." She obviously loved hearing that.

The next day, she flew to San Francisco to visit her dad and see some old friends. Without Daniel.

Daniel was scared. He had visions of Kim hooking up with other men, San Francisco men, men who probably couldn't spell but who could give women orgasms just by looking at them. His best friend suggested he try to distract himself by getting back to work on a novel he'd started in college and had long ago abandoned. He decided to drink bourbon instead.

The Problem: Confirmation Bias

Daniel was the yin to Kim's yang. She was the Yoko to his John. They were so happy together that they frequently felt, and even said aloud, that it must be hard not to be them.

Which was a problem. Because ever since their first date, all they could see were the facts that confirmed their relationship was on a plane above all others, a tendency economists call "confirmation bias."

"A month after we got married, we were having breakfast in a romantic hotel in Istanbul and looking at every couple sitting around the garden," Kim said. "And I remember thinking that we were the most in-love couple there."

They confirmed their perfectness at home, too. At dinner parties or out at restaurants, they watched other couples and felt sorry for them. They were conventional, predictable, co-dependent. Kim and Daniel, on the other hand, were invigorated by their relationship, motivated to be their best selves. Wherever they looked, Kim and Daniel were seeking confirmation of what they *wanted* to believe rather than seeing the whole picture, which included the fact that they were human and had flaws and weren't perfect.

Think about the last time you debated politics with your father-in-law. Did you search for all the evidence to undermine your point or everything to confirm it? We're guessing the latter. When you bought a house in a not-yet-gentrified part of town, did you focus on the empty lots and crack vials or on the one yuppie café selling Fair Trade coffee? We're going to guess you spent a lot of time talking up that café to your buddies when they accidentally stepped on a crack vial on the way to your house.

In Kim's case, once she stopped seeing Daniel as perfect professor guy, she started seeing only the qualities that confirmed he was paternalistic-suffocating-dull-as-a-doorknob professor guy. She disregarded any information that weakened her case, such as:

- She had been happy with him for almost two years.
- His "paternalism" had landed her some jobs she had thoroughly enjoyed.
- His only complaint about trips like the one she took to Bolivia was "I miss you"—not exactly the definition of "suffocation."

Confirmation biases obscure the whole picture, leading to self-fulfilling prophecies.

"Daniel started to represent everything I had avoided all my life," said Kim. "Stability. Sameness. And I did find university life stifling. Tenure meant jail to me. The rest of our lives in the same, everyone-knows-your-business town? No thanks."

When smart stock managers or policy makers want to test their ideas, they don't assemble a group of like-minded thinkers to confirm those ideas; they find the sharpest dissenting minds available and ask them to pick their ideas apart. Then they come up with better ones. Tech companies hire hackers to help them understand how to protect against security failures, army generals conduct elaborate war games to find the soft spots in their battle plans, and savvy CEOs plan for success while preparing for disaster.

This might all sound like a horribly unromantic approach to relationships (though at this point, you should be used to that from us). What's wrong with falling in love and thinking your other half is perfect? Nothing, except for the fact that in doing so, you're risking a bubble. You will be utterly crushed when you realize he won't always be built like Hercules and she won't always greet you at the door in nothing more than an apron and crotchless panties.

With their bubble burst, Kim and Daniel's first step toward saving the relationship was for Kim to start seeing the whole picture again. At least, that's what her dad told her: He's not an economist, but he's clearly a smart guy.

During her visit, Kim's dad took her to a bar in the Mission and made the Daniel case for her all over again, based on facts (Daniel's actions) and not feelings (Kim's confirmation biases). He reminded her of the time she had called home and talked about how smart and sure of himself Daniel was. What a perfect match he was for her. Kim's dad reminded her that Daniel was hardly the noose-around-his-wife's-neck kind of guy. He had bought Kim tickets to Bolivia, visited her while she was there, and even suggested that she stay longer when the film she was working on ran over schedule. He was patient, not overbearing. "You've had that kind of guy, Kim, you know what they're like," her dad said.

Kim went home, ready to give the relationship another shot. But talking about it all with Daniel only made things worse. "I felt like I was on *Dr. Phil,* trying to 'express' myself and listen to him with an 'open heart.' But none of that made me excited to be married again."

The Solution: Creative Destruction

In 1942, an Austrian economist, equestrian, and ladies' man named Joseph Schumpeter published a book in which he offered up a theory: Those who innovate in the face of change flourish, and those who play it safe wither. And it is through this process of death and re-birth, turmoil and innovation—a cycle Schumpeter called "creative destruction"—that the economy revitalizes itself. Bust-ups in the economy are not only good, said Schumpeter, they're necessary.

During a lecture he gave at Harvard during the Great Depression, Schumpeter said in his heavy Viennese accent: "Chentlemen, you are vorried about the depression. You should not be. For capitalism, depression is a good, cold douche."

Recent bubbles have ended with bouts of creative destruction. Out of the savings-and-loan crisis of the 1980s came much-needed regulation of the industry. Out of the tech bubble emerged a more powerful and wide-reaching Internet, along with a handful of innovators

Joseph Schumpeter, Renaissance Economist

 Schumpeter didn't just espouse creative destruction, he lived it. As one of his biographers said about him: "For capitalism and for Schumpeter personally, nothing was ever stable. Uproar was their only music." Schumpeter wrote books in his twenties, became the Austrian minister of finance in his thirties, switched over to banking, made a fortune, lost it all in the stock market crash, moved to America, took a job at Harvard, and became something of a sensation (the capes he liked to wear didn't hurt). According to Thomas McCraw, his biographer, Schumpeter said he aspired to be the best economist, best horseman, and best lover in the world, but admitted things didn't work out so well when it came to horses.

like eBay, Amazon, and Google. In the wake of the housing crisis, Congress took steps to regulate the mortgage industry, and Americans, reminded that the economy is not a one-way bet, started to save a little money.

The process of creative destruction isn't always pleasant. Companies have to lay off tens of thousands of employees as they figure out how to reinvent themselves in the face of rivals. In 1920, for example, 2.1 million Americans worked for railroad companies. Today, there are fewer than 200,000. "Sawyers, masons, and miners were among the top thirty American occupations in 1900. A century later, they no longer rank among the top thirty; they have been replaced by medical technicians, engineers, computer scientists, and others," wrote Federal Reserve economist W. Michael Cox and journalist Richard Alm.

But creative destruction is also what keeps economies vibrant and productive. That's hardly going to make the nearly two million out-of-work railroad workers feel better. But it's great news for the twenty-something computer geeks who are revolutionizing human communications. Evolution is inevitable: Imagine the CEO of Sony saying, "This HDTV is the best ever. Let's stick with this one for the next ten years and call it a day."

In other words, you can't spackle the holes in the wall and cover them with pictures—sometimes you need to tear the wall down entirely and rebuild it from scratch.

Daniel continued to mope for a few weeks after Kim returned from California, but eventually, after too many World War II documentaries, he turned off the TV, put down the bourbon, and engaged in an act of creative destruction: He went back to his novel. He reoriented his life around the book, getting up early to work on it, going for walks to clear his head, and hanging out with friends to get new ideas. He started living like a person who wasn't catatonically depressed. "Writing gave me something to do that I could control," said Daniel. "Because I couldn't control anything else in my life, definitely not my marriage."

It also gave Kim some breathing room. As uncertain as she felt coming back, the fact that Daniel was immersed in his book meant he wasn't trying to corner her into any decisions or therapy or work. Their marriage was in a new place, eerily peaceful but not out of the woods.

One morning a few months after she had the talk with her dad, Kim woke up to find Daniel in his office downstairs, furiously typing away. She made a cup of coffee and sat next to him as he told her about the plot twist he was hatching.

It was the first time since her return they'd had a pleasant moment without once thinking about their problems. "It reminded me what it was like when we started dating, just having conversations about the things we were interested in," said Kim. "This was the Daniel I remembered, but the feelings I had were more grounded. Like here's a guy who's not perfect, who has issues. Are these issues I can live with? I think so."

It took months before Kim admitted that what largely drove her away was insecurity and jealousy. And Daniel admitted that he had gone overboard trying to "save" Kim, instead of letting her find her own way. "I spent a lot of my time worrying about Kim and planning for Kim, when she's perfectly capable of handling her own life," he said.

The rose-colored glasses have stayed off, but Kim and Daniel both consider the marriage they have today to be better than the one they had in that first whirlwind year. "It was great while it lasted," Daniel said. "But it wasn't real."

Or as Winston Churchill put it, "Difficulties mastered are opportunities won," and he knew a thing or two about both.

CASE STUDY #2

The Players: Leila and Jake

Remember limerence, from chapter 2 on loss aversion? That period of intense romantic desire, of blind passion, of blissed-out, in-love-for-the-first-time jitteriness? Well, that's how Jake and Leila remembered their marriage before she decided to quit her job and hate her husband. But we're getting ahead of ourselves.

Jake and Leila met in their late twenties, training for the Boston Marathon. She looked good in spandex, Jake told us, so he sidled up to her during a twenty-mile practice run.

"At least it helped the miles fly by," said Leila, who spent the last five of those miles listening to Jake talk about his cow-tipping youth in Kansas, his dad's brief stint selling cosmetics door-to-door, and the software company he had recently founded. "Jake was just weird enough to be interesting," said Leila.

They went out on a nonrunning date the next day. The date lasted into the evening, and they capped the night at Jake's place, talking ("not just talking," said Jake) until four a.m.

Pretty soon they were spending weekends together, alternating holidays with each family, and attending mandatory family functions such as Jake's socially inept brother's annual clambake in Topeka. When they moved in together and bought a car, Leila's friends freaked out. "They assumed people got married first, and then bought cars together," Leila said. "But we wanted a car, and we didn't want to get married yet."

Leila was finishing a master's in modern art, with the goal of becoming a curator. She spent her nights studying and her days scouring magazines and websites and going to galleries, hoping to find small-bit artists she could one day make big. "She was incredibly ambitious," Jake told us. There were nights when they would go to bed at the same time and an hour later he'd wake up to find Leila in her office, crashing an article for some eclectic art journal. "She needs about twenty minutes of sleep a night."

They got married. She landed a job as an assistant to a big-deal New York gallery owner. Jake started talking about taking his company public. They traveled. They got pregnant. They never discussed the possibility that Leila would stay home with the baby because Leila wasn't the kind of person to drop her dreams to slice grapes in half and read *Pat the Bunny* a thousand times a week.

They lined up a day care slot before the kid was even born.

While she was on maternity leave, Leila started hanging out with some new people: Alex from her birthing class; Liz with the skinny legs from the playground; her mother, who suddenly came to visit every forty-five seconds. Invariably, the conversation would bounce from the best breast-feeding aids (definitely the Boppy, no definitely My Brest Friend) to sleep-training techniques (definitely let them cry it out, no definitely comfort them) to whether or not Leila should go back to work.

"Won't you miss watching Jasper hit all his milestones?" asked her oh-so-subtle mother.

"Have you verified that the day care has never been involved in a lawsuit?" asked Liz.

"You work late all the time," her mother piped up again. "Isn't it going to be hard?"

"I hear their first year of life is magical. Not that I would know. I had to work the whole time," said the dry cleaner.

Leila's mother-in-law, the one with two paying jobs and three volunteer jobs, said she took a few years off when Jake and the boys were little. "They grow up so fast," she said.

Even the parenting blogs were stressing her out: One mentioned a study that found kids who went to day care had higher levels of stress and more aggression than kids who stayed home with a parent. Yikes.

Leila started to wonder if maybe working wasn't such a good idea. Maybe Jasper would be a failure if she didn't stay home with him. Maybe she was selfish for wanting to be a mom *and* an art world wunderkind. Why couldn't she go part-time, like some moms she knew? Or try staying home for a few years? So far, she was enjoying being a mom, way more than she'd expected to. She could always jump back into the fray later. The art world wasn't going anywhere.

She asked Jake what he thought of her not going back to work. He told her to go for it. "It would be great for Jasper," he said. What about the money? she asked. Did he think they could make it on one salary? "We'll make it work," he said.

Leila called her boss and told her she wasn't coming back.

Finally, she'd made a decision. The right decision. The decision that would be good for her soul and her son. She went to Mommy & Me yoga and found a music class that advertised something about teaching kids how to distinguish Bach from Beethoven. She learned baby sign language and managed to teach Jasper the sign for milk. Her art magazines piled up in a basket by the door, unread.

Leila had jumped headfirst into a stay-at-home bubble.

And then, by about month eight, the bubble burst.

The Problem: Herd Behavior

Herd behavior: Following the crowd, even when the crowd's information is unreliable, biased, or wrong.

Herd behavior: Being overly influenced by the noise of the market—Twelve Stocks to Watch! Money Tips for Women! Get Rich Fast!

Herd behavior: Keeping up with the Joneses.

Herd behavior: Deciding to be a stay-at-home mom because other people say your kid will be damaged goods if you don't. Even though you know in your gut that's baloney. And even though you love your work.

Herd behavior: One reason bubbles happen.

Think back to the late 1990s, when everyone decided Internet companies were worth billions of dollars, even though Internet companies weren't actually making a dime. The hordes bought untested companies for absurdly high values. Every buyer pushed prices higher, fueling a spectacular bubble that eventually popped in 2000. Pets.com: Raised $82.5 million when it went public, then crashed less than a year later. Kozmo.com: Blew through $280 million before going bust. Webvan.com: From $1.2 billion to zero.

Two years later, as the market was recovering from the hangover of the tech boom, the herd was already forming behind the next big thing: housing. Spurred on by cheap mortgages, commentators, and Wall Street wizards who claimed house prices always rose, a wide swath of the country started buying and selling houses as if they were stocks. Prices soared—until they stopped soaring in 2006. Then the bubble burst, leaving the herd (the country) with a mountain of debt.

This is what Warren Buffett has to say about herd behavior: "When the price of a stock can be influenced by a 'herd' on Wall Street with prices set at the margin by the most emotional person, or the greediest person, or the most depressed person, it is hard to argue that the market always prices rationally. In fact, market prices are frequently nonsensical."

For Leila, the decision to stay at home was unduly influenced by the herd of moms, moms-in-law, and mom bloggers surrounding her during her maternity leave. She definitely loved her time with Jasper, and she thought more of it was better than less of it. But she also loved her work. "If you had asked me when I wasn't jacked up on hormones and really, really tired whether I had the patience, tolerance, and temperament to be home with a baby, I would have told you no way," said Leila. Yet she quit her job after consulting, among others:

- Her mother, who had always wished she'd worked but for some reason encouraged Leila to stay home.
- A sister and cousin who stayed home and believed, religiously, that moms who didn't were neglecting their children.
- A group of new mom-friends who were smart and funny, and who had made the decision not to work, and who seemed happy.

Not exactly an objective crowd.

Leila's stay-at-home bubble lasted exactly five months after she was slated to go back to work. At the time, Jake's company was preparing to go public and he was traveling every week. She missed having another grown-up around, started to despise the tedium of board books and homemade baby food. She missed reading about, talking about, and learning about art. She felt cobwebs forming in her head.

So she took out her frustration on the closest person to her: Jake.

When was he coming home? she'd ask. Because she hadn't signed up for single motherhood. Why didn't he ask more questions about their day? Was he not curious? Did he not find his son's day an interesting topic? Why did his conference calls always take place during dinner?

She got paranoid. Why didn't Jake ask her opinion about anything anymore? Did he think she wasn't as smart as the women he worked with? Did he think she was going a little crazy? *Was* she going a little crazy? She read the papers, too, you know, she was aware of what was going on in the world. And on it went, in an endless feedback loop.

"I was always in the doghouse," Jake said. "If I traveled, I was abandoning her. If I was around, I wasn't doing enough." One Sunday,

IN PLAIN ENGLISH:

Feedback Loop

A chain reaction that doubles back on itself. Stock market falls, so...
you sell off stocks, which makes... stock market fall further. Husband
acts like jerk, so... you wonder why he always has to be such a jerk,
which makes him... seem like a jerk the next time (even if he shows up
with flowers).

when Jake told her he had a three-hour conference call later that afternoon, Leila lost it.

"Why did you encourage me to stay home?" she said. "I am not cut
out for this."

Jake remembered it differently: "You asked my opinion, and I said
you should do what felt right. If you hate being home, go back to
work. But don't make me the bad guy."

"*I'm not making you the bad guy*," said Leila, not using her library
voice. "I'm just *saying* you could've helped me think this through
more before I quit my job."

Jake was sick of being the fall guy. Leila was sick of being the mom.

The Solution: Look in the Mirror

One day, soon after Jasper started crawling, Leila found herself rifling
through her closet, looking at all the clothes she hadn't worn in more
than a year, including suits, cocktail dresses, and silk blouses. Who was
the woman who wore those clothes? Leila wondered. She looked
down at the outfit she had on: one of Jake's old wife beaters, denim
shorts, Tevas. Tevas—so it had come to that.

She had a few minutes before she had to leave for Jasper's tumbling class at the Y. She quickly changed into a cute little pencil skirt, a low-cut blouse, and a pair of alligator heels she'd bought two summers ago at a sample sale. She put on some jewelry—a novelty. Let the other moms at the Y think what they will. Leila looked in the mirror: She still had it.

When Jake came home that night, Leila was decked out as if she were hosting a gallery opening. "Wow, you look nice," he said. "What's the occasion?"

"The *occasion*?" Leila said, not using her library voice again. "Does there have to be an *occasion* for me to look nice?"

Jake got some crackers from the kitchen cabinet and ate them in silence while he helped Jasper put together a puzzle.

The next day, Leila had a playdate with Alex and Liz. This time, she put on one of her sexy-secretary shirt-dresses and spent some quality time with her makeup while Jasper crawled around the bathroom floor, probably wondering who had kidnapped his mom.

The moms immediately noticed Leila's transformation. "What's the occasion?" they asked, practically in unison.

"Christ, why is everyone obsessed with occasions? I'm tired of looking like a mom, okay?" Leila said. "No offense."

On her walk home, she tried to imagine how it would feel if she were at work at that very moment instead of pushing Jasper down the sidewalk and worrying that the cherry Popsicle juice he'd dripped on her earlier would never come off her sexy-secretary shirt-dress. The stroller hit something on the sidewalk, tipped forward, and sent Jasper rolling out onto the concrete. He banged his head and screamed his lungs out. Leila screamed, too. Had she in all honesty forgotten to strap the little guy in? What the hell was the matter with her? She tried to calm him down, holding him tight and examining every part of him until she concluded that there was no blood and probably no concussion.

Nonetheless, Leila was up all night, checking Jasper's breathing every hour on the hour, going over all the evidence proving she was a sorry excuse for a mother. She couldn't sing. Her mind tended to wander, which meant bad things happened like Jasper falling out of his stroller. Swings made her nauseated, riding them and pushing them. She hated the term "mom-friends." Breast-feeding bored her. Being a mom made her resent her husband.

"I should have known better," Leila said to Jake the next morning. "*You* should have known better."

"What exactly *should* I have known, Leila?" asked Jake, this time ready for the attack. He'd woken up so many times to daggers being thrown his way from the other side of the bed, the breakfast table, or the telephone that he had his shields up practically before Leila opened her mouth.

"That I shouldn't have quit my job."

"I see. I should have been psychic. I should have told you to leave our new baby in the hands of strangers because I'd rather you sit around looking at art all day."

"*Aha!*" said Leila. "I knew it! You don't take my work seriously. 'Stand around looking at art all day'? That's what you think I do? I should be sitting in front of a computer all day or kissing investors' asses for start-up money?"

"That's not what I mean, and you know it," said Jake, flailing now. Damn! His shield had failed him—what an idiot! "That came out all wrong. Of course I take your work seriously. I take *you* seriously. I just don't know what to do anymore to make you happy."

Leila recounted all the harm she'd done herself while Jake sat back and watched. Jake, in turn, told Leila over and over again that he'd done nothing wrong, that he was an easy target.

Leila would have been wise to stop railing at Jake and listen to our friend Warren Buffett, who once said: "My idea of a group decision is to look in the mirror."

We think the idea of making a decision by looking in the mirror is also great marriage advice. When you're panicking about the amount of sex you're having—or not having—or despairing over the fact that other couples seem to be happy and it must be because she stays home to manage it all, ask yourself: Is that what you want, or is it what the herd says you should want?

The people giving Leila advice wanted her to make the same decisions they had made. Liz with the skinny legs had given up a career as a lawyer, but she hated law and loved yoga. Alex gave up a career in fashion, but her career had been foundering and she was waiting for another lightning bolt to strike. Leila, by contrast, loved her work. She had labored hard to get where she was and never planned to get sidetracked.

Buffett's Mirror

Warren Buffett is one guy who can take his own advice. For example, in 1987 he started thinking about investing in Coca-Cola. He liked the  product, thought the company had sound financials, and loved that everyone else in the market at the time thought the stock was a dud. Coke's war with Pepsi had driven the price down to $38 a share. Buffett loaded up: He started with $600 million in shares and then upped it to $1.2 billion. His stake would eventually be worth more than $17 billion.

Buffett did pretty much the same thing with the Washington Post Company, American Express, and Goldman Sachs. Ignore the crowd, make a killing. Words to live by.

During Jake's next business trip, Leila opened an email. It was an email she got every week, filled with art industry job postings from a Listserv she was on. Since Jasper was born, she'd deleted these emails without opening them. What was the point? But that day, she was curious. Reading through them depressed her. It was that same feeling: Now that she was out of the loop, getting back in would be too hard. She forwarded the email to Jake, adding—with a touch of the dramatic—"Check out the life I could have had."

That was it for Jake. When he came home, he sat Leila down and told her enough with the pity party and the husband bashing. "I have an idea," he said, and suggested she make one simple call—to her old boss to ask whether she was free for lunch. "You had a good relationship with her. Take advantage of it. Pick her brain, tell her you're ready to jump back into things."

Leila was unconvinced. She was scared. "The woman's busy," she said.

"She's gotta eat," Jake said.

Leila caved and put in the call. Her boss sounded happy to hear from her and agreed to lunch the following week. When the day arrived, Leila wore her most un-mom-like clothes, prayed the woman wouldn't judge her too harshly for flip-flopping so soon after quitting, and asked if she had any career advice.

"No," said her boss. "But I do have some work I need done, and if you're willing to settle for part-time freelance, you're hired."

Leila took it. Less pay, no perks, but it was a foot in the door. And if a full-time spot did open up, she'd be in the right place to snag it.

Soon after she was back at work, the tension in Jake and Leila's house started to evaporate. Leila began reading again (adult books) and going out to networking events when Jake was in town to watch Jasper. She took on more and more work at the gallery until her part-time gig turned into full-time. She stopped blaming all her problems on Jake. True, she had fewer problems, but she also had the head space to see him clearly again—as a guy who had her best interests at heart.

"I wish I had the genes to stay home," Leila said. "But I'm a better mom when I get to go to work every day."

When we met them, they were preparing to send Jasper to kindergarten. The herds were already gathering. Private was better than public. Progressive better than traditional. This teacher better than that teacher. Leila and Jake swore they were drowning it all out. And yet . . . "Liz told me about this great school run by a group of former actors," Leila told us. "It sounds amazing."

Good luck, Leila.

CASE STUDY #3

The Players: Martha and Phil

In some ways, Martha and Phil spent the first twenty-five years of their marriage in a bubble. They raised three kids together, bought and renovated two houses, and while they watched friends' marriages sputter and fall apart, theirs remained strong.

Their only real source of friction was church. As the kids got older, Martha got more and more involved, attending services every weekend, participating in prayer groups, pot lucks, and game nights. Phil was fine going to services, but that was about it. "There are plenty of games I like playing," he told us. "But bingo with the kooks from the choir is not one of them."

In 2005, the last of their kids went off to college. "We didn't think a lot about what life would be like after they left," said Phil. "We never had time. If you'd asked me to predict how I would feel, I would have guessed lonely."

But it wasn't lonely. It was spectacular.

They slept in on Saturdays, had surprising amounts of sex, read the books they'd been talking about reading forever, went to whatever movie they wanted whenever they wanted, and even road-tripped across the country in a rented RV. Martha, who had given up working as a hospital administrator when their first son was born, took a philosophy class at the senior citizen center. She learned to cook food other than hamburgers and Tater Tots. And after reading a book about the genocide in Rwanda—which had been on her nightstand for "probably eight years"—she became interested in Africa. She started to follow the events unfolding in Darfur as if it were the town next door. "There were a lot of things happening in the world that I hadn't had time to care about," she said. "Now I could care."

Phil was busy, too. He signed up for classes in business at the local community college, thinking that some basic finance skills might give him the confidence he needed to finally start his own business. He spent a lot of time thinking about what a business would look like and talking to his in-laws about investing. He stayed up late at night poring over *Real Estate Finance,* a trade publication that he told us cost "eight hundred dollars for a subscription. Can you believe that?" It would be worth it, he said, when he started his new business.

Newly liberated Martha and Phil were still riding their bubble.

In 2006, Martha went with a church mission to visit a refugee camp for Sudanese victims of the Darfur conflict. She encountered women who had watched their husbands being executed and their children being raped. "I met a four-year-old orphan caring for her one-year-old brother," she said. "Their parents were slaughtered in front of him. It's hard to explain what seeing things like that does to you. These people had nothing. No home, no family, no food. Nothing. I felt an obligation to help."

It never occurred to Martha and Phil that pursuing these new passions could hurt their marriage. "We were together for so long, I took for granted that everything would be okay," said Martha. "My mom always said the key to a good marriage is supporting each other, and that's what we were doing. We'd been nothing but supportive of each other for decades. Why would that change because the kids were gone?"

But a couple of years after the empty-nest high, Martha and Phil's bubble burst. With every trip to Africa—they were now happening every few months—Phil seemed less and less interested in Martha's human rights crusade. And the busier Martha got, the less she noticed how hard Phil was working with his job and the classes he was taking. To Phil, it seemed that everything Martha did was focused on people halfway around the world. "Why Africa?" he said. "I mean, why not the bad parts of Minneapolis, where we *live*?"

Martha barely noticed that Phil no longer asked about her work. (Here's a tip: If you come back from a two-week trip to Darfur and your husband doesn't ask you how the trip was, call a marriage EMT.) She was constantly busy, organizing fund-raisers and book drives, planning trips, or returning from them. "It didn't feel to me like my life was all that different," said Martha. "I was putting the same amount of energy into other people, they just weren't the people living in my house."

What she overlooked was how her confidence in Phil and their marriage was leading her to take their marriage for granted. She believed that she and Phil would be together forever, no matter what, that things would continue to tick along without much work, and that their happiness index would continue to trend upward. Martha's relationship, in her mind, was too big to fail. "I loved the security of marriage," Martha said. "But I got complacent. I missed the warning signs."

One morning, Martha walked in the door, threw her keys on the table, and let out a deep breath. She'd just come from the airport after a twenty-four-hour trip. She was beat.

When she walked into the kitchen, Phil was waiting for her. "This marriage isn't working for me anymore," he said.

Two years later, after many thousands of dollars' worth of therapy, they divorced.

The Problem: Overconfidence

Martha isn't the kind of person you meet and think: "Overconfident." She's modest and soft-spoken and has spent the better part of her life taking care of other people. But when it came to her marriage, Martha was guilty of the kind of confidence that gets couples in trouble.

"It probably sounds crazy," she told us. "But the idea of divorce never entered my mind until I came home and Phil said he was leaving me."

Studies show we are, as a rule, wildly overconfident creatures. In one survey of more than 3,500 American teens, respondents predicted, on average, that they had a 72.5 percent chance of having a college degree by age thirty; at the time, only 30 percent of thirty-year-olds actually had college degrees. In another, slightly more informal survey, 82 percent of Harvard Business School students said they were better-looking than the rest of their classmates. And in a survey of 137 people who had recently applied for a marriage license in Virginia, most said they were aware that about half of all marriages end in divorce but put the likelihood of them one day getting divorced at zero percent.

Zero percent? We're glad people are confident when they get married. But *zero percent*? We're some of the most confident people we know—and we love our husbands—but we would definitely put our chances of divorce above zero.

In our own Exhaustive, Groundbreaking, and Very Expensive Marriage Survey, 84 percent of respondents chose the answer "confident" or "completely confident" when asked to rate the likelihood that their spouses would never cheat on them, and 78 percent were confident they and their spouses would "always be together."

Certainly, some confidence is good. In business, it helps entrepreneurs who have to believe against all odds that they will succeed. It helps salespeople who are paid to convince others that they are on to something big. In life, confidence is what gets us out of bed in the morning.

But in high doses, confidence can mess with our heads, hearts, and bank accounts. It can prevent people from preparing for the future as they assure themselves that since everything is going swimmingly today, everything will go swimmingly tomorrow, too. The more people see the world as they would *like* to see it—not as it really is—the more overconfident they become.

Disastrous displays of overconfidence can be found in everything from chief executive suites (no surprises there) to extreme sports. On May 30, 2002, a group of climbers reached the 11,249-foot peak of Mount Hood in Oregon. They took in the beauty. They celebrated. They felt, probably, that the worst was over. And then they started their descent. As they made their way down the mountain, the sun came up and the temperature rose. The lead climber, Bill Ward, was the last to go down. But because this was considered an easy climb, he didn't take the extra step of anchoring himself to the mountain, a precaution that can prevent disaster in case of a fall. So when he did slip and fall, he took all the other climbers who were tethered to him down, too. Three of them died.

The climbers' "mental model of this beginner's mountain did not match the reality of that fateful day, resulting in their tragic accident," wrote economists Andrew Lo and Jeremiah H. Chafkin in a blog post about managing risk in the corporate world.

Most of us won't be summiting any mountains anytime soon, nor are we captains of industry, but that doesn't mean we don't fall prey to overconfidence. When we borrow more than we can pay back, buy securities we don't understand, or purchase houses we *just know* will appreciate in value, we're putting an awful lot of faith in things we can't control.

Freek Vermeulen, an associate professor at the London Business School, compares business managers who get overconfident to Icarus, whose wax wings melted when he flew too close to the sun: "This is what we often see very successful companies do, too: They become successful doing something, but this makes them overconfident and blind to the dangers that other developments pose to them. This behavior often leads to their downfall."

The same can be said for Phil and Martha. "We had such an amazing couple of years, it didn't occur to me that Phil could be unhappy," Martha said. "We started on the empty-nest journey together, had our joyride, and then I took a detour and didn't realize he wasn't with me."

The Solution: Couples Confidence Index

If you knew there was a decent chance a hurricane was going to hit your town tomorrow, you would stock up on water and Kit Kats and board up your windows, correct? You'd be a fool not to. Why not take the same precautions to prepare for a marriage emergency?

Let's take the weather analogy one step further: The reason you know there's a decent chance a hurricane is going to hit your town tomorrow is that Joe, the local weatherman, has been regularly checking up on certain key indicators, many of which are not looking good. Technology allows Joe to see hurricanes coming, which allows us to prepare for them before they land in our backyard.

You can do the same for your marriage. As unromantic as it might sound, you can develop some indicators that help you gauge what's in store.

Economic indicators are metrics that reflect the health of the economy. Important ones include unemployment, the change in gross domestic product, inflation, and the number of new houses built in a given period. One well-known indicator is "the consumer confidence index," which gauges overall household consumption and people's opinions about the future; if you start consuming a lot less and report that you think the world is ending—meaning that your confidence is waning—the index drops.

Another economic indicator comes care of economist Robert Shiller. He developed something called "the crash confidence index," which looks at how confident people are that there won't be a stock market crash. It shows that when the market rises, people believe passionately that the party will continue and their confidence that there will be no crash also rises. Shiller's index reached its all-time high in 2006, as the market was still soaring but right before it was headed for a crash. It reached its all-time low at the beginning of 2009, even as the next stock market rally was taking hold.

We think Shiller's a smart guy, and we like the idea of warning signs that go beyond, "He's not talking to me, I wonder what happened." So we developed our own Couples' Confidence Index. Think of it as a way to take the temperature of your marriage without having to fill out the workbook at the end of most relationship books (not that we have anything against relationship books or workbooks). Consider it an excuse to check in with each other.

When you're in a relatively good place—not euphoric, not despairing—draw up a baseline index. Answer the following questions. Tally the total. Then ask yourself the same questions six months later. Is the total higher (more euphoric) or lower (more despairing)?

Getting a handle on where you are in the cycle may help you see the boom, enable you to anticipate the bust, or force you to acknowledge that you two need some help before you end up like Martha and Phil.

THE COUPLES' CONFIDENCE INDEX

♥ On a scale of 1–5, how would you rate your satisfaction with your marriage right now? (**5**=You are currently thinking of things you could do to make his life better, like taking the kids to your parents for a weekend so he can play golf with his buddies. **4**=You like spending time with her and wish you could do it more often. **3**=Things are fine, you're not arguing as much as you used to. **2**=You're getting drunk and hitting on the bartender. **1**=You're cursing your mother for failing, for once in her life, to warn you that your taste in men left something to be desired.)

        1   2   3   4   5

♥ On a scale of 1–5, how much quality time are you spending together? (**5**=Joined at hip, **4**=Nights and weekends, **3**=Sunday afternoons, **2**=Once a month you have dinner together, assuming one of you remembers to show up, **1**=You may have exchanged words in the past 48 hours but you can't be sure.)

        1   2   3   4   5

♥ On a scale of 1–5, how much sex are you having? (**5**=Lemurs in heat, **4**=Every other day, **3**=Not keeping track, but enough, **2**=You'll have to think about it for a second, **1**=Born-again virginity.)

        1   2   3   4   5

♥ On a scale of 1–5, what's the tenor of the most recent argument you had? (**5**=We disagreed, made up, and had five hours of tantric sex, **4**=It was a pretty heated discussion, but nothing too terrible was said, **3**=Hurtful words were exchanged, but we found a way to resolve it, **2**=We yelled, it was awful, and now he's in a time-out, **1**=Went to a dark place.)

1   2   3   4   5

♥ On a scale of 1–5, how many nice things have you done for your spouse this week? And by "nice things," we don't mean saying hello and goodbye, but things like installing shoe shelves in her closet or asking how his day was and listening to the answer for a change. (**5**=Too many to count (but he deserves it!), **4**=A few, **3**=One or two, **2**=I think none, but I don't have time to think about it, **1**=What's "nice"?)

1   2   3   4   5

♥ On a scale of 1–5, when you lie in bed at night and think of your spouse, what kinds of thoughts run through your head? (**5**=All positive, including gently swaying fields of lilies and the two of you picnicking naked among them, **4**=Mostly positive, you'd kill for a night out to catch up and give him that "special surprise" you promised him on his birthday, **3**=A mix of positive and negative, as in he's not perfect, but he's better than most, **2**=Mostly negative, a business trip would be nice right about now so you could stop listening to her incessant bitching about the renovation, the car, and the doormat—who gets angry about doormats?—you forgot to get, **1**=Given the chance, you'd export him to China.)

1   2   3   4   5

KEY

If you scored 25-30: Bubble alert! Things are very, very good, but be-ware: A crash could be around the corner.

If you scored 15-24: Keep on keeping on. Work to show your apprecia-tion of your spouse and hope the good karma rubber-bands back your way.

If you scored 6-14: Start reading this book from the beginning.

Now, dog-ear this page. Every few months, come back to this quiz and run through it again. If your score is falling, maybe it's time to peel back a few layers and figure out what's wrong. Maybe it's time to have an honest conversation about why you're angry or feeling ne-glected or getting lazy. If your number is rising, take stock of what's working (praise, appreciation, affection) and be conscious of keeping it up. And if it's a perfect score every time and you are patting yourself on the back, we'd refer you back to Icarus and his melted wings.

THE BOTTOM LINE

1. **Drown out the noise.** Don't let yourself be overly influenced by what everyone else is doing. Do what our friend Warren Buffett does: Look in the mirror and figure out what's right for you, regardless of what the herds are doing.

2. **Reinvent yourselves.** Rough patches don't mean you're doomed. They mean you're married. Fifty years is a long time, and there are going to be bumps along the way. Use them as an opportunity to get creative and evolve.

3. **Assess.** It's easy to wake up every morning for decades and do the same thing, over and over again, oblivious to the subtle changes in your partner and in your relationship. Then you're surprised when you wake up one day and things just aren't so great anymore. Check in with each other on a regular basis, see if you're both getting what you want out of the relationship, and if not, fix it *before* it breaks.

4. **Be confident, not overconfident.** Of course you have high expectations of your marriage, otherwise you wouldn't have said "I do" in the first place. But overconfidence is a different animal altogether. That's when you start ignoring problems and assuming you're invincible. You're not. Instead, invest constantly in your marriage and stay on the ball.

10

GAME THEORY

Or, Know Your ~~Enemy~~ Spouse

THE PRINCIPLE

The Cuban missile crisis ring a bell? When the United States and the Soviet Union nearly nuked each other to smithereens? Vaguely? Here's a quick refresher: In the fall of 1962, the U.S. discovered that its archenemy had been secretly building missile installations in Cuba capable of launching nuclear warheads. What's more, Soviet ships loaded with missiles were already en route to Cuba.

The U.S. had a number of issues with this—namely, that Cuba is just ninety miles off its coast, so Americans would have zero time to respond if a nuke was suddenly headed their way.

Upon receiving this news, President Kennedy, rather than reaching for his football, pushing the red button and incinerating Cuba, opted for a more measured approach. He deployed naval forces to stop the Soviet ships from reaching Cuba. The blockade, he said, would remain in place until Khrushchev agreed to turn back and dismantle the Cuban sites.

The rhetoric quickly became overheated. Khrushchev told Kennedy he better stand down or he'd be sorry. Kennedy told Khrushchev *he* better stand down or *he'd* be sorry. Khrushchev didn't budge. Kennedy went all DEFCON 2 on Khrushchev.

For several days, the world held its breath as neither side appeared to back down. Americans loaded up on Spam, prayed for enough bomb shelters, and awaited their doom.

As the two leaders kept their fingers on the trigger—just in case!—secret negotiations were under way, and by the end of nearly three weeks, the Soviets finally agreed to turn their ships around and dismantle their missile silos in exchange for guarantees that the U.S. wouldn't invade Cuba.

It was a close call—the closest call of the Cold War.

And it's now used as a classic case study in game theory, a branch of mathematics that analyzes how people, companies, and governments interact and make decisions in strategic situations. The Cuban missile crisis is what's known in game theory as "the game of chicken": Two players push each other to the brink, hoping the other one will back down first.

Now replace Kennedy and Khrushchev with Joel and Lisa. And replace the nuclear missiles with Joel and Lisa's refrigerator, which has been empty for three days. Husband and wife are in a standoff, neither one backing down. They've been ordering in from Gino's Pizza every night this week, and they've never had such indigestion in their lives. But god help Joel if he's going to go to the supermarket; he's gone food shopping the last five Saturdays while Lisa played tennis. Lisa's not going, either—she does everything around the house, including folding Joel's underwear and paying the bills, which means unless Joel wants to start paying the bills *on time* and digging his dirty clothes out from under the bed, he's going to be the one hauling his sorry self to the ShopRite. She can wait. She's waited this long.

Maybe you and your spouse are more mature than Joel and Lisa. Maybe you never stand tough and wait for the other to back down. Maybe you don't do all sorts of other things like guilt him into doing something you don't feel like doing or twiddle your thumbs until she gives in and does a job for you.

Maybe.

But what's more likely is that you each have a little Joel and Lisa in you, a little Khrushchev and Kennedy, and that when it comes to your marriage, you're not above engaging in some brinksmanship, or scheming to win an ongoing battle, or strategizing to get what you want—in fact, you do it more than you probably admit.

Which is why we think you could use a lesson in game theory. See, we don't think being strategic is bad. It might *sound* cold and calculating, but it's reality—and you might as well own it. If your friends invite you for a weekend away, no spouses, and you want to go, you naturally start thinking about how you can make it happen with minimal fuss, right? You think about what you can offer your spouse in exchange, how to bring it up, when to bring it up, and what type of flowers to present as graft when you're in the midst of bringing it up.

That's called "strategizing," and game theory can help you get a lot better at it.

We've saved game theory for the end because it's slightly more complicated and slightly more wonky than the other concepts in this book. But we think you're ready for it.

Here are a few things game theory and marriage have in common:

- In game theory, as in marriage, there are two players (actually, there can be more than two players in game theory, but since we're not advocating polygamy, we're sticking to two-player games).
- In game theory, as in marriage, each player is trying to do the best he can for himself but is limited by the fact that he's not alone. There's always someone else in the equation—a competitor, a foreign rival, a wife—trying to do the best for herself, too.

- In game theory, as in marriage, there are "cooperative" strategies in which the two parties work together to come up with a solution that's best for both of them, and there are "noncooperative" strategies in which each party is out for number one.
- In game theory, as in marriage, it's usually the noncooperative strategy that proves most appealing and hardest to resist.
- In game theory, as in marriage, it's usually the cooperative strategy that makes everyone happier in the end.

THE PEOPLE SPEAK . . .

About Cooperation

Many of the people who took part in our Exhaustive, Groundbreaking, and Very Expensive Marriage Survey said cooperating was a huge challenge. Here, some answers to the question "What's the hardest part about being married?"

- "Learning to live with another person in the house."
- "Having to compromise."
- "Different points of view."
- "Making myself less of a priority."
- "Not always getting my way."
- "Agreeing to disagree."
- "Seeing eye to eye in raising children."
- "Negotiating different goals."
- "I can't do everything I want when I want to."
- "Toilet seat."

Who invented game theory is an open question. Some say credit goes to the Jews, specifically the authors of the Talmud, a massive compendium of Jewish law written on or about the year AD 200 by the great rabbinical scholars of the age. The legal debates in the Talmud range from whether Jews are supposed to be vegetarians (unclear, though they are instructed to keep their animals well fed before sending them to slaughter) to what happens to circumcised men who attempt to put their foreskins back on (they definitely do not make it to heaven).

But we digress.

The Talmudic discussions that involve game theory include how to divide a dead man's estate among his angry creditors when his fortune is less than his debts; how to divide a garment when one person insists the whole thing is hers and another person claims half of it; and this doozy: what to do when a man marries his brother's widow, who gives birth to a son *eight months later,* and then the man dies, too, leaving that son of dubious parentage plus two sons who are definitely his, and then the grandfather subsequently dies, and everyone else is left to figure out how to divide his estate (answer: 41⅔ to the mystery son and 58⅓ total to the two legitimate sons—don't ask us to explain).

Fast-forward some seventeen hundred years to the 1944 publication of *Theory of Games and Economic Behavior* by John von Neumann and Oskar Morgenstern. Von Neumann, considered the greatest mathematician of the twentieth century, had developed something called "the minimax theorem" a few years earlier, which in extremely simple terms shows how to minimize potential losses in a two-person game, or how to make the best of a situation when you can't have it all. In their book, von Neumann and Morgenstern expanded on minimax, laid out a bunch of other strategic games, and introduced the world to game theory. Ever since, economists have used game theory to develop, among other things, antitrust policies, nuclear deterrence strategies, optimal baseball salaries, and matching programs for medical students and hospital residencies.

Whether it's a minimax problem or the game of chicken, game theory tackles situations in which you can't have it all. The goal instead is to find strategies you can use to achieve the best results possible, considering the likely strategies of the other players.

Note those three magic words: *best results possible.*

That's not the same as "getting what I want" or being "right" all the time, two scenarios many of us would prefer. But if game theory teaches us anything, it's that relationships aren't about having it all, they're about having all you can *under the circumstances.* In your marriage, those "circumstances" include the obvious, though often overlooked, fact that there's another person involved: your spouse—a spouse who also happens to be after his own best results.

As the economist Thomas Schelling says of game theory (and which could easily be confused with a definition of marriage): "Two or more individuals have choices to make, preferences regarding the outcomes, and some knowledge of the choices available to each other and of each other's preferences. The outcome depends on the choices that both of them make. . . . There is no independently 'best' choice that one can make; it depends on what the others do."

With that in mind, here are three general strategies game theory offers for improving the outcomes of potentially sticky spousal situations:

1. Think ahead. How will he react to what I'm about to do or say? And how should that reaction influence my behavior?
2. Learn from the past. How did she react the last time I did this? How can I do things differently now to avoid the same outcome?
3. Put yourself in his shoes. This doesn't mean considering what *you* would do if you were him, but what *he* would do if he were him, which he is.

That's it right there—the essence of strategic thinking in whatever "game" you're playing. It sounds like such solid advice, and yet so many people routinely do the opposite when it comes to relationships. You tell your buddies a guys-only fishing trip is a go even though you have a newborn at home and you haven't run it by your wife. In the midst of a silly argument, you accuse your husband of being "dense" even though last time you pulled that card, he (rightly) went postal on you. You expect she'll put out after you bring her breakfast in bed and are shocked when she says thanks, wolfs it down, jumps in the shower, and heads for the office without even a kiss goodbye (news flash: When is she *not* in a rush to get to work?).

We think the economists Avinash Dixit and Barry Nalebuff summed up game theory beautifully: It is "the art of finding ways to cooperate. . . . It is the art of convincing others, and even yourself, to do what you say. It is the art of interpreting and revealing information. It is the art of putting yourself in others' shoes so as to predict and influence what they will do."

Below, four couples, four games they unwittingly played, and four strategies they employed to turn mutually assured destruction into a win–win marriage.

CASE STUDY #1

The Players: Ariel and Ryan

The Problem: Strategic Polarization

Ariel and Ryan agreed on one thing: They needed to move. Their 850-square-foot apartment wasn't big enough for the two of them and Hank, their very active two-year-old. The place had charm and their pretty Brooklyn neighborhood was filled with amenities, but the stress of living on top of one another was taking a toll.

"We had a shoes-off policy in the house, but no place to put the shoes, so the first thing you saw when you walked in was a pile of dirty shoes—and if they were Ryan's, then smelly, too," said Ariel.

They set out to find a new apartment. They assumed this would be relatively painless since they had similar tastes. But after a couple of weeks of looking, they hadn't come close to agreeing on anything. A troubling pattern had emerged: Most of the listings Ariel sought out were in the same trendy neighborhood they already lived in. Most of the listings Ryan came up with were in neighborhoods that were more affordable, but less trendy and farther from Manhattan, where both of them worked. What this meant: Every viewing involved exchanging fake pleasantries with the real-estate agent, followed by a tense trip home either in silence or in heated discussion about why each insisted on ignoring what the other wanted.

Ariel wanted to stay in the same neighborhood. Hank had day care friends around the corner, the markets had organic food, and the commute to work was manageable. Ryan insisted they'd get a lot more for their money if they were willing to move a few subway stops away. "I wasn't talking about Long Island, just a neighborhood that didn't have grass-fed beef at every corner deli," said Ryan.

Their differences of opinion grew starker the more apartments they saw. They would check out a cute place Ariel had picked in a manicured prewar building, and Ryan would notice how narrow the hallway was or how little storage space the kitchen had—failing to acknowledge the views or the tree-lined street. Running to meet Ryan at an apartment he had picked out, Ariel counted the minutes it took to get there from the office, then complained about the police presence on the corner.

"Police are a good thing!" Ryan said. "Don't you want to see the streets protected?"

"I'd rather live in a place where the streets don't *need* to be protected," said Ariel.

What had started out as somewhat different preferences soon grew into entrenched, immovable opinions.

"We argued every night," Ariel told us. "It was horrible. I would look at him and I could feel myself getting annoyed. He had always been stubborn, but this was ridiculous. Willing to put a third bedroom ahead of our son's safety? Come on!"

You won't be surprised to learn that that's not how Ryan saw things.

Ariel, he said, was being way too dramatic about the safety issue. For one thing, the homicide rate was only a tiny bit higher than in their current neighborhood (and yes, he checked). But Ariel's real problem, said Ryan, was that she was scared to live next door to people who didn't look like her: "She's a snob."

You won't be surprised to learn that Ariel disagreed with that.

Ariel and Ryan were living in a state game theorists call "strategic polarization." Each had become totally inflexible, polarized, firmly rooted at opposite ends of the spectrum. What's interesting about a situation like this is that the two players don't start out in opposition—rather, they get that way over time. Ariel and Ryan used to be in agreement about what they wanted: nice apartment, more space, Brooklyn. Even at the point of polarization, if we had given Ryan a few cocktails, he would have confessed to enjoying the amenities of his neighborhood and being perfectly happy to stay there. Similarly, Ariel would have conceded that she would make the most of moving to a new area and that a ton more space—especially if it meant a home office for her *and* a room for Hank—might have made life easier. They were able to have empathy and put themselves in each other's shoes if they tried (one of the skills of a smart game theorist), but they chose not to. Instead, their strategies were to remain fixed in their positions and wait for the other to give in.

Adam and Ehud Kalai (son and father, respectively), the game theorists who first gave this game a name, offer the example of two very persnickety people who each like the thermostat set at slightly different temperatures, 71 degrees Fahrenheit and 69 degrees. They have adjoining rooms and their own thermostats, so whatever temperature one sets will mix with the other's and become an average. At 71 and 69, the overall temperature becomes 70. But that's too cool for her and too warm for him, so they each adjust their thermostats by a degree, to 72 and 68. Same problem with the 70-degree average, so they adjust again, to 73 and 67. Before you know it, they've each gone as far apart as they can, to 140 and 0 (these are fancy thermostats) and they're no better off than they were at the outset: 70 degrees.

"What starts out as a minor difference ends up as a vast polarization," says Ehud Kalai.

Complete polarization is a type of "Nash equilibrium," so-named for the Nobel laureate John Forbes Nash (who was later the subject of the film *A Beautiful Mind,* in which he's played by Russell Crowe). Very, very simply, a Nash equilibrium is a situation in which neither side has an incentive to change strategies because doing so won't make either one any better off, given what the other side has chosen to do.

For example: Two airlines are selling $500 tickets on a flight from New York to Rome. To win more customers, Cheapo Air decides to lower its fare to $400. Cut Rate Air now has no choice but to lower its fare to $400 or risk losing its business to Cheapo Air. As long as Cheapo keeps its fares at $400, Cut Rate has to do the same. If Cheapo does decide to change strategies and return to a $500 fare, it will lose customers to Cut Rate, which will suddenly become the more affordable carrier. Both airlines are now stuck selling $400 seats and raking in much lower profits than before. Even more annoying is what happens when Cut Rate then decides to drop its fare to $300 so it can finally trounce its rival: Cheapo follows suit.

Frustrating, right?

Part of the reason this happens is that both sides are acting independently. They're not cooperating. If they did cooperate, they might be better off. (Though in the airlines' case they'd get in trouble with the feds for collusion, but that's another story—they're not married.)

Back to Ariel and Ryan. Given Ariel's insistence that they stay in the neighborhood, Ryan felt he had no choice but to insist right back at her that they leave. Caving would mean losing the argument completely. And given Ryan's insistence that they move to god knows where, Ariel felt she had to stay firmly rooted in her position, too.

"There was no room for negotiation," said Ariel. It was an all-or-nothing battle.

The Solution: Collusion

Or was it?

Realistically, Ariel and Ryan's argument had to end some way, somehow if they wanted to stay married, which they did. What to do?

When we ran their situation past Ehud Kalai, he offered his two-cent solution: Communication and cooperation. Kalai said when two people are headed toward polarization, they first need to recognize that it's happening. Then they need to come up with a compromise and commit to it. "That's where communication comes in," says Kalai.

And what should each person communicate?

"Information," says Kalai.

Aha!

Remember in chapter 7, how we told you information is a great economic tool for communicating better? Well, in Ariel and Ryan's case, neither had the information needed to reach a compromise. Ariel, for example, hadn't told Ryan (though she did tell us) that she would consider moving farther out if they could find a pretty block and maybe get a car so she could still shop at her favorite stores. She was worried if she let on that she was open to doing it his way, there would be no going back. And Ryan hadn't told Ariel (though he did tell us) that one reason he wasn't giving in was that he worried it would set a bad precedent: In future disagreements, Ariel would think he'd always give in.

But if Ariel and Ryan shared the information they'd been hiding, each of them might have softened, somewhat, to the other's position. They might have found a way to cooperate.

In the business world, sharing critical information, under certain circumstances, is considered collusion. And in the business world, collusion is illegal. When companies that are supposed to be competing with each other—like Cut Rate and Cheapo Airlines—share information, the consumer is usually the one who gets the bum deal, paying $2,000 for a flight from New York to Boston. Of course, that's also why it's hard to find a big difference in the price of an airline ticket—because each airline is required to set prices independently, each one reacts to the other's pricing almost instantaneously.

But in a marriage, collusion isn't only legal, it's good strategy. And that's exactly what Ariel and Ryan did—not because they do whatever we tell them to do, but because eventually, after seeing dozens of apartments and running out of mean things to say to each other, they had no choice but to start thinking strategically.

Ariel, inadvertently behaving like a game theorist, wondered how Ryan would react if she changed strategies. What if she threw him a bone—if she admitted that he had a point—that maybe moving out of the neighborhood would have *some* upsides, like saving money that they could one day use to buy their own home instead of renting, or to pay for Hank's college education? "Ryan loves to be right," said Ariel. "And I've noticed over the years that sometimes being right is enough. That's all he needs. If I just say, 'Ryan, you have a point,' he gets so excited that he'll agree to anything."

Ryan, meanwhile, was busy figuring out how he could salvage a speck of what he wanted. He knew Ariel well enough to know that she had the *ability* to compromise—she'd compromised by moving to New York to begin with when she wanted to stay in California. He decided to suggest—just suggest—that he was open to staying where they were, if they could find something for the same price they were already paying. "The minute I told her I had started considering it, I could see her softening up. She's so predictable," said Ryan. As he expected, once he suggested he would compromise on the neighborhood, she was more than willing to let him have a bigger say in which apartment they finally chose.

Here's where they ended up: in a bigger apartment in the same neighborhood. It was cheaper because it was on a less desirable block. But it had plenty of room for all three of them, and because it happened to be a recession and a renter's market, they were able to negotiate with the owner for an even lower rent than they were paying for their old place. As an added bonus, the owners were hoping to sell it in about a year, and Ariel and Ryan would have first dibs. By colluding, they achieved the *best results possible*—and they'd never even heard of game theory before we came along.

CASE STUDY #2

The Players: Heather and Pradeep

The Problem: Prisoners' Dilemma

Heather and Pradeep had a son named Zach who hated doing his homework. He was a smart kid with a warm smile—when he chose to smile. But homework, as he said over and over, was not his "thing." Since Zach was fifteen, and his parents wanted him to go to college, this was an issue.

Problem was, neither parent wanted to be the bad guy when it came to policing Zach's homework. Heather and Pradeep had stressful jobs and worked long hours, and the last thing they wanted when they came home was an unpleasant and frustrating argument with Zach. It was easier to give in.

"He's a good kid," they'd reassure each other, both secretly fearing that someday he would blame them for not being hard enough on him.

To tackle the problem, Heather and Pradeep mapped out a good cop/bad cop strategy. Every night during dinner, the "good" cop would ask what Zach's assignments were for the evening and offer to help.

Then at nine p.m., the "bad" cop would go into Zach's room and check if he'd done his work. If he hadn't, he had to stay put: no TV, no Internet, no video games. The bad cop would offer to help but also enforce the law.

Being the bad cop was not a fun job. It invariably turned into an exhausting conversation about how much Zach hated his teachers and his dumb school and why couldn't his parents leave him alone and who wants to go to Harvard anyway and when was he ever going to need algebra in real life?

So Heather and Pradeep decided to alternate bad cop duties. That worked for a while, until one night after Heather came home from a particularly brutal day at the office. It was her turn to be the bad cop, and five minutes after the nine p.m. check-in, she walked out, with Zach. Pradeep watched as Zach bounded downstairs to watch TV and Heather poured herself half a bottle of pinot grigio. "That's great," Pradeep whispered to Heather. "He got his work done?"

Heather paused, taking a swig of wine. "Well, no. But I couldn't deal with it tonight."

Pradeep was floored. "Wait a second," he said. "We had a deal."

"I don't see *you* forcing him back to his desk," Heather said.

"That's because it's not my night," said Pradeep. "And guess what? It won't be my night tomorrow, either, or the night after that!" Pradeep figured if he couldn't trust Heather to play by the rules, he shouldn't have to play by the rules, either.

Heather and Pradeep had inadvertently walked into a game called "the prisoners' dilemma." In the game, each player's best option under the circumstances is to *not* cooperate with the other player even though they'd both be better off if they did cooperate.

The example from which the game takes its name involves two suspected criminals, let's call them Pat and Joe. Each is detained in a separate interrogation room and pressed by the police to rat the other one out. Since they're not allowed to see or speak to each other, they have to make their decisions without knowing what the other one will do. They face three possible scenarios:

1. If one rats the other out and the other keeps quiet, the rat goes free and the silent one gets the full ten-year sentence.
2. If they both keep quiet, they'll both get only one year for a lesser offense, since the police still won't have enough evidence to convict on the bigger charge.
3. If they both rat each other out, they'll both get leniency and receive only half the full sentence, or five years.

This is what it comes down to:

	Joe says nothing	Joe snitches
Pat says nothing	*1 year*, 1 year	*10 years*, freedom
Pat snitches	*freedom*, 10 years	*5 years*, 5 years

We've put Pat's results in italics to distinguish them from Joe's. Clearly the move that will have the best result for Pat—if Joe says nothing—is to snitch. And clearly the best move for Joe—if Pat says nothing—is to snitch. The second-best result for both will come from both saying nothing. The problem is that neither can risk saying nothing for fear that the other will talk. Remember, if one says nothing and the other snitches, the silent one gets the full ten-year sentence. This means that no matter what the other one does, each guy's *best* move is to snitch (and pray that the other one doesn't). So that's what they do—and they both spend five years in jail. There's no way around it. Why? Because snitching is their best strategy when they consider what the other is most likely to do.

The prisoners' dilemma offers some valuable insight into what happens during certain types of standoffs: The true best move—what economists call "the first best"—is the cooperative one. But when two people are operating independently, they can't trust each other to cooperate, so they have to adopt a strategy of kill or be killed.

When it came to handling the homework problem, Heather and Pradeep were clearly in noncooperative land. They were the Pat and Joe in their own prisoners' dilemma. Note the two signs that the game had commenced: 1) Each adopted a noncooperative strategy to avoid fighting with Zach, knowing it meant the other would do the same (oh, and that Zach wouldn't do his homework); and 2) Each would have been better off had they cooperated because it would assure the other's cooperation, while ensuring that Zach did his homework.

Remember the trap of every prisoners' dilemma: The noncooperative move might *seem* better to one player at the time, but it ultimately leaves both players worse off. Here were Heather and Pradeep's options and outcomes:

	Pradeep plays bad cop	Pradeep slacks off
Heather plays bad cop	Zach does homework	Zach does homework
	Spousal peace	Spousal discord
Heather slacks off	Zach does homework	**Zach doesn't do homework**
	Spousal discord	**Spousal discord**

The optimal strategy is clearly the one in the upper left, but Heather and Pradeep landed in the lower right because Heather wanted a night off from arguing with Zach even though it was her turn to be bad cop, which caused Pradeep to vow he wouldn't be the bad cop, either.

Fortunately, Heather and Pradeep weren't Pat and Joe. They weren't stuck in separate rooms and barred from communicating. They also had more than one chance to cooperate, whereas Pat and Joe had only one shot to make the right choice—meaning rather than being a "onetime" game, Heather and Pradeep's marriage was what's called a "repeated" game.

"One of the things about a repeated game is that you have a history with each other," Harvard economist Al Roth told us. "In a marriage, you want to invest in that history. You and your husband should be the most devoted historians of your marriage."

Still, given how tempting it can be to not cooperate, how could Heather and Pradeep commit to cooperating no matter what? How could both players triumph in this prisoners' dilemma?

The Solution: Commitment Device

One way was to impose a commitment device, a strategy we talked about in chapter 8 on intertemporal choice. Commitment devices are ways to ensure you act in your long-term interests—locking the freezer door, for example, and giving your wife the key so you can't binge on ice cream every night. A commitment device is a binding incentive. Create a commitment device that motivates you to cooperate and eliminates the option of cheating, and you can avoid the trap of the prisoners' dilemma. The temptation to defect might still be there—we're only human—but the option to do so will be gone.

After each defected a few times, Heather and Pradeep decided they needed a commitment device if they were ever going to give Zach a fighting chance of getting into a decent college. They didn't call it a commitment device, they just called it a "new plan."

This new plan involved consequences. Whoever shirked bad cop duties would have to be the bad cop every night for a week. The other person, on good cop duty for the week, would get to go out after work as much as he or she wanted, leaving the bad cop stuck at home with Zach—making sure he had dinner, did his homework, and was in bed by ten. Not that Heather and Pradeep didn't love their son with all their heart, but a fifteen-year-old boy was a handful, and those days, going out to the bar was often much more appealing.

Which is why the plan worked. Each one knew ahead of time what the other person's next move would be. No guesswork required.

"I knew if I cheated, Pradeep would have no qualms about making me be bad cop for a week," Heather told us. "That's the kind of guy he is."

CASE STUDY #3

The Players: Ingrid and Mike

The Problem: Free Riding

Ingrid and Mike had been married less than a year, and already Ingrid had had it up to here. Like Mike, she had a demanding job. She worked in crisis communications for big corporate clients, while Mike had just started his own hedge fund. Like Mike, she had to do a fair bit of after-work schmoozing. And like Mike, she had plenty of things she wanted to do in her spare time, including get to the gym once in a blue moon, watch bad TV, and see friends.

Yet unlike Mike, Ingrid was the one who found herself playing the role of 1950s housewife. She did the laundry. She made the bed, emptied the kitty litter, picked up the dirty glasses from the coffee table, and organized their weekend plans. Mike enjoyed clean laundry, a tidy bed, a fresh-smelling litter box, an uncluttered coffee table, and weekends that magically filled up with fun activities and get-togethers with friends. "Must be nice to be Mike," Ingrid would say.

Mike's a free rider, economists would say.

Free riders stay home and enjoy the peace while the enlisted guys go off to war. Free riders drive SUVs and let the hybrid owners worry about the environment. Free riders don't vote, yet they get the benefits of the democratic process. And when someone else organizes a cleanup campaign of their local park, free riders can stop worrying about the trash—without lifting a finger.

In Ingrid and Mike's still-young marriage, it had become second nature for Mike to sit back and let Ingrid take care of the housework. That was his strategy—and to be honest, it was a smart one, since he knew that whatever he didn't do, she would. And she did, which only perpetuated the free ride. "I'm very quick to feel I'm being taken advantage of," Ingrid told us. "But that doesn't seem to stop me from doing everything anyway."

Would the house fall into disarray if Ingrid went on strike? Would weekends be spent playing Parcheesi at home? "If it wasn't for me, we'd be living in squalor," Ingrid told us.

But Mike argued that eventually he'd clean up, empty the kitty litter, and even make some social plans—just not on Ingrid's boot camp schedule. "She's anal," said Mike. "Why is that my fault?"

The Solution: The Mixed Strategy

To resolve the situation (not win it, mind you, but resolve it to the best extent possible), we needed to convince Ingrid to start thinking strategically. We suggested she ask herself two questions:

1. What was her *ideal* outcome and what was an *acceptable* outcome?
2. What kind of strategy would get Mike to do enough work to meet her acceptable outcome?

Ingrid told us her ideal would be Mike doing half of all the work, in exactly the way she did it, and on her timetable. "A girl can always dream," she said.

Her acceptable situation involved Mike doing half the work, on his time and in his way, even though that would mean waiting longer than she wanted for clean water glasses and potentially ending up at Hooters for dinner. And more cat poop than she was comfortable with.

Another scenario Ingrid felt she could probably live with was Mike doing some of the work some of the time, or even Mike taking on more responsibility in other areas in exchange for her continuing to do what she was doing. We told her that might mean accepting that she has the comparative advantage in certain tasks (remember the lessons from chapter 1!) and so might have to do them herself. She grudgingly agreed that we were right.

It might seem apparent, yet in the heat of the moment, couples often don't approach negotiations in terms of ideal versus acceptable. They want ideal, period. But as game theory shows us, the best result in a two-person interaction is, by definition, the *best result possible under the circumstances,* taking into account the other player's own strategies.

Once Ingrid figured out some acceptable outcomes, she could concentrate on a strategy to achieve them. For starters, we told her, she needed to remove the temptation for Mike to free ride. She could do this by shifting from a "pure strategy"—clean *all* the time, make *all* the social plans—to a "mixed strategy"—clean *some* of the time, make *some* of the plans.

A mixed strategy means you mix things up in order to keep the other party on his or her toes. The strategy is used in all sorts of contexts, not only as a solution to free riding. It's the same strategy employed by soccer players who intentionally vary the direction they aim their penalty kicks, and by tennis players who try to be unpredictable about their forehand and backhand serves. Similarly, the Internal Revenue Service audits some of the people some of the time but is unpredictable about whom it audits and when. Keeps taxpayers on their toes. Most people have never been audited, yet they continue to file their taxes honestly. Or at least mostly honestly.

How to implement a mixed strategy? Like this: The weekend after we met with Ingrid, she made plans for herself and left Mike home to fend for himself. Then, the next week, when she had plenty of clean clothes in her own closet, she skipped doing the laundry, leaving Mike with no underwear and no socks. Another week, she decided to live with a cluttered coffee table. She chose what she would stop doing at random, to keep him guessing.

Ingrid was doing a little thinking ahead, counting on the fact that Mike would be thrown off balance and, hopefully, respond by picking up some slack. And to Ingrid's delight, that's what happened (sometimes). Mike responded by occasionally picking up the slack or even picking up the phone to make a plan with one of his buddies. He did the laundry when he realized he was about to run out of underwear. Somehow, the water glasses got clean.

Even Ingrid had to admit that given who Mike was, her new strategy led to the best result possible. Mike didn't suddenly morph into the superhusband of her dreams, but by mixing things up, she at least turned him into the acceptable husband of her dreams.

"That game theory stuff really works!" said Ingrid.

Okay, so she didn't actually say that. But she did say she was happy to be our guinea pig and she's been enjoying coming home to a clean litter box to this day.

CASE STUDY #4

The Players: Marcus and Gary

The Problem: Battle of the Sexes

Marcus and Gary were two retired academics who rarely went out on weekends. Even retired, Marcus was a workaholic, happy to spend all day Saturday *and* all day Sunday in the library working on his last great opus on the medieval popes. Gary, an expert on the Romantic poets, was pretty passionate himself about Wordsworth and Blake, but was also blessed with the awareness that there was more to life than academia. He wanted them to go out and *do* stuff on weekends, go swimming, take little trips, enjoy life once in a while.

Gary would bug Marcus to work less and go out more, but he couldn't get any traction. "I never knew anyone as stubborn as Marcus. You'd think I was asking him to come with me for a night out in a hospital cafeteria followed by a colonoscopy."

"What should we do this weekend?" Gary might ask on a Thursday, all innocence and charm.

"Do?" Marcus would say.

"Why don't we go to a movie?"

"Maybe Sunday, if I get enough done."

Then Sunday would arrive and Marcus would complain it was too hot outside, or too cold, or his knee was still sore from the last walk around the block. So Gary would force himself to work, too, or putter around the garden, or look online for cheap airfares to Europe. Marcus, meanwhile, would hole up in his study, angrily rewriting Wikipedia entries on great medieval thinkers.

What's wrong with this picture?

A lot of things, but for our purposes, we'll point out one: the fact that Gary *wanted* to go out but didn't. And the reason he didn't go out is that Marcus didn't want to go out. If Gary wanted to hang out with Marcus—which he did—he'd have to stay home.

Gary and Marcus were playing a game called "the battle of the sexes." In this game, two players want to do different activities, but they want even *more* to be together than apart. (Don't be confused by the fact that Gary and Marcus are both men and the battle of the sexes implies a man and a woman—it's just game theorists being hetero-normative.)

Anyway, say you love to watch *Deadliest Catch,* and she (or he) prefers *Project Runway.* You cave to her because as much as Heidi Klum makes your stomach turn, you don't like the idea of going to the basement to watch your crab show all by yourself. You guys are acting out the battle of the sexes.

This is how a game theorist would plot it:

	Gary stays home and works	*Gary goes to the zoo*
Marcus stays home and works	3, 2	0, 0
Marcus goes to the zoo	0, 0	2, 3

The numbers represent how happy Marcus and Gary are in each situation, with 0 being the saddest and 3 being the happiest. When they do different things, like one goes to the zoo while the other stays home, they're both sad and lonely. But if they both stay home and work, Marcus is at peak happiness since he's doing what he wants with the guy he wants to be with, while Gary is at level 2, happy enough in Marcus's company but still wishing they were at the zoo. Similarly, Gary will be superhappy at the zoo with Marcus, while Marcus will be happy enough enjoying Gary's company but wondering what he's missing back home on the Internet.

Unlike some other games, the battle of the sexes starts out with players who truly want to cooperate. Yet whichever activity they choose, one person will be slightly less happy than the other. One solution that could work is flipping a coin. Seriously. The idea was tossed out by Robert Aumann, a Nobel Prize winner who said when two players can't make a binding contract to determine what to do, they can allow the solution to be determined at random by a third party. That third party could be a coin toss or a mediator.

So that's it, the solution to all your problems: Toss a coin! We told you economics was the easiest route to a happy marriage.

Solution: First-Mover Advantage

It never occurred to Gary to toss a coin, and even if it had, Marcus would never have agreed to leave his fortune to the winds of fate. What Gary did do was change strategies—he took control of their weekends.

One Saturday, Gary got up and made the coffee as usual. Marcus joined Gary in the kitchen as usual, and the two read the paper as usual. Then Gary announced he'd booked a guided hike in a nature preserve about an hour out of town and they needed to be ready to go in thirty minutes. He didn't give Marcus advance notice because he didn't want to give him a chance to protest.

"I knew if I framed it as a question, Marcus would say no," said Gary. "He'd find an excuse to stay home." He told Marcus whatever work he'd planned to do that day could wait until Sunday, assuring him that "nothing is going to happen to the medieval era while we're out."

To Gary's relief, Marcus agreed, though not without a little protest.

"Wait, we're going to a nature preserve?" asked Marcus. "That means mosquitoes. Did you buy repellent?"

"Yes," said Gary.

About Giving In

Gary and Marcus weren't the only couple we met who found themselves in this kind of pickle. A few other complaints we heard along
these lines:

- We only have sex in the morning, when she likes it best.
- We spend more time hanging out with his buddies than with mine.
- We always go to the same three restaurants.
- All our vacations are spent with family. Why can't we ever take
  one alone?

Notice that in all cases the aggrieved spouse is choosing to go with
the other person's preference rather than going off on his or her own.
That's classic battle of the sexes, since they're forgoing their first
choices to spend time with their partners.

"Do I have time to go to the bathroom?"

"Yes, but hurry up."

"Will we get back in time for *Dancing with the Stars*?"

"We'll do our best."

What Gary had done was to take the "first-mover advantage,"
which is a strategy akin to calling "shotgun" for the front seat. In game
theory, the "first mover" has an advantage over the other players because he moves first. Israel had the advantage in the Six-Day War because it attacked Egypt preemptively. Netflix had the advantage in the
online DVD rental market because it was the first major player in the
game. Marcus had long had the first-mover advantage by planting
himself at his desk every day and barely moving. Gary, who liked

being around Marcus, had gone along with it—until the day he woke up and made himself the first mover.

Gary didn't stop there. To ensure continued outings, he bought season tickets to the ballet and to the local black box theater company. One thing that Marcus hated even more than a sloppy Wikipedia entry was wasting money. Once the tickets were bought, he wouldn't let them go to waste.

"Gary knows me well," Marcus told us. "Which isn't always a good thing."

That's what worked for Marcus and Gary. But there's one more solution to the battle of the sexes that we think is worth telling you about: changing the rules of the game. Contrary to what the name suggests, the battle of the sexes isn't limited to romantic partners. It gets played whenever two people want different things but at the end of the day also want to work together. For example, consider two authors who want to write a book together. One likes to write about economics, the other about marriage. If they each go with their preferences, they can't write the book together. But neither one wants to go it alone. That means one of them has to give in to the other.

If they're smart, they'll change the rules of the game, much as Captain James T. Kirk did when he faced the dreaded *Kobayashi Maru* scenario during his training at Starfleet Academy. (Did we just insert a reference to *Star Trek*? Yes, we did.) No other student had ever won this game—it was, in fact, a no-win situation—until Kirk came along and reprogrammed the game entirely. Similarly, the two authors who want to write a book together might agree to do something completely unexpected: combine their passions and write a book about economics *and* marriage.

If you look hard enough, there's usually a plan C that can resolve any battle of the sexes—whether it's two vacations a year, sex in the afternoon, or the book you've just finished reading.

THE BOTTOM LINE

1. **Think ahead.** Before you tell your spouse everything he did wrong in the past week, consider how he will react to the onslaught. Is he likely to nod his head, agree completely, and apologize? Or will he more than likely tell you to put a sock in it? If the latter, rethink your approach.

2. **Think backward.** How did he react the last time you went away for a weekend with friends, leaving him alone with two kids, and only gave him an hour's notice? Did he get kind of upset? If so, consider giving him some advanced notice, or even—and this is crazy—asking if it's cool with him.

3. **Be realistic.** You can't have everything you want, when you want it, and how you want it—if there's someone else in the equation, that is. And since there's always someone else in the equation in a marriage, you're going to need to compromise and be willing to settle sometimes for what's acceptable, versus ideal.

4. **Put yourself in his shoes.** In order to really know what's going to get him on board, you need to imagine what it's like to be him, including his preferences and dislikes. It's called empathy, and it goes a long way.

5. **Give an inch.** You'd be surprised—or maybe no—how quickly two people can become completely polarized, on opposite sides of the fence and unwilling to compromise. Giving an inch, which might mean just saying something as simple as, "I see your point," is the first step in meeting each other halfway.

Acknowledgments

This book was made possible by nearly two thousand people, including economists, psychologists, friends, friends of friends, colleagues, parents, siblings, complete strangers, research assistants, babysitters, editors, spouses, and babies.

A huge thanks goes to Gary Becker for his early encouragement. David Laibson, David Hirshleifer, and Howard Rachlin also helped point us in the right direction. Our other professors included Alvin Roth, Shelly Lundberg, Claudia Olivetti, Raymond Fisman, Ulrike Malmendier, Casey Mulligan, Bart Lipman, Andrew Postlewaite, Devin Pope, Sergiu Hart, Ehud Kalai, Robert Frank, Betsey Stevenson, Justin Wolfers, Ernst Fehr, Uri Gneezy, Colin Camerer, Robert Shiller, Emir Kamenica, Allen Parkman, Daniele Paserman, Claudia Goldin, and Daniel Hamermesh.

On the marriage side of the equation, John Gottman and Julie Schwartz Gottman gave us a weekend that proved invaluable to both our book and our spouses. (Paula continues to work on her patience, Jenny her tone). Thomas Sexton, Peter Kramer, Stephen Konscul, Jonathan Bloch, David Tannenbaum, Connie Feutz, Gerald Weeks, Lois Braverman, and John Buri taught us further lessons on love and compromise.

Our Exhaustive, Groundbreaking, and Very Expensive Marriage Survey was a result of the hard work of Mike Brezner and Gil Bugarin at United Sample, and by all the people who answered 63 inexcusably nosy questions about their private lives. Michael Luca, our unflinching research assistant, never met an economic mystery he couldn't solve. We've already filed our recommendation with the Royal Swedish Academy of Sciences to get Luca shortlisted for the Nobel Prize.

Our agent, Amy Williams, dragged herself out of maternity leave and sold the hell out of this book amid the worst financial crisis since the Great Depression. Susan Kamil chose us and believed in us, and she didn't hesitate to remind us of that fact every time we needed reminding (which was often).

Andy Ward—editor, therapist, savior, visionary, funny man, friend. You made it happen.

PAULA THANKS ...

Tom Weber, who mentored, inspired, titled, and schlepped to deep Long Island to meet the game theorists. Charles Duhigg, who tempted fate and made the introductions. Mia Steinberg, psychological adviser. Jessie Knadler, discerning reader and ecstatic trance dancer. Nathan Lump, who said it was a no-brainer and was half right. Shirley Nord, Nancy Cuervo, Alice Proujansky, Natalie Hall, Laurie Saft Ginsberg, Stacy Lewin-Farber, Dan Farber, Marisa Milanese, Mo Lee, Rob Baedeker, Laura Scholes, Bunny Finley, Gale Wilson, and Michael Williams helped provide the infrastructure.

Jeff and Sonya, my Middle East correspondents, subtitlers, videographers, and role models.

My parents, Lenore and Mark, whose marriage blows every other marriage out of the water.

Nivi, for inadvertently giving me a book idea, for waking up with me at 5:30 in the morning, for pushing me, for marrying me, for loving me.

Ida, sweet as apple cider, who has always been here. And Noa, who arrived just in time.

JENNY THANKS . . .

John Leonard, for the room I could call my own, Alex Michel, provocateur extraordinaire, Hal Lux, wise man, incisive editor. Charles Duhigg, for the killer blind date. Emily Miller, Amy Noonan, Laura Lafave, and Amy Williams, for having great friends and offering them up.

Ben and Tickie, Richard and Charlie, and Ben and Jackie, for making us feel welcome whenever we turned up.

To Larry Ingrassia, and *The New York Times,* for giving me time off, even though my timing left much to be desired.

Susana, you are the calm to every tempest we create. We are blessed to have you in our lives.

To my parents, for showing me what it takes to make marriage work: love, hard work, two sinks. To Imogen and Richard, the consummate team whose hard work I get to enjoy every day.

Thorold, for your boundless goodwill toward this book. For making an adventure out of every rock pool and parking lot: She's a lovely and lucky hen. For loving me the way I need to be loved and taking a flyer on marriage.

To Ella, a light brighter than the sun. I love being your mom. And to Tess (a.k.a. "Boris"), for waiting long enough that we could finish.

WE BOTH THANK . . .

The people who shared their stories with us. You all are the beating heart of this book. We knew when we started on our Spousonomical journey that marriage involved trade-offs. But you taught us that the hardest trade-offs, when handled wisely and with love, also produce the greatest rewards.

Notes

Chapter 1: Division of Labor

7 **Or they might be**   James Brooke, "New Zealand Finds Isolation Is an Asset," *New York Times*, October 6, 2002.

8 **England had to put in only**   We're keeping things fairly simple, but there's an additional calculation economists would make here—one that would lead to the same conclusion—and that's the opportunity cost of making knickers and wine, meaning the cost of what each country gives up to make each good. For Portugal, the opportunity cost of a pair of knickers is two bottles of wine—that is, for every pair of knickers the country produces, it's not producing two bottles of wine. For England, the opportunity cost of a pair of knickers is only half a bottle of wine.

Similarly, the opportunity cost of a bottle of wine is half a pair of knickers in Portugal and two pairs of knickers in England.

England is the clear knicker leader.

15 **Marriage, as the economists**   Betsey Stevenson and Justin Wolfers, "Marriage and the Market," *Cato Unbound*, January 18, 2008, http://www.cato-unbound.org.

15 **Sharing household chores**   "As Marriage and Parenthood Drift Apart, Public Is Concerned About Social Impact," Pew Research Center, July 2007, http://pewresearch.org/assets/social/pdf/marriage.pdf.

18 **"The upshot is quite extraordinary"**   Lauren F. Landsburg, "Comparative Advantage," *Library of Economics and Liberty*, http://www.econlib.org/library/Topics/Details/comparativeadvantage.html.

22 **Both assumed, because of the way** In their paper, "Mothers and Sons: Preference Development and Female Labor Force Dynamics" (*Quarterly Journal of Economics* 119, no. 4 [November 2004]: 1249–1299), economists Raquel Fernandez, Alessandra Fogli, and Claudia Olivetti found that men were more likely to marry working women if their own mothers had worked. This evidence is consistent with a growing literature in economics on role model effects, meaning how children (and, later, adults) are influenced by the behavior of their role models, from teachers to politicians to parents.

25 **Create a market for air** Steven Landsburg, *The Armchair Economist: Economics and Everyday Life* (New York: Free Press, 1995), 81.

27 **His first wife dumped him** Werner Stark, "In Search of the True Pareto," *British Journal of Sociology* 14, no. 2 (June 1963): 103–112.

27 **He and his second wife shared** Manon Michels Enaudi, "Pareto As I Knew Him," *Atlantic Monthly,* http://www.carloalberto.org/files/michels35.pdf.

34 **"It is as if the design"** Jagdish Bhagwati, "A New Vocabulary for Trade," *New York Times,* August 4, 2005.

Chapter 2: Loss Aversion

38 **Economists have quantified the difference** Amos Tversky and Daniel Kahneman, "Loss Aversion in Riskless Choice: A Reference-Dependent Model," *Quarterly Journal of Economics* 106, no. 4 (November 1991): 1039–1061.

40 **He spent the next year** David Gauthier-Villars and Carrick Mollenkamp, "How to Lose $7.2 Billion: A Trader's Tale," *The Wall Street Journal,* February 2, 2008.

40 **As summed up by Andrew Lo** Jenny Anderson, "Craving the High That Risky Trading Can Bring," *New York Times,* February 7, 2008.

40 **In the late 1970s** Daniel Kahneman and Amos Tversky, "Prospect Theory: An Analysis of Decision Under Risk," *Econometrica* 47, no. 2 (March 1979): 263–292.

42 **This time, 92 percent of the students** According to probability theory, a game that gives you an 80 percent chance of winning $4,000 (and a 20 percent chance of getting nothing) means you will win an average of $3,200 (80% × $4,000 + 20% × $0 = $3,200). If you play once, you will end up with either $4,000 or $0. However, if you keep playing throughout the night, your luck starts to even out, and your winnings should be $3,200 per game (on average). An 80 percent chance of losing $4,000 means that your losses will average out to $3,200 per game if you consistently choose that option. Oh heck, just trust us.

42 **Yet the minute gas goes up**   David Leonhardt, "Seeing Inflation Only in the Prices That Go Up," *New York Times,* May 7, 2008.

53 **The second group**   Daniel Kahneman, Jack L. Knetsch, and Richard H. Thaler, "Experimental Tests of the Endowment Effect and the Coase Theorem," *Journal of Political Economy* 98, no. 6 (December 1990): 1325–1348.

53 **Once they'd bought into the bells**   C. W. Park, S. Y. Jun, and D. J. MacInnis, "Choosing What I Want Versus Rejecting What I Don't Want: An Application of Decision Framing to Product Option Choice Decisions," *Journal of Marketing Research* 37 (2000): 187–202.

54 **In another experiment that tested**   Amos Tversky and Daniel Kahneman, "The Framing of Decisions and the Psychology of Choice," *Science* 211, no. 4481 (1981): 453–458.

59 **Scientists have found that people**   D. Marazziti, H. S. Akiskal, A. Rossi, and G. B. Cassano, "Alteration of the Platelet Serotonin Transporter in Romantic Love," *Psychological Medicine* 29:3 (1999): 741–745.

62 **"The significant carriers of utility"**   Richard H. Thaler, *The Winner's Curse: Paradoxes and Anomalies of Economic Life* (Princeton, N.J.: Princeton University Press, 1992), 70.

63 **Meanwhile, the next day**   Martin Weber and Colin Camerer, "The Disposition Effect in Securities Trading: An Experimental Analysis," *Journal of Economic Behavior and Organization,* 33:2 (1998): 167–184.

64 **On the other hand**   Philip A. Fisher and Ken Fisher, *Common Stocks and Uncommon Profits* (New York: John Wiley & Sons, 1997), 100.

Chapter 3: Supply and Demand

73 **According to the Pew Research Center**   "As Marriage and Parenthood Drift Apart, Public Is Concerned About Social Impact," Pew Research Center, July 2007, http://pewresearch.org/assets/social/pdf/marriage.pdf.

73 **And according to the General Social**   Tom W. Smith, "American Sexual Behavior: Trends, Socio-Demographic Differences, and Risk Behavior," GSS Topical Report No. 25, National Opinion Research Center, University of Chicago, March 2006, http://www.norc.org.

73 **"Happy couples have more sex"**   Tara Parker-Pope, "When Sex Leaves the Marriage," *New York Times,* June 3, 2009.

74 **The good news is**   Stacy Tessler Lindau, L. Philip Schumm, Edward O. Laumann, Wendy Levinson, Colm A. O'Muircheartaigh, and Linda J. Waite, "A Study

of Sexuality and Health Among Older Adults in the United States," *New England Journal of Medicine* 357, no. 8 (2007).

74 **As the critic**   Caitlin Flanagan, "The Wifely Duty," *Atlantic Monthly,* January–February 2003.

81 **No one knew who owned**   Gretchen Morgenson, "It's Time for Swaps to Lose Their Swagger," *New York Times,* February 27, 2010.

87 **There's a theory in economics**   Gary S. Becker and Kevin M. Murphy, "A Theory of Rational Addiction," *Journal of Political Economy* 96, no. 4 (1988): 675–700.

89 **They paid some people**   Gary Charness and Uri Gneezy, "Incentives to Exercise," *Econometrica* 7, no. 3 (2009): 909–931.

97 **Economists have shown that the *U.S. News & World Report***   Michael Luca and Jonathan Smith, "Why Is First Best?: Responses to Information Aggregation in the *U.S. News* College Rankings," working paper, 2010, http://ssrn.com/abstract-1472129.

Chapter 4: Moral Hazard

102 **These could be deliberate**   Tom Baker, "On the Genealogy of Moral Hazard," *Texas Law Review* 75, no. 2 (1996): 237.

105 **According to the General Social Survey**   Tom W. Smith, "Altruism and Empathy in America: Trends and Correlates," National Opinion Research Center, University of Chicago, February 9, 2006, http://www.norc.org.

110 **Here's proof—proof from the other**   Sebastian Galiani and Ernesto Schargrodsky, "Property Rights for the Poor: Effects of Land Titling," *Journal of Public Economics* 94, nos. 9–10 (2010).

116 **Research shows that marital satisfaction**   John M. Gottman and Clifford I. Notarius, "Marital Research in the 20th Century and a Research Agenda for the 21st Century," *Family Process* 41, no. 2 (2002).

116 **"It is one of life's great ironies"**   John W. Jacobs, *All You Need Is Love and Other Lies About Marriage* (New York: HarperCollins, 2004).

119 **Even a whopping salary**   For a deeper dive into baseball and moral hazard—specifically, the increase in the number of days players spend on the disabled list after they sign a guaranteed contract—see Kenneth Lehn, "Property Rights, Risk Sharing, and Player Disability," *Journal of Law and Economics* 25 (October 1982): 343–366.

119 **They could, in theory, stipulate**   Theodore Bergstrom, "Economics in a Family Way," *Journal of Economic Literature* 34, no. 4 (1996): 1903–1934.

121 **They compared hunting accidents** Michael Conlin, Stacy Dickert-Conlin, and John Pepper, "The Deer Hunter: The Unintended Effects of Hunting Regulations," *Review of Economics and Statistics* 91, no. 1 (2009): 178–187.

128 **Pitchers in the AL** John-Charles Bradbury and Douglas Drinen, "The Designated Hitter, Moral Hazard, and Hit Batters: New Evidence from Game-Level Data," *Journal of Sports Economics* 7, no. 3 (2006): 319–329.

Chapter 5: Incentives

132 **You've got a big office** Monica Langley, "Parting Shots: In the AIG Divorce, a Battle over Who Gets What—Former Chief Threatens Suit over Files and Mementos; A Push to Choose Sides—Snowball's Health Records," *The Wall Street Journal,* May 4, 2005.

132 **Your corporate jet has a StairMaster** Devin Leonard, "Greenberg & Sons," *Fortune,* February 21, 2005.

133 **And now that the brass ring** Gretchen Morgenson, "Behind Insurer's Crisis, Blind Eye to Web of Risk," *New York Times,* September 27, 2010.

133 **Joe's personal compensation** Serena Ng and Thomas Catan, "We Were 'Prudent': AIG Man at Center of Crisis," *The Wall Street Journal,* July 1, 2010.

133 **"A cornerstone of personnel economics"** Edward P. Lazear, "Performance Pay and Productivity," *American Economic Review* 90, no. 5 (2000): 1346–1361.

136 **Starting in 2007, the U.S. credit crisis** For more on Mr. Cassano's role in the financial crisis, see Michael Lewis, "The Man Who Crashed the World," *Vanity Fair,* August 2009.

137 **In one recent experiment** Carl Mellström and Magnus Johannesson, "Crowding Out in Blood Donation: Was Titmuss Right?" *European Economic Association* 16, no. 4 (2008): 845–863.

137 **Which led to an *increase*** Michael G. Vann, "Of Rats, Rice, and Race: The Great Hanoi Rat Massacre, an Episode in French Colonial History," *French Colonial History* 4 (2003): 191–203.

137 **But the threat of punishment** Radha Iyengar, "I'd Rather Be Hanged for a Sheep than a Lamb: The Unintended Consequences of 'Three-Strikes' Laws," *National Bureau of Economic Research,* Working Paper 13784, February 2008, http://www.nber.org.

143 **However, he doesn't totally shake down** Ernst Fehr and Bettina Rockenbach, "Detrimental Effects of Sanctions on Human Altruism," *Nature* 422 (March 2003). (In the experiment, Fehr and Rockenbach worked with "monetary units," not dollars, but we used dollars to keep things simple.)

149 **The rival responds**   Avinash K. Dixit and Barry J. Nalebuff, *The Art of Strategy: A Game Theorist's Guide to Success in Business & Life* (New York: W. W. Norton & Co., 2008), 76.

159 **Subjects were put into three groups**   Dan Ariely, Emir Kamenica, and Dražen Prelec, "Man's Search for Meaning: The Case of Legos," *Journal of Economic Behavior and Organization* 67, no. 3 (2008): 671–677.

Chapter 6: Trade-offs

161 **The city's politicos**   Mayor's Office of Management and Budget. Figure is 2008 gross city product. http://www.nyc.gov/html/omb/downloads/pdf/eco710pdf.

162 **Luckily for us**   R. B. Ekelund Jr., "Jules Dupuit and the Theory of Marginal Cost Pricing," *Journal of Political Economy* 76, no. 3 (1968): 462–471. Jules Dupuit, a nineteenth-century French engineer, is credited with inventing the cost-benefit analysis itself. But there is debate over whether Dupuit fully grasped the concept of marginal utility, which is key to economists' understanding of cost-benefit analyses. That's why we're giving Marshall credit. That, and we like his story better.

165 **Like we said**   Feel free to read Brent R. Hickman's "Effort, Race Gaps and Affirmative Action: A Structural Policy Analysis of U.S. College Admissions" (working paper) if you want to know more about this particular cost-benefit analysis. In a nutshell, Hickman looks at the costs high school students pay to do well in school (all the fun stuff they could be doing instead of studying, like playing World of Warcraft) versus the benefit (upping their odds of getting into college).

177 **In 2008, the agency**   Alan Stern, "NASA's Black Hole Budgets," *New York Times,* November 24, 2008.

178 **"Remembering the irrelevance"**   http://gregmankiw.blogspot.com/2006/06/jd-vs-phd-my-story.html.

186 **Only four in one hundred**   Karl Sigmund, Ernst Fehr, and Martin A. Nowak, "The Economics of Fair Play," *Scientific American,* January 2002.

186 **The authors chalked this up**   Joseph Henrich, Robert Boyd, Samuel Bowles, Colin Camerer, Ernst Fehr, Herbert Gintis, and Richard McElreath, "In Search of Homo Economicus: Behavioral Experiments in 15 Small-Scale Societies," *American Economic Review* 91, no. 2 (2001): 73–78.

187 **As the economist**   Richard Thaler, *The Winner's Curse* (Princeton, N.J.: Princeton University Press, 1992).

Chapter 7: Asymmetric Information

194 **Akerlof thought complete information**   George A. Akerlof, "Writing 'The Market for Lemons': A Personal and Interpretive Essay," November 14, 2003, http://www.nobelprize.org.

203 **Subjects were asked to read two**   Larry D. Rosen, Nancy A. Cheever, Cheyenne Cummings, and Julie Felt, "The Impact of Emotionality and Self-Disclosure on Online Dating Versus Traditional Dating," *Computers in Human Behavior* 24, no. 5 (2008): 2124–2157.

208 **Indeed, only 27 percent**   Jeffrey M. Jones, "In U.S., More Would Like to Lose Weight Than Are Trying To," Gallup, November 20, 2009, http://www.gallup.com.

216 **Only 3 percent**   Sheena S. Iyengar and Mark R. Lepper, "When Choice Is Demotivating: Can One Desire Too Much of a Good Thing," *Journal of Personality and Social Psychology* 79, no. 6 (2000): 995–1006.

216 **Gottman says when a spouse feels**   The Art and Science of Love: A Weekend Workshop for Couples Presented by Drs. John and Julie Gottman (Seattle, June 2009).

Chapter 8: Intertemporal Choice

222 **Ring up thousands of dollars**   Automated Access to Court Electronic Records. The sixty-four hundred figure cited represents the number of bankruptcies per day in 2010, through the month of May. http://www.aacer.com.

222 **His interests included geology**   R. Warren James, "The Life and Work of John Rae," *Canadian Journal of Economics and Political Science* 17, no. 2 (1951): 141–163.

222 **"The actual presence"**   Shane Frederick, George Loewenstein, and Ted O'Donoghue, "Time Discounting and Time Preference: A Critical Review," *Journal of Economic Literature* 40 (June 2002): 351–401.

224 **Bag the gym**   Adapted from Craig Lambert, "The Marketplace of Perceptions," *Harvard Magazine,* March–April 2006.

227 **"When one is not hungry"**   George Loewenstein, "Hot-Cold Empathy Gaps and Medical Decision Making," *Health Psychology* 24, no. 4 (2005): S49.

229 **Creepy**   Dan Ariely and George Loewenstein, "The Heat of the Moment: The Effect of Sexual Arousal on Sexual Decision Making," *Journal of Behavioral Decision Making* 19, no. 2 (2006): 87–98.

236 **One group was told**   Daniel Read, George Loewenstein, and Shobana Kalyanaraman, "Mixing Virtue and Vice: Combining the Immediacy Effect and the

Diversification Heuristic," *Journal of Behavioral Decision Making* 12, no. 4 (1999): 257–273.

236 **Deep down, we know** This experiment played out in the real world a few years later when Slate conducted a poll to determine what Netflix movies were languishing on readers' shelves the longest. More than one thousand people admitted to "having sat for days, weeks, months, and even years on everything from *All About Eve* to *Z,* the Oscar-winning French drama starring Yves Montand."

Chapter 9: Bubbles

248 **It's the story of a tulip** Our version of the tulip mania was adapted from Charles Mackay's 1841 bestseller, *Extraordinary Popular Delusions and the Madness of Crowds.* We embellished on his account, which has been questioned by some and discredited by others. Not being experts on seventeenth-century Netherlands, we can only say that Mackay's tome is still a must-read among smart financiers. Having lived through a few of our own bubbles (of the economic variety), we don't think his tale sounds far-fetched. Michael Lewis, who edited *The Price of Everything: Rediscovering the Six Classics of Economics,* included Mackay's tulip tale. And Lewis is a smart guy.

252 **"If we speak frankly"** John Maynard Keynes, *The General Theory of Employment, Interest and Money* (Classic Books America, 2009), 124.

253 **In 1999, *Time*** Robert Reich, "John Maynard Keynes," *Time,* March 29, 1999.

255 **As Francis Bacon put it** Francis Bacon, *Novum Organum* (Charleston, S.C.: Forgotten Books, 2010), 28.

255 **In some instances** As Charles Mackay, the British journalist who brought us all that stuff about the tulip craze, wrote in *Extraordinary Popular Delusions and the Madness of Crowds,* "Men, it has been well said, think in herds. It will be seen that they go mad in herds, while they only recover their senses slowly, and one by one."

261 **Bust-ups in the economy** Joseph Schumpeter, *Capitalism, Socialism and Democracy* (New York: Harper Colophon Books, 1975): 82–85.

261 **"For capitalism, depression"** Robert L. Heilbroner, *The Worldly Philosophers* (New York: Touchstone, 1999), 291.

261 **As one of his biographers** Thomas K. McCraw, *Prophet of Innovation: Joseph Schumpeter and Creative Destruction* (Cambridge, Mass.: Belknap Press of Harvard University Press, 2010), 6.

261 **According to Thomas McCraw** Ibid., 4.

262 **A century later** W. Michael Cox and Richard Alm, "Creative Destruction," *Concise Encyclopedia of Economics,* Library of Economics and Liberty, http://www.econlib.org/library/Enc/CreativeDestruction.html.

267 **"In fact, market prices"**   Warren Buffett, "The Superinvestors of Graham-and-Doddsville," speech to commemorate the fiftieth anniversary of the publication of *Security Analysis* by Benjamin Graham and David Dodd, May 17, 1984. http://tilsonfunds.com/motley_berkshire_superinvestors.php.

271 **"My idea of a group"**   Mary Buffett and David Clark, *The Tao of Warren Buffett* (New York: Scribner, 2006), 20.

272 **His stake would eventually**   Alice Schroeder, *The Snowball: Warren Buffett and the Business of Life* (New York: Bantam Books, 2008) 551–552 and 674.

277 **In one survey of more**   Baruch Fischhoff, Andrew Parker, Wandi Bruine De Bruin, Julie Downs, Claire Palmgren, Robyn Dawes, and Charles F. Manski, "Teen Expectations for Significant Life Events," *Public Opinion Quarterly* 64, no. 2 (2000): 189–205.

277 **In another, slightly**   We say "informal" because the figure comes from a conversation we had with Whitney Tilson, a money manager, who told us, "I was sitting in the room eleven years ago at my fifth reunion in June 1999 and they showed the results of the class survey done for the reunion. I'm sure of the number—it was so hilarious that everyone laughed." But, he said, that's as official as the 82 percent gets.

277 **And in a survey of**   Lynn A. Baker and Robert E. Emery, "When Every Relationship Is Above Average: Perceptions and Expectations of Divorce Around the Time of Marriage," *Law and Human Behavior* 17, no. 4 (August 1993).

278 **The more people see**   Perhaps one of the best historical examples is the defeat of the British armies at Gallipoli, in Turkey, during World War I. For an entertaining summary of that, see Malcolm Gladwell's *New Yorker* article: http://www.newyorker.com/reporting/2009/07/27/090727fa_fact_gladwell.

278 **The climbers'**   http://freakonomics.blogs.nytimes.com/2009/08/04/scaling-the-heights-of-corporate-greed-chafkin-and-lo-on-risk.

279 **"This behavior often leads"**   http://blogs.harvardbusiness.org/vermeulen/2009/03/businesses-and-the-icarus-para.html.

280 **Shiller's index reached its all-time**   Shiller's index is based on survey data from institutional investors. For individual investors, the crash confidence was slightly higher in 2003 than it was in 2006.

Chapter 10: Game Theory

289 **The Talmudic discussions**   Robert J. Aumann, "Game Theory in the Talmud," *Research Bulletin Series on Jewish Law and Economics,* http://dept.econ.yorku.ca/~jros/docs/AumannGame.pdf.

290 **"There is no independently"**   Thomas Schelling, *Choice and Conse-*

quence: Perspectives of an Errant Economist (Cambridge, Mass.: Harvard University Press, 1995), 214.

290 **This doesn't mean considering** See Adam Smith's *Theory of Moral Sentiments*: "What should we do if we find ourselves as a spectator reacting in a very different way than our companion who is suffering? We should try to empathize, to understand his situation more deeply."

291 **"It is the art of putting"** Avinash K. Dixit and Barry J. Nalebuff, *The Art of Strategy: A Game Theorist's Guide to Success in Business and Life* (New York: W. W. Norton & Co., 2010).

308 **That third party** Len Fisher, *Rock, Paper, Scissors: Game Theory in Everyday Life* (New York: Basic Books, 2008), 85.

310 **No other student had ever won** A classic subject in the *Star Trek* canon, the *Kobayashi Maru* is a simulation test given at Starfleet Academy. Students have a choice of rescuing the crew of the *Kobayashi Maru,* a crippled fuel carrier in a no-fly zone, but getting destroyed by the Klingons in the process, or saving themselves but abandoning the crew of the fuel carrier. The test is a no-win situation intended to force cadets to learn how they would deal with losing. Only Kirk managed to beat it—by reprogramming the simulation so it was possible to rescue the ship and survive. "I don't believe in the no-win scenario," says Kirk in *Star Trek II: The Wrath of Khan*. Sadly, Kirk's game theory chops did him no good when it came to love: In the movie, he learns that he has a twenty-year-old son his old flame never told him about because she considered him such a deadbeat.

Image Credits

Index

ABOUT THE AUTHORS

PAULA SZUCHMAN is the deputy managing editor of *Newsweek*. She was previously a Page One editor at *The Wall Street Journal,* and a features reporter. She lives with her husband and two daughters in Brooklyn.

JENNY ANDERSON is a *New York Times* reporter who spent years covering Wall Street, and won a Gerald Loeb Award for her coverage of Merrill Lynch. She currently writes on education and lives with her husband and two daughters in Manhattan.